The Character of Justice

Rhetoric and Public Affairs Series

The Character of Justice

Rhetoric, Law, and Politics in the Supreme Court Confirmation Process

TREVOR PARRY-GILES

Michigan State University Press
East Lansing

Michigan State University Press
East Lansing, Michigan 48823-5245
Printed and bound in the United States of America.

12 11 10 09 08 07 06   1 2 3 4 5 6 7 8 9 10

LIBRARY OF CONGRESS CATALOGING-IN-PUBLICATION DATA

Parry-Giles, Trevor, 1963–
    The character of justice : rhetoric, law, and politics in the Supreme Court confirmation process / Trevor Parry-Giles.
        p. cm.—(Rhetoric and public affairs series)
    Includes bibliographical references and index.
    ISBN 0-87013-769-7 (cloth : alk. paper)
    1. United States. Supreme Court—Officials and employees—Selection and appointment—History. 2. Judges—Selection and appointment—United States—History. 3. Political questions and judicial power—United States—History. I. Title. II. Series.
    KF8742.P37 2006
    347.73'2634—dc22

                                                                2006002234

Cover and book design by Sans Serif, Inc.

g green press INITIATIVE Michigan State University Press is a member of the Green Press Initiative and is committed to developing and encouraging ecologically responsible publishing practices. For more information about the Green Press Initiative and the use of recycled paper in book publishing, please visit www.greenpressinitiative.org.

Visit Michigan State University Press on the World Wide Web at:
www.msupress.msu.edu

To Shawn

Contents

Acknowledgments

Sometime in the late 1980s, I attended a brown-bag lunch event hosted by Indiana University's Department of Telecommunications and featuring James Carey, then at the University of Illinois. Carey spoke about the recently concluded Supreme Court confirmation hearings of Judge Robert Bork, noting that such hearings have become media rituals with significant importance for the United States and its political culture. That brown-bag event began a research endeavor that culminates with this book.

Along the way, many people have read, edited, commented upon, supported, and criticized various versions of this research. I am grateful to them all. As reviewers, panel respondents, or editors, David Henry, Jim Jasinski, Catherine Langford, Bill Lewis, John Lucaites, Eileen Scallen, Jan Schuetz, Mary Stuckey, Mari Tonn, Barbara Warnick, and William Wiethoff have offered insights and criticisms that I hope have made the conclusions stronger and the arguments better. Verna Corgan deserves special mention, having willingly and cheerfully served as a respondent on three separate occasions, each time providing useful assessments. The reviewers for Michigan State University Press gave of their time and effort to put forth detailed evaluations of the manuscript, and I am indebted to them for their careful readings. Thanks also to the Southern States Communication Association and the National Communication Association for their permission to include material previously published in the *Southern Communication Journal* and the *Quarterly Journal of Speech* as portions of chapters 3 and 4.

Since commencing this research in the early 1990s, I have worked at several institutions, and I am grateful for the support received at each. Colleagues, chairs, deans, and students at St. Ambrose University and Western Illinois University readily listened as I discussed the vagaries of the Supreme Court confirmation process. Librarians at these institutions, and especially Irene Herold at Monmouth College, were very helpful as I repeatedly submitted interlibrary loan requests or asked for old congressional hearings. I am also grateful for a St. Ambrose University Faculty Development Grant that supported research travel to Washington, D.C., and I acknowledge the Central States Communication Association, which awarded me their Federation Prize in 1995 in support of this research.

My colleagues at the University of Maryland are uniformly supportive of my research efforts, and I value their friendship and encouragement. I am particularly pleased that I work among a group of dedicated rhetorical scholars—Robert Gaines, Kathy Kendall, Jim Klumpp, Joe McCaleb, Shawn Parry-Giles, and Mari Tonn—who are committed to scholarship and teaching and who enliven the rhetorical inquiry that we all pursue in positive and productive ways. I was also helped by the research efforts of two dedicated undergraduates—Evan Pitler and Joe Matukonis—and their efforts are appreciated. Led by our chair, Edward Fink, we strive in the Department of Communication to study the strategic use of discourse in the public sphere, and I hope that this project contributes to that worthy mission in some small way.

The entire community of scholars who study and write about rhetoric and public affairs owes a great deal to Marty Medhurst. With indomitable entrepreneurial energy, Marty shepherds our projects from draft to revision to publication in the journal he edits or the book series he guides. I am grateful to him for both his professional interest in my research efforts and for his personal kindnesses and courtesies. I am also grateful to the professionals at the Michigan State University Press for their diligence and patience while guiding this book toward final publication.

Three friends—Jim Aune, Marouf Hasian, and John Murphy—have, at various times in the development of this book, offered their support and enthusiasm. A citation, a kind word, a critical insight, an expression of encouragement, an invitation to a conference—whatever the means, each of these generous individuals contributed to this project's continuation and culmination.

Finally, as always, I am so thankful for the support of my family. My parents and in-laws are always interested in my work and dutifully say they will read every word, and I thank them for their encouragement. Two great kids, Sam and Eli, endure their parents' constant discussions of rhetoric and politics with only minimal annoyance. I am very proud of both boys and thankful for their patience with me. And Shawn's endless support and love are foundational to this project and to all that I do. For that, I dedicate this book to her.

1

Character and the Constitution

Politics in the Supreme Court Confirmation Process

It is not easy to conceive a plan better calculated than this to produce a judicious choice of men for filling the offices of the Union; and it will not need proof that on this point must essentially depend the character of its administration.

Alexander Hamilton, *The Federalist Papers*

The Supreme Court is not worth it. No job is worth it. . . . This is a circus. It is a national disgrace.

Judge Clarence Thomas, *Nomination of Judge Clarence Thomas to be Associate Justice of the Supreme Court of the United States*

On December 13, 2000, Americans of every political hue, from all parts of the nation, across cultural and class lines, learned once again of the U.S. Supreme Court's singular importance in the American government. Asserting in rather remarkable language their belief in the need for judicial restraint, the Court's slim majority in the case of *Bush v. Gore*[1] decided, nonetheless, to grasp their "unsought responsibility to resolve the federal and constitutional issues the judicial system has been forced to confront" and halt the recounting of ballots in the disputed Florida election for president. With only their credibility to support them, five justices of the Court resolved what the votes of over 100 million of their fellow citizens had made so complicated.

1

As it has done so many times before, the Supreme Court in 2000 inserted itself into a critical and ongoing national debate. Slavery, property rights, abortion, individual privacy, freedom of religion—all of the great issues that have confronted the United States have come before the Supreme Court for resolution.[2] In *Bush v. Gore*, the Court again addressed issues fundamental to the American democracy—the value of votes, federalism, the essence of republican governance. And, as in the past, their pronouncements angered many, pleased many, and set the stage for further debate and dialogue.

One consequence of the *Bush v. Gore* case, and the Supreme Court's ongoing pivotal role in American society, is an intense interest in Supreme Court nominations. Such scrutiny, however, is a relatively new phenomenon. For much of American history, Supreme Court nominations attracted little *public* attention. The rancorous public hearings that characterize some contemporary confirmation struggles were unheard of prior to the twentieth century.[3] Because of a Senate procedure in place until 1929 that prohibited floor debates about nominations, there is little recorded public discussion in the Senate concerning Supreme Court nominees prior to the last century. In the case of most nominations to the Court before 1916, the process of confirmation (or rejection) was simple, uncontroversial, and quick.[4] Unsuccessful or rejected nominations to the Supreme Court in the early years of the Republic were chiefly the result of partisan bickering, unpopular or lame-duck presidents, or simple incompetence.[5]

Many observers are highly critical of the contemporary Supreme Court confirmation process. Stephen L. Carter, for instance, suggests that the confirmation process for presidential appointees is broken and that public confirmation debates "run from the sublime . . . to the ridiculous."[6] Mark Silverstein worries that the current "disorderly, contentious, and unpredictable" Supreme Court confirmation process is so democratized that figures of high stature (such as Brandeis, Marshall, and Holmes) may be disinclined to accept nomination to the High Court.[7] Such criticism is the result of a series of divisive nominations in which extremely personal and highly volatile reasons were offered for the selection of candidates or the confirmation/rejection of presidential appointees.

Nominations to the Supreme Court are relatively rare and have become more so as justices live longer and retire later. As such, the disputes over judicial nominations have spread to the lower courts, with several of President George W. Bush's appellate court nominees facing increased scrutiny in the Senate. Though the vast majority of Bush's nominees have been

confirmed by the Senate, numerous high-profile cases have resulted in renewed attention to the confirmation process. Senators have threatened to
filibuster nominees to prevent floor votes on their confirmation, and the
White House has responded with recess appointments of particular appellate nominations and calls for reform in the confirmation process.[8] Much
of this conflict anticipated future Supreme Court vacancies, portending
possible, indeed likely, controversy when such vacancies occur.

Recent controversial Supreme Court confirmation debates happen in a
political culture dominated by the presence of the mass media as a source
of information and entertainment. The contemporary media environment
is premised upon discovery of the most unsavory and intimate details in
the lives of public officials,[9] and such an environment alarms those who
find fault with the system of assessing Supreme Court nominees.[10] The televised hearings on the nomination of Robert Bork in 1987 were viewed
with such disdain by some that proposals calling for private hearings and
written assessments of nominees soon appeared.[11] The highly mediated
clash between Clarence Thomas and Anita Hill in 1991, and the ensuing
outrage, resulted in closed-door executive sessions of the Senate Judiciary
Committee to consider personal matters of subsequent nominees Ruth
Bader Ginsburg and Stephen Breyer.

Criticisms of the Supreme Court confirmation process, though, mistak-
enly deflect attention from the power and impact of this process to its procedures and lack of civility. The result is a series of efforts that explore the
"proper" role for the Senate,[12] or offer reform proposals designed to restore
some mythical sense of decorum and privacy to these confirmation proceedings,[13] or construct quantitative models to measure and predict the patterns
and/or procedures of Supreme Court confirmations.[14] While such efforts are
noteworthy, of more profound interest are the larger social and political consequences of the confirmation process for the American community.

My concern, therefore, is with the cultural and political significance of
the Supreme Court confirmation process in the twentieth century. I pay
particular attention to the debates—in committees, in the Senate, and in
the news media—concerning nominations to the Court, emphasizing their
lingering legacy as public enactments of the struggle to give identity and
meaning to American law and jurisprudence. Contemporary public debates
about Supreme Court nominees are not solely partisan struggles or diver-
gences between judicial philosophies; they are moments of constitutive
formation for American conceptions of law, justice, and democracy. Specifically, the Supreme Court confirmation process rhetorically manifests and

enacts the shift of the adherence to civil and human rights in twentieth-century American law while simultaneously personalizing American conceptions of justice with particular nominees to the High Court. Through an examination of several confirmation struggles, I hope to indicate the importance and gravity of this process for the very constitution of American democracy and law. Before turning to the specific confirmation debates, though, it is necessary to explore the rhetorical and constitutional roots of the process itself.

The Rhetorical Nature of American Law

Systems of law and legal practice are decidedly rhetorical. Of course, at its most basic levels, the law requires that those who practice it engage in persuasion and advocacy. But the rhetorical nature of the law is deeper and richer than simple courtroom speaking; it defines its very ontology.[15]

The primordial function of rhetoric, according to Michael Hyde and Craig R. Smith, is "to 'make-known' meaning both to oneself and to others."[16] This meaning-making function defines the epistemological dimension of the relationship between rhetoric and the law. As Gerald Wetlaufer suggests, rhetoric bears, for those in the practice of law, "not just upon how we say the things we say but also upon *what* we say, on what we are able to *see*, on what we are able to think, on what we are able to know and believe, and on who we are able to be."[17] For law, thus, rhetoric is also an ontological essence, the very telos of law's existence and relevance for the community rooted in its dependence upon language for its very currency.

The relationship between rhetoric and law is also ideological. The law attempts to make known and demarcate the nature of human communal behavior. It strives to determine what is acceptable and unacceptable, which behaviors are permitted and which are forbidden. As such, it tries to provide some rationality to the contingency of human conduct in communities. In the process of providing that rationality, the law also works to rhetorically define the very nature of the community itself. This process occurs in a variety of settings that bear upon and express the law, from trials and legal opinions to television programs and Supreme Court confirmation hearings. James Boyd White puts it most clearly when he maintains that "the law is an art of persuasion that creates the object of its persuasion, for it constitutes both the community and the culture it commends."[18]

Consistent with this understanding of American law, my goal here is to explore the Supreme Court confirmation process's ideological role in the public expression of the law and, by extension, on the discursive formation of the American polity. In this discovery, I seek to "seriously engage the political implications of the relationship between rhetoric and law for *life-in-society*."[19] That exploration pays particular attention to the commitments expressed in a variety of discourses and by a variety of voices in the confirmation process. Such commitments play a significant part in the articulation of American law, be they "property rights," "liberty," "civil rights," "reproductive freedom" or "privacy." Analyzing the manner in which such commitments are implicated and expressed in Supreme Court confirmation debates demonstrates our use of these public debates for understanding the fundamental American commitment to justice.[20]

The origins of the confirmation process for Supreme Court justices are found in the constitutional provisions of Article II that require the president to nominate and, with the advice and consent of the Senate, to appoint justices of the Supreme Court. The precise meaning and historical derivation of that provision are matters of some dispute.[21] Rather than revisit that debate, and its accompanying preoccupation with the framers' intent,[22] I offer an interpretation of the Constitution that, in part, explains the evolving personalization of the Supreme Court confirmation process.

The Constitution, among its various confluent motives, is a characterological document compelling repeated and vigilant monitoring of the individuals chosen as the guardians of its republican liberty.[23] This interpretation also locates in the Constitution the roots of what I term "ideological embodiment," or the fusion that occurs between individual character and the communal demarcation of ideology.

Characterology and the Constitution

"A written Constitution," Kenneth Burke suggests, "which is continually referred to as a basis of decision, is a *calculus* of motives."[24] For Burke, such motives express the "Constitution-beneath-the-Constitution," or the expression of an environment, a context for the enactment of future acts and behaviors.[25] Burke's understanding motivates a multilayered reading of the Constitution, a sense of the document as it exists on different levels to manifest the American government.

Burke concludes that the American Constitution was crafted primarily as a capitalist instrument designed to offer protection from the abuse of governmental power and to instantiate property rights.[26] His economically driven reading of the Constitution would view the appointments process as designed solely to assure that like-minded elites were selected to office via procedures that limited the franchise and restricted popular access to government. I do not deny this reading, though I believe it is reductionistic to assert that such a reading is the *only* way to interpret the complex text of the Constitution and its accompanying rhetorical justifications. Similarly, readings of the Constitution that rely singularly on its institutional or procedural meanings are also limited. The Constitution exists instead, I maintain, on several different levels, and I want to suggest that the Constitution might also be read as a *characterological* document.

By characterology, I am referring to the study and evaluation of individual character and personality.[27] This reading of the Constitution sees a focus on character and persona as one of the important dimensions of the Constitution, operating alongside its institutional, or economic, or political levels, and yielding a political culture in the United States that is similarly multifaceted. Moreover, this reading reflects the preoccupation during the founding period with character and explores how that preoccupation might work within the Constitution. Forrest McDonald maintains, for instance, that an understanding of the founders' sense of republican virtue emerges from the personality of George Washington, a man "ever concerned, almost obsessively, with creating and then living up to what he called his 'character'—what in the twentieth century would be called his reputation or public image."[28] Indeed, rooted in the cultural ethos of the period, Washington "strove, therefore, not only to act honorably, but to cultivate a reputation for doing so."[29] John Adams was also preoccupied with questions of character and fame. In his classic collection of treatises on the subject, the *Discourses on Davila*, Adams concluded that "a desire to be observed, considered, esteemed, praised, beloved, and admired by his fellows, is one of the earliest, as well as keenest dispositions discovered in the heart of man."[30]

This conception of characterology contributes to the long-standing concerns about character and ethos in rhetorical theory and political decision-making. Isocrates noted that "the man who wishes to persuade people will not be negligent as to the matter of character,"[31] while Aristotle theorized the importance of ethos as a form of artistic proof to demonstrate the moral character of a speaker.[32] The discussion of character delineation in the *Rhetorica ad Herennium* also reveals the importance of this dimension of rhetoric and argument for the classical theorists.[33] In the realm of constitutional interpretation, ethos was appropriated by Philip Bobbitt in his discussion of constitutional theory. Seeking a broader, social sense of ethos, Bobbitt writes of ethical arguments as those "whose force relies on a characterization of American institutions and the role within them of the American people. It is the character, or ethos, of the American polity that is advanced in ethical argument as the source from which particular decisions derive."[34]

To study character, Jerry Frug maintains, the critic must engage the literary, psychological, and sociological overtones characteristic of leadership in a community where public people embody "cultural and moral ideals."[35] The Constitution's emphasis on character and leadership manifests the power of such ideals for the American polity and implicates these aspects of public life with the formation and perpetuation of the communal foundations of the American polity. This power is noted by Alasdair MacIntyre when he maintains that a society's characters are "the moral representatives of their culture and they are so because of the way in which moral and metaphysical ideas and theories assume through them an embodied existence in the social world."[36] The characterological nature of the American Constitution permits, indeed compels, a character/leader-based politics. The result is the embodiment of ideology, and the commitments that constitute ideology, with particular individuals facing scrutiny as they attempt to lead. This phenomenon is similar to the concept of characterization defined by Celeste Condit as "universalized descriptions of particular agents, acts, scenes, purposes, or agencies," and their most "important feature rhetorically is the powerfulness of their meanings."[37]

Characterology therefore works as a "Constitution-beneath-the-Constitution," or an additional explanation of the substantial nature of America's constitutional framework. It is a political style, to use the language of Robert Hariman. "Politics is an art," writes Hariman, and the analysis of politics must account for political style, or "a coherent repertoire of rhetorical conventions depending on aesthetic reactions for political effect."[38] In many ways, the characterology I define here is a fusion of what Hariman calls the courtly style (concerned with "the body of the sovereign, [that] displaces speech with gesture, and culminates in immobility")[39]—a style in resurgence in the contemporary mass mediated environment—and the embodiment characteristic of a republican style (a characteristic that "epitomizes the republican identification of politics and persuasion, for embodiment is a rhetorical accomplishment that in turn fuses speech and action, speaker and subject, technical artistry and political status").[40]

An elucidation of the characterological dimensions of the U.S. Constitution requires an exploration of its emergence from the Articles of Confederation as well as the actual rhetoric of character found in the document

itself and in the discourse urging its ratification by the several states following the Constitutional Convention of 1787.

Constitutional Origins/Constitutional Texts

The Constitution was drafted in a symbolic and political environment dominated by the Articles of Confederation, a maligned and misunderstood
foundation of the American constitutional experiment. According to the
conventional interpretation, the Articles of Confederation were a failed effort at a loose affiliation of states that remained essentially sovereign and
independent. This confederation did not allow for a strong national government, denied that government a reliable income source, and was resist-
ant to change.[41]

Revisiting the Articles of Confederation, some historians argue for the
more central role of this document in the formation and intellectual origins
of the American Constitution. Understanding the theoretical orientation of
the Articles of Confederation "is useful, perhaps essential, to understanding
better the full range of competing and interacting principles within American democracy," according to Robert Hoffert.[42] Indeed, much of the Constitution is simply an adaptation of provisions found in the Articles of
Confederation. The supremacy, privileges and immunities, and full faith
and credit clauses of the Constitution are drawn directly from the Articles
of Confederation, and "many of the additional textual powers granted to
the new government [under the Constitution] were ones that the old government had been exercising in practice."[43]

Because the framers of the Constitution were revising the Articles of
Confederation, it is no surprise that much of the language of the Articles
survives in the Constitution.[44] Of equal significance, though, are those provisions in the Constitution that are *not* found, or even suggested, in the Articles of Confederation. Such provisions mark the significant modifications
in government that are formative of the American constitutional experiment because it is in this modification process that the unique character
and substantiality of the Constitution is located.

While the Articles provided for a loose federal government comprised
primarily of a Congress, the Constitution constructs a governing structure
that is sophisticated and delicately, almost precariously, balanced between
branches with largely separate powers. Notably, however, while both documents construct governmental structures, only one, the Constitution, is
significantly concerned with the individuals serving in that government.
Only Articles V and IX of the Articles of Confederation address the staffing

of the federal government, and the rhetoric of these Articles is decidedly different from the provisions of the Constitution framing similar concerns.

Article V of the Articles of Confederation sets the term limits and representation parameters of a state's representatives in Congress.[45] Article IX establishes the power of Congress to select commissioners and judges from the states to settle intrastate disputes and a "Committee of States" from among their ranks for purposes of executive and judicial functions.[46] These provisions are formulated with reference to balanced representation between states, with some mention of terms and compensation. There is no sense in these provisions of the qualifications or character required of the individuals chosen to fill the offices of the federal government. Indeed, the Articles of Confederation are silent about the nature, quality, or requirements for individuals who people and operate its federal government. Such is not the case with the Constitution, marking a significant evolution in the rhetorics of government and political philosophy circulating at the time and in the formation of the American polity.

The U.S. Constitution expresses and contains two constitutions: "a constitution of power, and a constitution of limits," according to John Leubsdorf's reading. A constitution of power "exists to make governmental action possible [and] it trusts those who govern," while a constitution of limits "exists to prevent governmental abuse, and distrusts those who govern."[47] The characterological nature of the Constitution is trapped by and expresses the tension between a constitution of power and one of limits. While it establishes the nature of individual qualification and power within the governmental structure enacted, the Constitution simultaneously provides limits and tests for the exercise of individual authority. Put differently, while the Constitution establishes elaborate procedures to ensure the character and quality of the officials who people the government, it also seeks to limit their powers, to restrict what they can do, and thus manifests a suspicion of its own capacity to produce leaders of character and repute.

To "establish justice" and to secure the "Blessings of Liberty,"[48] the Constitution's framers constructed a government in the first three articles of the document they drafted in 1787. Each article consists of two parts: a specification of who shall be allowed to hold public office along with the conditions of their selection/election, and a designation of powers possessed by each of the three branches of government. Interestingly, the descriptions of election/selection procedures precede the specification of powers granted to the three branches. In so doing, the Constitution limits the exercise of power by first indicating who shall be allowed (and, by implication, not allowed) to exert power and authority with its governmental system.

Article I specifies the age and residency requirements for members of Congress while also prescribing the methods of election and terms of office for representatives and senators. Section 5, clause 2, allows that "each house may determine the rules of its proceedings, punish its members for disorderly behaviour, and, with the concurrence of two-thirds, expel a member."[49] Before discussing the presidential role as commander in chief or the specific executive powers of the presidency, the Constitution devotes a nine-clause section of Article II to the construction of an elaborate scheme for selecting and replacing the president of the United States. To ensure the fidelity of the executive, the framers commanded that the person elected president recite a public oath assuring a commitment to the Constitution and a willingness to "preserve, protect, and defend" it.[50] The president is also given the authority to nominate "and by and with the advice and consent of the Senate" to appoint ambassadors, justices of the Supreme Court, and "all other officers of the United States."[51] Article III establishes a judiciary whose officers are guaranteed steady compensation and an appointment for life and "during good Behaviour."[52] Impeachment of any officer of the U.S. government is an arduous process, ensuring that the results of the election/selection procedures are respected.[53] Of the amendments added to the Constitution, seven deal directly with selection/election methods to public office (the Twelfth, Fourteenth, Seventeenth, Twentieth, Twenty-second, Twenty-third, and Twenty-fifth)—well over a fourth of the twenty-seven amendments.

On one level, then, the dialectic of the Constitution is organized according to Leubdorf's power/limits dichotomy. My reading, however, suggests another dialectic, organized according to a character/power dichotomy that shapes the nature of the American government. Each of the formative articles of the document directly commands specific procedures for the selection of individuals given power in the constitutional system. While it is also concerned with the specific powers of the federal government, the Constitution's rhetorical structure suggests the critical importance of character in the framework and operation of the government it establishes. Arguably such concerns are, by virtue of the structure of the document, even paramount to the granting of powers and the separation of those powers.

Justifying the Constitution

The Federalist Papers, as a specific, historicized rhetoric, is of tremendous importance for understanding the U.S. Constitution. Issued as a series of essays in support of ratification, *The Federalist Papers* is still used contemporaneously to give meaning to the Constitution, and the essays "carry an enormous weight of authority."[54] They are, according to George Carey, "the single most authoritative source for understanding the character of our constitutional system."[55]

In terms of their format, the first fifty-one essays in *The Federalist Papers* address theoretically the need for a revision of the Articles of Confederation and the necessity of ratifying the proposed Constitution.[56] *Federalist Paper* No. 52 begins the justificatory rhetoric of the particular governmental scheme proposed in the Constitution, and such justification frequently regards the proposals for the selection of congressional representatives, presidents, and judges. Moreover, these proposals are viewed as essential to the protection of liberty within the constitutional formulation. As James Madison argues in No. 52, "it is essential to liberty that the government in general should have a common interest with the people, so it is particularly essential that the branch of it under consideration [the House of Representatives] should have an immediate dependence on, and an intimate sympathy with, the people."[57] Such dependence comes from the means of election specified in Article I.

The theme that the Constitution's selection/election procedures protects popular liberty recurs regularly throughout *The Federalist Papers.* Madison, writing in No. 62, claims that an unfortunate consequence of republican government may be the tendency "that those who administer it may forget their obligations to their constituents and prove unfaithful to their important trust." For this reason, the Senate is constituted, argues Madison, as a "salutary check on the government [that] doubles the security of the people."[58] Alexander Hamilton, writing as Publius in No. 68, maintains that the system for selecting the president "affords a moral certainty that the office of President will seldom fall to the lot of any man who is not in an eminent degree endowed with the requisite qualifications," fulfilling the true test of a good government, or "its aptitude and tendency to produce a good administration."[59]

As quoted above, Hamilton concludes in No. 76 that the advice and consent requirement will allow for the appointment of "judicious" individuals who will manifest the "character of its [the Union's] administration."[60] Finally, as to the structure of the judicial branch, Hamilton in No. 88 justifies its separation from the other branches by arguing that "liberty can have nothing to fear from the judiciary alone, [and] would have everything to fear from its union with either of the other departments." It is upon this basis that he advocates the system established by the Constitution allowing for judicial service during good behavior.[61]

The Consequences of a Characterological Constitution

As the foundation of the American civil religion,[62] the Constitution is a multifaceted text that issues specific commands and forms the substance of the American republican system. One primary motive of this text is its concern for the character of the individuals who occupy public office and who dominate public life. As it emerged from the Articles of Confederation, the Constitution sought to ensure that people of high caliber occupied its offices and that the selection procedures for those individuals protected and manifested that virtuous character. The system of government proposed by the Constitution depended upon that virtue for success, *The Federalist Papers* suggests, and the maintenance of that virtue allowed for the protection and expansion of republican liberty. The contemporary focus of political life on the character and image of political figures, therefore, is not altogether surprising given its ideological origins in the founding document of the Republic.

The Constitution's concern for character encourages political rhetorics that are driven in large measure by concerns of individual merit or malevolence. Kathleen Hall Jamieson documents this tendency throughout the history of presidential campaigning, noting that advertising the character and quality of presidential aspirants is as old as the Republic.[63] The process of nominating and appointing Supreme Court justices is similarly dominated by concerns of qualification and character.[64]

Another significant consequence of a characterological Constitution is the tendency for the demarcation of the American community to emerge from image-based rhetorics concerning the character and quality of those who occupy public office. In the American context, collective life as defined rhetorically is frequently organized and referenced by particular individuals via the narratives that tell their (and the community's) stories. Examples abound, from the log cabin myths we tell about our presidents to stories of wartime heroism and straight-talking moderation that surround Senator John McCain to the legendary struggles of Martin Luther King Jr., Susan B. Anthony, and César Chávez. These stories and so many others are dominant in the rhetorics that shape the American sense of national identity and communal values.

The fusion of collective identity with individual character has profound implications. The study of ideology involves the "interpretation of symbolic forms which seeks to illuminate the interrelations of meaning and power," in order to understand the exercise and maintenance of power.[65] Rhetorically, ideology is defined by the commitments (sometimes called values, ideographs, ideas, or touchstones) that organize and express the political language controlling public behavior and giving meaning to collective experience.[66] Examining ideology in this way attends to a community's "discursive record [as that record] chronicles the social changes that have taken place in that society."[67] The characterological orientation of American government motivates the definition of such commitments according to their relationships with particular public characters. The political language of the American community, therefore, is often a language of character and personality such that the foundations of that language achieve their primary meaning through their embodiment with particular public characters.

Ideological Embodiment and the Supreme Court Confirmation Process

The critical scrutiny of Supreme Court confirmations thus offers an explanation for the material operation of ideology in public, political texts, recognizing the constitutive power of such rhetorics.[68] This book examines the confirmation process as a rhetorical one, as an articulation of the nature and substance of U.S. political culture. As such, the book attends closely not only to the public debates and hearings about Supreme Court nominations but also to the mediated translations of these encounters to the larger community.

Supreme Court confirmations offer the American community an opportunity to assess and delineate its commitments to justice, the law, and civil liberties. In most contemporary instances, a nomination to the Supreme Court entails intense scrutiny of a nominee through detailed public hearings. The nominee comes to embody an ideological stance, and the process, therefore, invites investigation into the very nature of American law. At bottom, the differentiation of communal ideology that occurs in the Supreme Court confirmation process is fundamental to the formation of the community itself.

Not all Supreme Court confirmation debates, though, enact or contribute to our ideological formation. Recall that ideology refers to the political language that a community uses to define communal beliefs and to
dictate or guide public behavior. For a Supreme Court confirmation debate
to have an ideological impact, the nomination would have to invoke and
involve profound public concerns. Some twentieth-century nominations
were quickly approved with little or no public hearings or debates and thus
little discernible ideological impact. For example, President Herbert
Hoover's nomination of Benjamin Cardozo in 1932 was approved by the
Senate with no debate or discussion ten seconds after its announcement.[69]
Other nominations were complicated for reasons other than the ideological
or political positions of the nominee.[70] While interesting, such nomination
moments are not my main concern here, given their relative rhetorical in-
significance to the ideological demarcation of American law.

My focus is on those confirmation debates that significantly enacted and
expressed ideological struggling, particularly about the nature of justice,
rights, and the role of the law in the U.S. polity. Some of these debates resulted in the Senate's consent to the nomination, while others ended in rejection and disappointment for the nominee and the appointing president.
Some were protracted, highly mediated debates that engulfed and motivated public attention. Others were more subdued, less public, but still
highly significant for the larger community. But all of these public deliberations in some way performed and manifested meaningful political tension
within the American community at various stages of the last century.

Antecedents to the
Twentieth-Century Confirmation Process

Despite contemporary rhetorics to the contrary that uphold a pristine, non-
political confirmation process for Supreme Court nominees, the process
has been highly political since the earliest days of the nation. In 1795,
Chief Justice John Jay resigned from the Supreme Court to become the
governor of New York. To replace Jay, President George Washington
turned to John Rutledge of South Carolina—a former associate justice on
the High Court who was chief justice of the South Carolina Supreme Court
at the time of his elevation. Though he served briefly as a result of a recess
appointment, Rutledge earns the distinction of being the first presidential
Supreme Court nominee to be rejected by the U.S. Senate.

Rutledge was an eminent jurist, a well-regarded patriot with solid credentials and an established judicial temperament. He was rejected by the

Federalist majority in the Senate for a straightforward, overtly political reason—he opposed the Jay Treaty. As reported in the *South Carolina State-Gazette* on July 17, 1795, Rutledge and other leaders from the state met in Charleston "to consider whether the impending treaty of amity, commerce, and navigation, between the United States and Great Britain, is not degrading to the national honour, dangerous to the political existence, and destructive of the agricultural, manufacturing, commercial, and shipping interests of the people of the United States." As reported by this newspaper and several others throughout the nation, Rutledge's opposition to the treaty was impassioned, as when he "declares he had rather, the President should die, dearly as he loves him, than he should sign that treaty." For Rutledge, the treaty "was an humble acknowledgement of our dependence upon his majesty; a surrender of our rights and privileges, for so much of his gracious favour as he should be pleased to grant."[71]

Among Federalists, Rutledge's speech was sacrilege, and because it was so widely reported, it caused a sensation in Philadelphia and New York. Edmund Randolph, for instance, wrote to President Washington on July 29, saying, "the conduct of the intended Chief Justice is so extraordinary, that Mr. Wolcott and Col. Pickering conceive it to be a proof of the imputation of insanity."[72] William Bradford also questioned Rutledge's sanity in a letter to Alexander Hamilton: "The crazy speech of Mr. Rutledge joined to certain information that he is daily sinking into debility of mind & body, will probably prevent him to receiving the appointment I mentioned to you."[73]

Upon Rutledge's rejection by the Senate on December 15, 1795, reactions poured forth in letters, all responding to the decidedly political nature of the Senate's decision. Eight days after the Senate vote, President Washington wrote to Edward Carrington, expressing no surprise or particular displeasure at the exercise of advice and consent. "It had been expected that the Senate wou'd not confirm the appointment of Mr. R——," the president wrote, "and so it has happened."[74]

Indeed, just six years prior to the Rutledge rejection, Washington noted in comments to the Senate that "as the President has a right to nominate without assigning reasons, so has the Senate a right to dissent without giving theirs." The first president also felt it important that the president refrain from attending debates on nominations: "nor for the Senate on the other hand to be under the smallest restraint by his [the president's] presence from the fullest and freest enquiry into the Character of the Person nominated."[75] Washington's immediate successors also commented on the Senate's move. John Adams, writing to Abigail Adams, noted the pain he felt for his friend John Rutledge but remarked that the negative vote could have positive consequences—"C. Justices must not go to illegal Meetings and become popular orators in favour of Sedition, nor inflame the popular discontents which are ill founded, nor propagate Disunion, Division, Contention, and delusion among the People."[76] Also appreciating the role of politics in the process, Thomas Jefferson wrote to William B. Giles at the end of the year that "the rejection of Mr. Rutledge by the Senate is a bold thing, because they cannot pretend any objection to him but his disapprobation of the treaty. It is of course a declaration that they will receive none but tories hereafter into any department of government."[77] None of these presidents expresses concern about the abuse of the Senate's power, a sense that the Senate passed its judgment on illegitimate grounds, or an argument for the president's preeminence in the appointments process. Instead, each of these founders articulates an understanding of advice and consent in all of its political meaning.

Few of the founders were more involved and more instrumental in forming and justifying the U.S. Constitution than James Madison, and his comments on the meaning of the advice and consent provision as the nation's fourth president are instructive of the early dynamics involving this constitutional power. In early 1811, Madison saw his nomination of Connecticut's Alexander Wolcott rejected by the Senate. Viewed as an extreme partisan by Federalists in the Senate, Wolcott was "an attorney of little distinction," who only received nine votes of the thirty-three cast.[78] At the time, Madison did not react, but two years later, in a message to the Senate, he responded to a request for meetings with senators preliminary to his appointment of an ambassador to Sweden. In his reaction, Madison noted "the Executive and Senate, in the cases of appointments to office and of treaties, are to be considered as independent of and coordinate with each other. If they agree, the appointments or treaties are made; if the Senate disagree, they fail." Madison defines the shared powers of Article II uniquely here, recognizing the consent dimension of the advice and consent clause as predominant and restricting the behavior of the Senate as concerns their advisory capacity. "The appointment of a committee of the Senate," Madison maintained, "to confer immediately with the Executive himself appears to lose sight of the coordinate relation between the Executive and the Senate which the Constitution has established, and which ought therefore to be maintained."[79] For Madison, the president and the Senate share power as a function of Article II, even as the advisory power of the Senate is limited, and there is little in Madison's exposition of Article II that envisions a presidential prerogative or primary right in the area of appointments and treaties.

Several presidents throughout the early nineteenth century reflected on the appointments power in Article II, usually arguing for the exclusive nomination power of the presidency. Facing a requested justification for the removal of a Tennessee surveyor from the Senate, Andrew Jackson refused to yield to what he saw as the Senate's "unconstitutional demands" that were an "encroachment on the rights of the Executive."[80] For Jackson, removal of appointed officials from office was a presidential prerogative. The Senate also possessed a constitutional prerogative, in Jackson's view, and he disclaimed all rights "on the part of the President officially to inquire into or call in question the reasons of the Senate for rejecting any nomination whatsoever" in a message to the Senate concerning appointments to the Bank of the United States. Even as he upheld the Senate's autonomy, though, Jackson also affirmed the president's independence: "As the President is not responsible to them [the Senate] for the reasons which induce him to make a nomination, so they are not responsible to him for the reasons which induce them to reject it."[81] From Jackson's presidency came a powerful expansion of the presidential prerogative in appointments and nominations, an expansion troubling to Jackson's opponents as the presidency became the preeminent site of federal appointment, patronage, and spoils.

One of Andrew Jackson's staunchest Whig opponents in the Senate was Virginia's John Tyler.[82] Upon his accidental elevation to the presidency with the death of William Henry Harrison in 1841, Tyler was forced to confront his views on advice and consent from a different perspective. At the outset of his term in office, as he sought to claim the presidency as his own, Tyler remained true to his Whig principles. In his Special Message to the Congress assembled in special session in June 1841, Tyler vowed "[w]ith anxious solicitude to select the most trustworthy for official station," even as he acknowledged that "I can not be supposed to possess a personal knowledge of the qualifications for every applicant [and] I deem it, therefore, proper in this most public manner to invite on the part of the Senate a just scrutiny into the character and pretensions of every person I may bring to their notice in the regular form of a nomination for office."[83] Tyler further invited the Congress's involvement in presidential appointments and promised that he "shall also at the earliest proper occasion invite the attention of Congress to such measures as in my judgment will be best calculated to regulate and control the Executive power in reference to this vitally important subject."[84]

President Tyler soon discovered that Congress was more than willing to encroach upon his nomination prerogative, and his position regarding advice and consent shifted noticeably as he "broke with the Whig leaders in Congress and found himself a President without a party."[85] The relationship between Tyler and Congress deteriorated fairly quickly, and by March 1842 the President was rebutting the House of Representatives's attempt to obtain background information about presidential appointees and the appointment process. In reply to the House, Tyler articulated an almost Jacksonian vision of presidential prerogative: "The appointing power, so far as it is bestowed on the President by the Constitution, is conferred without reserve or qualification. The reason for the appointment and the responsibility of the appointment rest with him alone."[86] For the rest of his term, particularly as concerned his Supreme Court nominations, Tyler learned quickly of the Senate's ability to "paralyze the constitutional functions of one or both of the other branches of the government,"[87] as it stalled, refused to act, or rejected outright several of his nominations to the High Court. But from his relatively untenable position as the first vice president to succeed to the presidency, Tyler nonetheless argued for a primacy in the executive's role over appointments.

Justice Henry Baldwin's death in 1844 offered Tyler another chance to fill a Supreme Court seat, though he was unable to secure assent to his choices—Tyler holds the distinction of having the most nominees to the Supreme Court rejected by the Senate.[88] The Baldwin seat remained open for many months, and the appointment of George Woodward to the seat by James K. Polk is another revealing instance in the history of advice and consent. Polk's primary consideration in making the Woodward appointment was party loyalty and geographical representation on the Court—he first offered the seat to his secretary of state, James Buchanan.[89] Buchanan rejected the offer, and some months later Polk turned to Woodward. Woodward was a nativist who incurred disfavor from Democrats and Whigs alike, including the powerful Pennsylvania senator Simon Cameron, and was rejected by the Senate on a vote of 20–29 in January 1846.

The most interesting aspect of the Woodward case was Polk's struggles with Buchanan over influence and advice in filling Baldwin's seat. The president's diary is a fascinating document for what it reveals about Buchanan's persistence. On Christmas Eve, 1845, Buchanan visited the

White House to lobby Polk on behalf of John M. Read, a Federalist from Philadelphia. Polk was reluctant to nominate a Federalist: "I have never known an instance of a Federalist who had after arriving at the age of thirty," the president wrote, "professed to change his opinions, who was to be relied on in his constitutional opinions." Polk further noted his resolve "to appoint no man who was not an original Democrat and strict constructionist."[90] The next day, Christmas, Polk reported no visitors except Buchanan, who claimed to have spent "two sleepless nights" worrying about the Woodward appointment. Polk reports that his secretary of state complained that the president should have only made the Woodward appointment upon consultation with his cabinet. "I promptly answered," Polk reported, "that as President of the United States I was responsible for my appointments, and that I had a perfect right to make them without consulting my Cabinet, unless I desired their advice."[91] An interesting moment, Polk here reacts not to the exercise of advice and consent by the Senate but to an assertion of advisory prerogative by a member of his cabinet. Reacting to rumors that Buchanan would leave the cabinet in January 1845, Polk recorded in his diary that Buchanan's "greatest weakness is great sensitiveness about appointments to office. He has repeatedly seemed to be troubled, and taken it greatly to heart when I have differed with him about appointments and made my own selections."[92] Indeed, throughout his diary accounts of the nomination and rejection of George Woodward, Polk never complains about the Senate's action, except to note the hypocrisy of a senator who feigned fidelity to Polk after voting against Woodward. Instead, Polk confronted a claim of advisory power by a member of his cabinet, and he upheld presidential authority in the process. Curiously, Buchanan faced his own conflict with the Senate when he sought to appoint Jeremiah S. Black in early 1861, just a few months before the end of his term. Black's nomination failed by one vote.[93]

For the remainder of the nineteenth century, presidents faced several contested and rejected nominations for the Supreme Court as the Senate exerted its advice and consent powers. During the Ulysses S. Grant administration, the Senate rejected the nomination of Ebenezer Hoar, and opposition in the Senate forced Grant to withdraw the nomination of George Williams to be chief justice. Many of Grant's correspondents express disappointment at the result.[94] In the case of Williams, numerous improprieties and allegations were raised about the nominee in the Senate. Williams wrote to Grant in January 1874 to lament that "my abilities have been disparaged, and my integrity brought in question, and it seems to me that a public opinion adverse to my appointment has been created which might hereafter embarrass your Administration, and, perhaps, impair my usefulness upon the bench."[95] The next day, Grant withdrew the nomination.

Twenty years following the withdrawal of the Williams nomination, President Grover Cleveland faced the rejection of two nominees to the Supreme Court in one year. Justice Samuel Blatchford died in 1893. Cleveland nominated William Hornblower to replace Blatchford, only to have that nomination stopped by New York senator David Hill. Hill was part of the anti-Cleveland faction in New York, and "Cleveland made no secret of his determination not to conciliate his party enemies."[96] After the Senate rejected Hornblower, Cleveland put forth Wheeler H. Peckham, only to have Hill block that nomination as well. Cleveland's reaction to the rejection was muted. He defended Hornblower's nomination, writing to Don Dickinson that "a man should not be rejected for the place simply because corporations are among his clients, and I hope you will agree with me that in these days of wildness, conservatism and steadiness should not be at a discount."[97] Again, a president thwarted by the politics of the confirmation process, seeing his will rejected by the Senate, withholds comment as to the propriety of the Senate's action or the legitimacy of its role in the advice and consent process.

A century passed from the Senate's rejection of John Rutledge in 1795 to its dismissal of Grover Cleveland's nominees in 1894, and presidential reactions to advice and consent changed little over that period. Presidents from James Madison on sought to preserve presidential independence in the appointments process, rebutting congressional attempts to encroach upon their power in the form of requests for consultation or justification. But missing from the presidential reactions of the eighteenth and nineteenth centuries were complaints about the politicization of the confirmation process or calls for a presidential prerogative in the appointment of justices or government officials. Eighteenth- and nineteenth-century presidents accepted the vagaries of a political confirmation process and in so doing confirmed the dual, coordinate nature of appointments as demarcated in the U.S. Constitution.

The Confirmation Debates of the Twentieth Century

The story of twentieth-century Supreme Court confirmations begins in 1916, when President Woodrow Wilson shocked Washington with his nomination of Louis Brandeis. Brandeis's nomination enacted the skirmishes of a young, industrializing nation grappling with new economic tensions and anxieties. Brandeis was a progressive reformer, a challenger of the status quo, and a Jew. Each of these factors contributed to the anxiety that his nomination elicited from elite circles in Washington and Boston society. Powerful forces sought to keep the "people's lawyer" off the Supreme Court, and the Brandeis nomination heralded the beginning of intense controversy and scrutiny of Supreme Court nominees. Brandeis embodied the ideological ideals of progressivism and reform in ways that threatened existing orthodoxies and political/economic establishments. In lengthy hearings and acrimonious public debate, the Brandeis nomination performed the beginnings of a rhetorical shift in the law, such that "social justice" earned a place, even if only in dissent, in the lexicon of American constitutional jurisprudence.

The Brandeis confirmation also represented a meaningful shift in the conduct and process of Supreme Court confirmations. For the first time, extensive hearings were held concerning the suitability of a nominee to the Court. Furthermore, the process was organized, substantially, around a legal metaphor—the nominee stood accused of specific actions or conduct to be investigated by a tribunal that would pass judgment upon such conduct, with the ultimate verdict rendered as to the nominee's suitability for the Supreme Court. As with any public conflict or controversy, the Brandeis confirmation generated considerable media attention and coverage, a relatively new phenomenon in Supreme Court confirmations. In short, with the Brandeis nomination, the Supreme Court confirmation process became a highly public, supremely rhetorical process, and the Brandeis hearings would establish the boundaries of this process for most of the twentieth century.

Herbert Hoover returned to a familiar figure in American law and politics when he nominated Charles Evans Hughes as chief justice in 1930. Despite initial support, the Hughes nomination evolved into an contest that again tested the limits of progressivism and laissez-faire jurisprudence. Progressives charged that Hughes was a tool of big business and capital, and they worked to prevent his nomination. Hughes was confirmed, but the legacy of his confirmation struggle would linger and doom Hoover's nomination, just three months later, of John J. Parker as an associate justice. Depicted as an enemy of organized labor and an economic reactionary, Parker's nomination was rejected by the Senate, the first Supreme Court rejection since 1894. The Hughes and Parker debates publicly expressed a shift away from "property rights" and "substantive due process" as dominant concerns of American law toward a jurisprudence that privileged a concern for equality and a sense of justice based not in accomplishment but in entitlement.

The Parker nomination was also a harbinger of the importance of race to the American jurisprudence of civil rights and the growing importance of vested interest groups as a rhetorical voice in the Supreme Court confirmation process. Citing speeches from his political campaigns, the National Association for the Advancement of Colored People (NAACP) and others constructed Parker as a racist reactionary, unwilling to accept the role and influence of African Americans in U.S. life and law. The Supreme Court was defined, in this context, as the institution to guard the civil rights and offer constitutional protection for African Americans. Parker's addition to the Court, his opponents suggested, would prevent the Court from achieving its goal of assuring a better life for African Americans through equal protection of the laws.

The issue of race would be a central factor in several nominations to the Supreme Court following 1930. Different nominees would come to embody competing ideologies of civil rights, justice, and equality within a legal system grappling with these complex commitments. In 1967, for example, Thurgood Marshall represented the progress that the civil rights movement achieved by the simple fact of his nomination to the Supreme Court. He was the incarnation of a sense of justice that was blind to color and ethnicity. His detractors, though, saw and characterized him as the apotheosis of all that was dangerous about civil rights, from the threats of activism to the dangers of desegregation. They viewed Marshall as a threat to "justice," which they saw as dependent upon "strict constructionism" and "law and order." Not surprisingly, his historic nomination was also one of the most mordant confirmation struggles of the century.

Only two years later, Richard Nixon sent to the Senate the names of Clement F. Haynsworth Jr. and G. Harrold Carswell, both southerners, as associate justice nominees. Both men faced harsh questioning about their racial views and their commitment to civil rights, along with the examination of their ethics and general qualifications. Both men represented

Nixon's "southern strategy" and thus embodied a perspective toward civil rights that was ideologically controversial. As such, these nominees exemplified the ideological pressures pulling at a United States in the midst of the fight to define civil rights and its meaning for the larger polity. Central to that controversy were the importance of race and the role of the law in upholding equality and justice for all citizens. The rejections of Haynsworth and Carswell resulted in the elevation of Harry Blackmun to the Supreme Court, a Minnesotan, who would gain fame less for his decisions on race and civil rights than for his authorship of the *Roe v. Wade*[98] abortion rights decision.

When Ronald Reagan nominated Robert Bork to the Supreme Court in 1987, many feared the onset of what Senator Edward Kennedy called "Bork's America." Such a country, Bork's opponents warned, would be a place where privacy would disappear as a constitutional principle and women would lose control of their reproductive freedoms. Indeed, much of the conflict concerning Robert Bork and his elevation to the Court addressed issues of individual privacy and autonomy, cornerstones of an evolving sense of constitutional rights and justice in the United States. The Bork nomination thus signaled a shift in ideological skirmishing that embraced issues of privacy and autonomy, along with civil rights and equality, that are most often contextualized within the abortion debate.

Bork's nomination is also significant for what it tells us about the evolving process of Supreme Court confirmations over the span of the twentieth century. Unlike any previous nomination, Bork's was a full-fledged political spectacle complete with dramatic hearings, committed interest groups, and high drama fueled by intensive media coverage. While other nominations received considerable media coverage and public attention, Bork's nomination shifted the confirmation process into the realm of political spectacle, where specific modes of conduct, means of argument, and postmodern grammars of image construction become critical to success or failure. As such, it can be said that political spectacles magnify the importance of character and persona and heighten the role of ideological embodiment in the deliberative process, creating a new framework for political discussion. In the end, these new grammars doomed Bork's efforts to become a justice and defined his role as an ideological and apocalyptic embodiment of New Right legal philosophy.

Just four years later, President George Bush nominated Clarence Thomas for the Supreme Court. A pivotal moment in twentieth-century politics, the Thomas nomination was another postmodern spectacle that reflected the ideological angst of a culture working to value equality, justice, and opportunity within a framework and a history that make such values difficult to manifest. Rhetorically constructed as a worthy nominee because of his emotive and affective personal narrative, Thomas faced scandalous charges about very personal behaviors and responded with powerful and racially charged accusations of his own. The end result was a bookend to the Brandeis nomination, highlighting the profound evolution of the Supreme Court confirmation process over the span of the twentieth century, from deliberative assessment and careful scrutiny of character and qualification to political spectacle, replete with advertisements, lobbying, intensive and constant news coverage, and truncated argument often rooted in image and persona rather than character and credibility.[99]

This book traces the evolution of American law as publicly enacted in the Supreme Court nominations of Brandeis, Hughes, Parker, Marshall, Haynsworth, Carswell, and Bork. It also considers the post-Bork confirmation process with particular attention to the Thomas nomination. In this sense, this work is an attempt to understand and chart the rhetorical trajectories of the Supreme Court nomination process, to examine how the process has evolved over the span of the twentieth century, and to reach the normative conclusion that a politicized, ideologically challenging, complicated, spectacularized Supreme Court nomination process is a good thing for American democracy as it opens up to dialogue and dispute legal ideologies and practices often kept hidden or remote from the larger community.

The century began with severe ideological tensions concerning class, capitalism, and reform. As the twentieth century closed, tensions still existed regarding commitments to equality, opportunity, and civil liberties. These commitments are rhetoricized in Supreme Court confirmation debates addressing complicated questions of race and gender. Through the Supreme Court confirmation process, such ideological commitments are tested, reconfigured, and demarcated. Moreover, they also are embodied in the person of the nominee. Indeed, as this rhetorical process seeks to confirm or reject a potential justice to the Supreme Court, it also significantly expresses the character of justice for the American community.

2

For the Soul of the Supreme Court

The 1916 Nomination of Louis D. Brandeis

There is probably no more important duty imposed upon the President in connection with the general administration of the Government than that of naming members of the Supreme Court; and I need hardly tell you that I named Mr. Brandeis as a member of that great tribunal only because I knew him to be singularly qualified by learning, by gifts, and by character for the position.

President Woodrow Wilson, *The Papers of Woodrow Wilson*

The undersigned feel under the painful duty to say to you that, in their opinion, taking into view the reputation, character and professional career of Mr. Louis D. Brandeis, he is not a fit person to be a member of the Supreme Court of the United States.

A petition signed by seven former presidents of the American Bar Association and presented to the Senate Judiciary Committee

When the name Louis D. Brandeis was announced on the Senate floor as President Woodrow Wilson's newest nominee for the U.S. Supreme Court, observers report that the gathered senators "simply gasped."[1] So notorious was Brandeis's reputation, so complete and well known his progressivism, that the possibility of his ascending to the highest court in the land sent shivers throughout the political worlds of Boston and Washington. His nomination became a signature moment in the early twentieth century, and it demarcated the parameters of Supreme Court confirmations for much of the century, altering this critical constitutional ritual in American political life and offering a new vision of American law for a new and challenging century.

In part, Brandeis's nomination was made more significant by its context, its historical circumstance. After all, the early part of the twentieth century was a time of significant social adjustment in the United States. Caught in the throes of rapid industrial growth and expansion, the United States struggled to reorder public life to adapt to uncertain forces that defied easy explanation. That reordering created a movement, a series of efforts on the part of differing sectors of U.S. society, that we now call progressivism.

Defining progressivism and isolating its particular characteristics are complicated by the complexity of its ideology and the variety of its adherents. Daniel Rodgers concludes that, despite its confusing heterogeneity, progressivism is united around three rhetorics that are constant: "the rhetoric of antimonopolism . . . an emphasis on social bonds and the social nature of human beings, and . . . the language of social efficiency."[2] At a time when business and capital were thriving, reform threatened to undermine corporate success in the name of "social justice" and a concern for "human rights." Progressives in politics, journalism, and academia worked to alter the existing social structures to better protect powerless members of society from an economic system run amok so as to ensure an equitable and just community. At bottom, progressivism sought to "end corruption, promote civil liberties, pass fairer tax laws, and facilitate cooperative enterprises."[3] It was the recognition "that rapid technological change had social consequences" as well as the mechanism by which the community sought to confront those consequences.[4]

Among the pantheon of progressive leaders, few figures stood out more significantly for reformist legal acumen than Louis D. Brandeis. In the early decades of the twentieth century, progressives encountered an increasingly hostile political environment, historian Barry Karl reveals, and they shifted their energies to the courts and litigation in order to achieve social reform.[5] Brandeis was instrumental in these endeavors. Central to his progressivism was a belief in the importance of individual liberty and privacy, a commitment to antimonopolism, and an adherence to the ideals of social efficiency.[6] Indeed, Brandeis's public advocacy "throws into high relief the clash between traditional American individualist values and the opposing tendencies of modernization in Western society."[7]

For many of his contemporaries, Brandeis was an embodiment of progressivism and reform. Numerous newspaper headline writers and editorialists employed the moniker "people's lawyer" as they described the nominee.[8] The *Washington Post* published a digest of editorial opinion from around the country, quoting the *St. Louis Dispatch*'s judgment that Brandeis was a "slashing critic of corporate abuses" and the *Detroit Free Press*'s view that the nominee was a "socialist or a progressive."[9] One letter writer to the *New York Times* called Brandeis "a man in the foremost rank of the makers of modern thought."[10] The *Washington Star* predicted a "big fight" over the nomination because of Brandeis's positions and progressivism, a fight the paper claimed was "not a question about race."[11] Brandeis was such a polarizing figure at the time that Thomas McCraw even likens him in 1916 to Ralph Nader or Jesse Jackson in contemporary times.[12] Given his role in the legal and political world of 1916, it is not surprising that his nomination to the Supreme Court by Woodrow Wilson represented the contemporaneous tensions better than any other single event.[13]

The immediate impact of the nomination was profound. A subcommittee was formed within twenty-four hours to investigate the nominee. The creation of such a subcommittee was unprecedented and signaled the decisive importance of the nomination to the Senate.[14] Indeed, biographer Melvin Urofsky notes, "Few episodes in American history shed so much light on their era, for the lineup of supporters and detractors was a clear demarcation of progressives and those opposed to the reform movement."[15]

The Brandeis confirmation hearings tell an ideological tale of American culture and U.S. legal politics in the Progressive Era. As the Senate assessed the character of Louis D. Brandeis and his fitness for the Supreme Court, it also publicly scrutinized the progressivism and reformism that the nominee embodied. As such, the conflict over his confirmation to the Court offers a historical glimpse into the tensions at work in the formation of an American commitment to progressive reform and the regulation of economic activity.

Brandeis represented a type of progressivism that threatened entrenched forces of capital and business. He sought dramatic reforms in American systems of free enterprise and social policy, holding to a commitment to "social justice." Social justice at the time was a complex concept, defined by Senator Thomas J. Walsh during the Brandeis nomination as the "movements and measures to obtain great security, safety devices, factory inspection, sanitary provision, reasonable hours, the abolition of child labor, all of which threaten a reduction of dividends. They all contemplate that a man's a man and not a machine."[16] In a legal sense, Charles Warren, writing in 1913, defines "social justice" legislation as those laws and regulations that uphold the rights of workers and the subaltern as opposed to those with power and wealth.[17]

Brandeis's opponents found legal refuge in provisions of the Constitution that they interpreted as guarantors of their property rights. As such,
the primary set of tensions that emerged from his confirmation included
conflicts between capitalism and progressivism, between "social justice"
and "property rights," and between reform and the preservation of the status quo.

Progressivism and "social justice" were emerging as legal and political
constructs of some rhetorical stature for the U.S. community by 1916.
When he was nominated to the Supreme Court, Brandeis's personification
of progressivism became a critical component of the debate about his nomination, signaling the developing role of Supreme Court nominees as the
individual and public incarnation of important ideological constructs. In
addition, these hearings are different from earlier Supreme Court confirmations in that they are rhetorically structured according to a trial
metaphor. The nominee stood accused of a series of charges impugning his
character—allegations that attacked his ethics as a lawyer and as a progressive reformer. Advocates represented both sides of the question, and the
"judges" were the senators sitting on the subcommittee. Witnesses and evidence were offered, and a final verdict was rendered.[18]

The forensic framework of these proceedings is of considerable significance for their ideological impact. Legal proceedings seek to establish guilt
or innocence, while deliberative discourse, such as Senate confirmation
hearings, works to determine the rightness or folly of particular social actions. The structuring of this debate according to a trial metaphor amplified
the importance of character during the deliberations and foregrounded
Brandeis's ideological embodiment of progressive reformism.

The hearings worked both structurally and symbolically, then, to enact
the struggle underway over the meaning of progressivism for American life
and jurisprudence. Through the ideological embodiment of progressivism
and reform in the character of Louis D. Brandeis, the American polity publicly disputed its adherence to progressivism and all that this movement
entailed. Moreover, because his confirmation hearings were structured
forensically, these hearings fused progressivism with the character of Brandeis. Ultimately, this confirmation controversy would not only have serious consequences for the nature of American progressivism but also would
profoundly influence the procedures and implications of the Supreme
Court confirmation process for the remainder of the twentieth century.

The "Trial" of Louis D. Brandeis

Louis Brandeis and Woodrow Wilson were, by all accounts, close. Brandeis was an important adviser to Wilson, seeking to influence his policies and to contribute to his thinking about significant social and political issues. Wilson adviser Josephus Daniels maintains that "their minds ran together,"[19] while Philippa Strum argues that Brandeis was of such significance in Wilson's philosophical thinking that he "altered Wilson's conception of the State."[20]

In 1913, newly elected President Wilson sought to appoint Brandeis to his cabinet, potentially as attorney general or secretary of commerce. The opposition to such a move was intense, and Wilson retreated. His nomination of Brandeis to the Supreme Court in 1916 was done with little fanfare and with almost no outside consultation. Wilson was apparently quite pleased with the nomination, and it served him politically as well. Entering the presidential election season of 1916, Wilson needed to assure progressives of his commitment to their cause, and with Brandeis's nomination, he did so "in one grand gesture."[21]

The controversy surrounding Brandeis's nomination was unusual, prompting the unparalleled move by the Senate to establish an investigatory subcommittee. The most recent rejected nominees to the Supreme Court were Grover Cleveland's choices of William Hornblower and Wheeler H. Peckham in 1893–94. Cleveland's nominees were rejected largely because of senatorial courtesy to New York's David Hill, who opposed Cleveland in the state.[22] Also in recent memory of those in government in 1916 was the struggle over the confirmation of Stanley Matthews in 1881, when the Senate consented to the nomination by only one vote. The Matthews confirmation was noted prominently in the majority report of the subcommittee that investigated Brandeis.[23]

The Judiciary Committee subcommittee charged with considering the Brandeis nomination consisted of five senators, three Democrats and two Republicans.[24] The subcommittee commenced its hearings on February 9, 1916, and heard testimony until late March, generating an extraordinary 1,590 pages of statements, documents, and questioning regarding the nominee. Because of the vast scope of these proceedings, outside counsel was hired to guide the subcommittee in its work. This decision on the part of the subcommittee reinforced the forensic nature of the proceedings, though they occurred in a decidedly deliberative setting. Retained to oppose the nomination was Austen George Fox, a New York appeals attorney.

In order to assure that Brandeis's perspective was fairly presented, the subcommittee appointed George Anderson to its staff. Anderson, in 1916, was
a federal district attorney in Boston and a long-standing associate of the
nominee.[25] The subcommittee issued its findings on June 1, 1916, and reported favorably on the nomination by a vote of 3-2 that split according to
party affiliation. As was the custom at the time, Brandeis never appeared
before the subcommittee, but his involvement in his defense was considerable, as he frequently provided documents, records, and advice to those in
Washington advocating his appointment.[26]

As the Republican minority noted in its report, twelve specific charges
were made against Brandeis that questioned his ethics and judicial ability
(although two of the charges concerned the same case).[27] John Frank carefully examined each of the complaints raised by the nominee's opponents,
and his understanding of this case is still resonant. He concluded that, of
the twelve charges, five were immediately discredited and warranted little
attention.[28] The seven remaining charges were elaborately and meticu-
lously set forth by those who opposed Brandeis in both written and oral
testimony. Each of the charges bears directly on the ethics and integrity of
Brandeis, and they call into question the propriety of seating him on the
Supreme Court. Insofar as such charges questioned Brandeis's character as
a progressive advocate, they also worked to challenge the very ethics of
progressivism as an ideological touchstone for the newly industrial United
States.

I focus on one set of charges made against Brandeis as well as the more
general assessments offered about the nominee's overall character and
reputation.

The United Shoe Machinery Case

Of all the charges put forth against Brandeis, the complaints about his conduct in the case of the United Shoe Machinery Company were the most
widely circulated at the time and speak most clearly about how the nominee powerfully represented progressivism and reform in these hearings.[29]
Brandeis served as a director at United Shoe from 1899 to 1906, acting as a
representative for the large stock holdings of a Chicago family. In 1906, he
organized and guided the company's opposition to pending legislation in
the Massachusetts legislature designed to restrict the company's leases.
After severing his connection with the company, Brandeis attacked the
monopolism of United Shoe. Specifically, he counseled a group called the

Shoe Manufacturer's Alliance that sought to break United Shoe's domination of shoe manufacturing in New England.

The switch in Brandeis's thinking about United Shoe, and his active and persistent advocacy against the company's interests after resigning his directorship, motivated the "indictments" against the nominee in this case. In a written statement read to the subcommittee, Sidney Winslow, the president of United Shoe, concluded:

> Mr. Brandeis has, at the instance of new clients, attacked as illegal and criminal the very acts and system of business in which he participated . . . [and] in so doing, his knowledge of our leases and business, acquired while acting as our director and counsel, has naturally been of value. . . . Mr. Brandeis, however, has made false and misleading statements as to our acts and business, both to committees of Congress and elsewhere.[30]

Winslow maintained that this behavior made Brandeis "guilty of unprofessional conduct and of conduct not becoming an honorable man."[31] Acting prosecutorially, Winslow offered many pieces of evidence to support his hostility toward Brandeis and to prove the allegations made against the nominee, including countless documents and transcripts.

Winslow's statement constructed Brandeis as an individual seeking to undermine and destroy a company for which he willfully worked for many years. On this level, Winslow argued that the nominee was dishonest. But the text of his statement also maintained that Brandeis lied to Congress, that he was unprofessional, and that he was dishonorable. The focus of Winslow's attack was clearly on the character of the nominee. Additionally, Brandeis's conduct occurred in a situation in which he sought progressive reform—the breakup of a monopoly. Because Winslow's attack was so personal, and because it was an assault on Brandeis's reform efforts, the text of the statement indicates specifically how ideological embodiment worked in these hearings. Indeed, Winslow drew primarily on Brandeis's own testimony before congressional and state legislative committees as his evidence for the nominee's ethical breaches.[32]

The same inclination to focus on the character and ethics of the nominee is found in the minority report of the subcommittee. As it addressed the United Shoe charges, the minority report found Brandeis wanting in professional propriety. Senator Albert Cummins concluded that "a due regard for professional propriety would have prevented Mr. Brandeis from accepting employment from anyone to attack his former client with respect to the very matters about which he had advised and defended it."[33] California Republican John Works maintained that Brandeis, in this case, was "far from commendable and shows a lack of appreciation . . . of the duty of an attorney to his client and a due sense of the proprieties so necessary to be observed by members of the profession."[34] Works noted that Brandeis "has defied the plain ethics of the profession and in some instances has violated the rights of his clients and abused their confidence."[35] Once again, the statements from his opponents were addressed to Brandeis's lack of "professional propriety" and his unwillingness to accept the "duty of an attorney."

The job of rebutting the charges put forth against Brandeis fell to Edward McClennen, a junior member of Brandeis's law firm and the nominee's chief spokesperson in Washington during the hearings. Concerning the United Shoe Machinery Company charge, McClennen offered detailed records and recollections about the various cases brought by the company in which Brandeis acted as counsel, the particular time frame of those cases, and Brandeis's involvement with the company, as well as pertinent memorandums concerning the matter obtained from Brandeis's files.[36] McClennen's main contention was that Brandeis had severed his official ties to United Shoe prior to advocating the dissolution of its monopolistic control of shoe manufacturing in New England.

Much of McClennen's testimony concerning the United Shoe charges provided a "defense" of Brandeis in this controversy. However, in the process of answering the specific charges, McClennen was also able to testify to the nominee's character and reputation. One of the questions surrounding Brandeis's involvement with the United Shoe Machinery Company concerned payment of fees to Brandeis by the Shoe Manufacturer's Alliance for his opposition to United Shoe. McClennen testified that when his law firm was paid $2,500 by the alliance, Brandeis returned the money to the alliance from his personal funds. As McClennen concluded:

> We [the law firm] are engaged in the practice of law and expect to be paid for practicing law. Mr. Brandeis has a definite percentage of the profits of that firm, and while we can stand it for him to give his time to public causes, he has thought that perhaps it was a little hard on the rest of us to ask him to give his time to public causes when there was a client ready to pay him for those same services.[37]

These remarks work not only to vindicate Brandeis of any wrongdoing but also to demonstrate his character as an individual concerned about fairness and equity. While McClennen, throughout his testimony, offered detail after detail to support Brandeis, he also rescued the nominee's character in the face of considerable assault. Along the way, he testified to Brandeis's ethics and judicial temperament.

McClennen's "defense" was persuasive with the majority members of the subcommittee. Senator William Chilton's majority report noted that "three and one-half years elapsed after his [Brandeis's] resignation from the [United Shoe Machinery] company before he advised any other client on the subject."[38] The report highlighted contradictions in Winslow's testimony and refuted conclusively the charge that Brandeis employed privileged information in his attacks against United Shoe. Chilton concluded:

> The most significant fact in this case is that Mr. Brandeis voluntarily and with no prospect of profit to himself gave up his connection with a profitable client as soon as and because he became convinced that the policy which it was pursuing and would not change was wrong. . . . It may well be asked, How long does an employment mortgage the lawyer's conscience?[39]

Unlike the portrayal of Brandeis offered by Winslow and the Republicans on the subcommittee, this statement defended the nominee as selfless, committed, and principled. Ultimately, his "defense" maintained, Brandeis's conscience would not be "mortgaged" when he confronted the genuine need for progressive action.

Of all the charges made against Brandeis, the United Shoe Machinery Company case elicited the most interest and coverage in the news media. As might be expected, the reactions to the charges were mixed. These reactions also tended to mirror the differing interpretations of the events in this case offered at the confirmation hearings. The *Nation*, which opposed the nomination, maintained that "it is impossible, in our opinion, to study the whole record in this case . . . without coming to the conclusion that his [Brandeis's] course was not only in clear violation of professional ethics, but was marked by a shiftiness and lack of moral delicacy which are hurtful to his reputation."[40] Those who supported the nomination were much more favorable in their discussion of this charge. William Hard, writing in the *Outlook*, defended Brandeis's conduct in the case at length, seeing the events as evidence of his "independence of mind."[41] The *New Republic*, recognizing the seriousness of the charges, devoted an entire editorial to them, concluding that this case proves that the nominee is "at once judicial, rarely courageous, possessed of an ardent and calm sense of justice which to him is truth in action." They maintained that the case "illustrates strikingly his unprejudiced love of truth, and his courage to pursue it."[42] And the *Literary Digest* quoted a *Philadelphia North American* editorial that defined Brandeis's behavior in the United Shoe case as an example of his commitment to "public duty," when he "force[d] the company to obey the law."[43]

The debate over the United Shoe charges reveals in stark relief just how these hearings ideologically tested progressivism as embodied by Louis Brandeis. Here was a situation that directly related to the basic concerns of progressivism. A large monopoly was controlling virtually all shoe manufacturing in the United States. United Shoe was a gigantic conglomerate, and its very existence, coupled with its monopolistic control over the industry, directly challenged many of the principles expressed by Brandeis as anathema to progressivism. Brandeis's actions, and the assessment of those actions in the confirmation debates, reveal how Brandeis came to personify progressivism. To his detractors, he betrayed the rules and mores of his society and his profession, and such a betrayal was a commentary not only on his personal ethics but also on the worthiness of his reformist cause. To his supporters, Brandeis gave up considerable profit in order to realize the achievement of principle and the betterment of society—the *New Republic* even defined this case as a demonstration of Brandeis's sense of "justice" and his courage in achieving reform.[44] As such, Brandeis's actions in the United Shoe case represented the progressive movement, and the interpretation given to those actions expressed the tensions present in the American community over the meaning and extent of economic and industrial reform.

Brandeis's Reputation and Judicial Temperament

All of the charges made against Louis Brandeis in his confirmation hearings turned on relatively delicate and subjective interpretations of facts and legal ethics. Together, though, they worked to promote a critique of Brandeis's character as ethically suspect, lacking in full legal or judicial propriety or both. Peppered throughout the endless legal documents and testimony in the hearings were comments that spoke directly to Brandeis's overall reputation and character. In an actual trial, such commentary would constitute character testimony—evidence presented to offer insight as to motive and state of mind. In these hearings, this testimony worked to malign Brandeis's motives, and, as such, it reinforced Brandeis's quintessence of progressivism.

Many members of the Boston establishment testified against Brandeis and assailed his overall reputation within that community. Attorney Edward Hutchins, for instance, offered that Brandeis's "general reputation at the bar is that he is a lawyer of great ability, but not straightforward."[45] Another Boston attorney, Francis Peabody, maintained that "he [Brandeis] is considered as a conspicuously able man; but, on the other hand, his reputation is that he is not always truthful, that he is untrustworthy, and that he sails under false colors."[46] A series of petitions from "citizens of Massachusetts" appear in the transcripts, asserting that "we do not believe that Mr. Brandeis has the judicial temperament and capacity which should be required in a judge of the Supreme Court."[47] The ultimate condemnation came from the minority members of the Senate Judiciary Committee in their final report:

> We regard it as a great misfortune and a distinct lowering of the standard heretofore maintained in making appointments to this high office that one should be selected for the place whose reputation for honesty and integrity amongst his associates at the bar has been proved to be bad, which reputation has been justified by his own course of conduct.[48]

What stands out most prominently in these comments is the question of "honesty." The charge that Brandeis was dishonest worked not only to reinforce many of the specific ethical charges that he faced but also to assail his overall qualifications for the Supreme Court. His alleged lack of honesty also impugned progressivism. Brandeis was extremely successful in his reform efforts, and the attacks on his honesty suggested that such success was not the result of principle or expert advocacy but rather came from subterfuge and manipulation.

News sources were quite interested in the question of Brandeis's reputation, and they were eager to offer their own editorial stance on the issue. Of course, conflict promotes coverage, and there was a pronounced discrepancy of opinion as to Brandeis's standing in his community. *Current Opinion*, for example, quoted the editor of the *Boston Common*'s judgment that the nominee was "the most liked and most hated man at the bar in America."[49] In its coverage of the hearings, the *Literary Digest* remarked that there was a "sharp contrast of view on the legal character" of Brandeis.[50]

Those media outlets opposed to the nomination portrayed Brandeis as an individual incapable of working with others and who was so politically committed as to preclude judicial qualification. The *Nation* concluded that Brandeis's reputation must be suspect because of the great number of

Boston lawyers willing to testify as such. The journal opined that "we must bear in mind that nothing could be more distasteful to a respectable lawyer than to give testimony adverse to the character of a fellow member of the bar."[51] The *New York Times* was more pointed. It editorialized that Brandeis lacked judicial qualities necessary for appointment to the Supreme Court and that his elevation to the Court was only an attempt to secure political advantage. Immediately following the nomination, the newspaper concluded that "Mr. Brandeis would take his seat upon the bench equipped with a variety of preconceived and firmly held opinions relating only remotely, if at all, to questions of law and the constitutional powers of Government." The paper argued that "the court needs no advocate, can never put itself in the position of pleading for any cause."[52] Two days later, the *Times* accused the Wilson administration of appointing Brandeis in order to win pending Sherman antitrust cases. It maintained that to "nominate and confirm with intent to 'pack' the court of the Government prosecutors would be as flagrant a breach of trust as to put upon the bench an avowed partisan and active advocate of the defendant corporations."[53]

The charge that Brandeis lacked a good reputation, that he was not of correct judicial temperament, was both an attack on the individual and an attack on the progressivism he represented. Joel Grossman and Stephen Wasby maintain that attacks on "judicial temperament" are generally designed to "mask criticism of the ideology [the nominee to the Court] is likely to pursue while on the bench."[54] Brandeis was assailed for his ethical improprieties, yet of all of the cases from his rather famous and lengthy legal career, his ethical lapses, according to his accusers, occurred only in those cases where he sought progressive reform. "Social justice" as an ideological principle is, therefore, discredited because of the means used to achieve it. Indeed, this line of argument against the nomination manifested what Max Lerner calls "a stiffening of the ranks, a closing of the gaps in the phalanx, [and] a call for a united front" from those opposed to progressivism. Lerner concludes that, fundamentally, the protest against Brandeis "was a crucial recognition by the old order that the new order was threatening."[55]

Amid the antipathy directed at Brandeis in the hearings were occasional, and eloquent, proclamations of his upstanding character and reputation. Most such declarations argued that those who assaulted the nominee were either his vanquished opponents from past legal battles or the forces of reactionary business interests working to prevent progressive reform and change. Moreover, in the process of testifying to Brandeis's character, his champions also upheld the power of reform for the betterment of American society.

One of the most articulate statements in favor of Brandeis occurred in testimony presented to the subcommittee on February 29, 1916. During hostile testimony concerning Brandeis's reputation in Boston, George Anderson entered into the record a letter from Boston attorney and Harvard Law School instructor Arthur D. Hill. Hill noted that Brandeis was unpopular with the Boston bar because "[h]e is a radical and has spent a large part, not only of his public, but of his professional career, in attacking established institutions, and this alone would, in my judgment, account for a very large part of his unpopularity."[56] Despite his unpopularity, Hill maintained that it was generally recognized that Brandeis was dedicated to public service and the public good. In a final, and powerful, conclusion, Hill reflected on Brandeis's fitness for the Supreme Court:

> Throughout his career he has shown unusual interest in and sympathy for those classes in the community upon whom economic conditions bear hardly, and has devoted a large part of his time and energy to measures he believed would help them. The work which he has done along these lines has been sanely planned and carefully worked out, and he has acquired in doing it an unusual grasp of those social and economic conditions which underlie many of the most important questions with which the Supreme Court will have to deal.[57]

Hill's letter went unchallenged in the subcommittee. His analysis was "candid," according to legal historian A. L. Todd, and as a Republican from Boston, "[i]f anyone had the right to examine the motives of the anti-Brandeis petitioners, this man did."[58] But this statement of support is more powerful than just an attack on Brandeis's opposition. Hill positioned Brandeis squarely in the radical progressive movement. But Hill also upheld that radicalism as precisely the quality that made Brandeis qualified for the Supreme Court. Brandeis's reform efforts, Hill maintained, gave the nominee the necessary knowledge and sympathies to be an effective justice on the Supreme Court.

Brandeis's opponents were also attacked by Roscoe Pound, a professor and soon-to-be dean of Harvard Law School, in a letter appended to the subcommittee report on the nomination. Pound maintained that Brandeis possessed the "judicial temperament" necessary for the Supreme Court and that those who dispute the nominee's temperament "know very little about him and base their opinions upon newspaper accounts of the vigorous battles which he has fought as an advocate."[59] Similar testimony came from a missive by Charles Eliot, emeritus president of Harvard, that was also included in the subcommittee's report. Eliot testified to Brandeis's abilities as a student while at Harvard Law School and argued that Brandeis's "professional career has exhibited . . . much practical altruism and public spirit." Eliot concluded by upholding the nominee's judicial qualifications: "He has sometimes advocated measures or policies which did not commend themselves to me; but I have never questioned his honesty or sincerity, or his desire for justice. He has become a learned jurist."[60] These commentaries, as with the Hill letter, rehabilitated Brandeis's reputation while simultaneously recognizing that his reform efforts encountered hostility from business and capital because of the nature of progressivism and not from some ethical lapse on his part.

Attacking Brandeis's opponents was popular with those news sources favorable to the nomination. The editorials of the *New Republic* are typical.[61] Its March 11, 1916, editorial maintained that Brandeis "has been a rebellious and troublesome member of the most homogeneous, self-centered and self-complacent community in the United States."[62] Two weeks later, the same magazine cited testimony from the hearings that called the Boston legal community an "aristocracy," offended by Brandeis's betrayal of "group loyalty," because of his progressive efforts concerning the United Shoe Machinery Company and the railroads.[63] The *Independent*'s condemnation of the "Brandeis heresy *trial*" concluded that the nominee had offended "great and powerful interests" in his work, and those interests were determined to "break him."[64] The ideological resonance of this vision of Brandeis for broader audiences is demonstrated in a letter printed in the *New York Times* from Alexander Lanier on February 1, 1916. Lanier calls Brandeis "a Socialist and an impracticable theorist, hostile to vested rights, and given to promoting class hatreds and social unrest." Such a progressive, in Lanier's view, had no place on the Supreme Court, an institution "justly regarded by our people as the bulwark of their property rights."[65] Moreover, Brandeis's alleged socialism and his lack of judicial temperament are identified as the chief reasons for opposition to his nomination in a review of editorial opinion in dozens of newspapers from around the country offered by the *Literary Digest*.[66]

Of course, by attacking the entrenched, reactionary opposition to Brandeis, his champions powerfully reinforced his image as the "people's lawyer." The *New Republic* maintained that Brandeis "is not often amiable in a fight" but that this lack of sociability derived from his commitment, his belief that the law "has not been a game . . . [and] the issues he has dealt with have been great moral questions."[67] Other writers worked to support Brandeis's potential as a judge and suggested that his prior advocacy on behalf of progressive causes did not disqualify him as a Supreme Court justice. The *Outlook* identified Brandeis's progressivism as the primary source of the controversy over his nomination and argued that such sympathies are the best reason for his confirmation because "[t]he rights of property are exceedingly well represented in all our courts."[68] Hamilton Holt, writing in the *Independent*, cited Brandeis's experiences as an arbitration judge in the New York garment industry and concluded that the nominee's mind "is the clearest, the keenest, and the justest I have ever known."[69] His supporters in the news media sought to reconcile the apparent opposition between Brandeis as the "people's lawyer" and Brandeis the possible Supreme Court justice. The *Independent* even featured an article noting the facial resemblance between Brandeis and Abraham Lincoln, complete with altered artist's renderings to illustrate the similarity.[70]

As an object of ideological struggle, Brandeis came to embody competing visions of progressivism. This public debate over Brandeis's ideological identity and relevance appears in a letter to the *New York Times* from Louis Jacoves, who responds to an attack on Brandeis from Alexander Lanier. Jacoves defended Brandeis's progressivism and argued that "a court composed of eight-ninths conservatism and one-ninth idealism—granted the one-ninth be impractical idealism—it is a craving subscribed to at least by the members of the labor unions of this country, and investors to railroads . . . and those represent one-ninth of the voting people and are entitled to a representation in our highest tribunal."[71] The diversity of editorial and public opinion about the Brandeis nomination, in a time before rampant public opinion polling and focus groups, speaks to the penetration of the Brandeis controversy into the larger public consciousness. Brandeis was the personification of different dimensions, competing valences, of progressive thought and action, and his nomination to the Supreme Court occasioned public discussion of this ideological challenge to prevailing orthodoxies of government and law.

A series of politically meaningful statements of support for Brandeis came from those senators on the subcommittee who advocated consent to the nomination. The subcommittee's chair, William Chilton, maintained that "there is more in the life of Mr. Brandeis as shown by this record to incline one to the belief that he has the qualities of a good judge than there is to the contrary." Chilton disputed each of the charges set forth against Brandeis, even remarking that the nominee's opponents presented "absolutely nothing to reflect upon Mr. Brandeis's character as a man or a lawyer."[72]

Senator Thomas J. Walsh of Montana took his advocacy of Brandeis to a different level and issued a spirited defense of Brandeis as a nominee and as a progressive. Walsh's statements manifested a truly progressive view of the law that was beginning to take hold in the early twentieth century. He worked from the premise that the "bar is still the bulwark of the liberties of the people." "To it," he continued, "they must look in the future as they have looked in all of our history for fearless champions."[73] The senator demonstrated how each of the ethical charges against the nominee were unfounded and then proceeded to issue a defiant defense of Brandeis as a progressive:

> The real crime of which this man is guilty is that he has exposed the iniquities of men in high places in our financial system. He has not stood in awe of the majesty of wealth. He has, indeed, often represented litigants, corporate and individual, whose commercial rating was high, but his clients have not been exclusively of that class. He seems to have been sought after in causes directed against the most shining marks in it. He has been an iconoclast. He has written about and expressed views on "social justice."[74]

The progressive rhetoric of this statement encapsulates the entire struggle over the Brandeis nomination. Brandeis was opposed by individuals who feared what he embodied—the encroachment of progressivism into all facets of American politics. Brandeis attacked the existing financial system and was vigorous in his assault. For his efforts, he was appointed to the Supreme Court and his nomination attacked. In the process, his reputation and character were also questioned. But as Walsh pointed out, the real reason for the opposition was because Brandeis embodied the ideological ideals of reform, progressivism, and "social justice." As the embodiment of these principles, he challenged the status quo and existing power relationships, and the threatened elites waged a powerful campaign to prevent his elevation to the Supreme Court. Ultimately, of course, they were unsuccessful.

Anti-Semitism and the Brandeis Confirmation

Louis D. Brandeis's "trial" was largely fought over questions of ethics, reputation, and an incredible volume of legal minutiae. Lurking beneath the entire proceedings with only an occasional public airing was the issue of Brandeis's religion. That Brandeis was Jewish only enhanced and magnified the alleged threats presented by the progressive forces to the established systems of business, government, and law. Brandeis's religion served, significantly, as a marker of his character as an outsider, as someone unworthy of membership on the Supreme Court.[75] Throughout the many pages of the hearings and reports from the Senate Judiciary subcommittee, Brandeis's religion occurs in the deliberations only once to any significant degree. Francis Peabody, a lawyer from Boston, was testifying as to Brandeis's reputation at the Boston bar on March 2 when he was asked by Senator Duncan Fletcher to recall any particular incidents that would demonstrate Brandeis's "disingenuity." The following exchange ensued:

> *Senator Fletcher.* Were any other cases brought to your attention to corroborate that adverse impression?
>
> *Mr. Peabody.* Then came this case of his denial of employment by the Illinois Central, and, although it made no particular difference to me in a way, yet, until within a number of years—I can not tell how many—I did not know he was a Jew. I would say that that had not been disclosed until a few years ago. That made no difference as far as my opinion of him goes, except so far as it was made prominent and before that had not been known.[76]

There were no follow-up questions, no additional probing concerning these remarks. "Peabody had ventured on ground where none in the room wanted to stay," notes A. L. Todd, "so the innuendo in his remarks was left unchallenged." Interestingly, Peabody was the final witness called to testify about Brandeis's reputation in Boston.[77]

The unseemliness of open discussion of Brandeis's religion did not lessen its importance in the struggle for his confirmation. Significant efforts were made to stifle open Jewish support for the nomination by Brandeis's allies. Attorney General Thomas Gregory tried to minimize Jewish activity on the nomination, preferring that its outcome be determined by party loyalty and affiliation.[78] McClennen maintained in retrospect that anti-Semitism was the primary reason for opposition to the nomination, particularly from the Senate's southern Democrats.[79]

While those involved in the congressional proceedings were reluctant to discuss the nominee's religion openly, the news media mentioned it frequently. Although Brandeis's Zionism was not a prominent news item, the simple fact that he was Jewish excited mostly positive commentary. The *Literary Digest*, noting some distress on the part of editorial writers nationally about the nominee's religion, concluded: "That President Wilson has chosen a Jew of high legal attainments to sit in the Supreme

Court is generally held wise and commendable."[80] The same journal featured an article that highlighted Brandeis's religion, observing the jubilation in New York City's East Side Jewish community when the nomination was announced. The article quotes extensively from a *New York Tribune* piece that reports the reactions of this community. Although generally complimentary, the account nonetheless highlights Jewish difference, with quotations in German and Yiddish. It describes a man "with long, black forelocks escaping from an over-sized hat-band" and gives the impression that Brandeis's true loyalties were with a Jewish Palestine, where he would like to be president.[81] The *Outlook* maintained that Brandeis's religion was a reason for confirmation because the Supreme Court needed to represent all religions.[82] *Current Opinion* labeled Brandeis a "Bohemian Jew" who fled Europe with his family following the revolutions of 1848.[83] In a pointed fashion, all of the descriptions of Brandeis mention his religion, and thus the media accounts reinforced alleged differences between Jews and Gentiles that bubbled beneath the public deliberations about his confirmation.

There is still considerable disagreement among historical observers as to the role of anti-Semitism in this particular controversy. Richard Friedman maintains that it played a "subsidiary role in the dispute,"[84] while Ronald Rotunda claims that the opposition to Brandeis "laced its rejection of his social activism with extensive anti-Semitic rhetoric."[85] The actual anti-Semitic rhetoric in the hearings and in the official congressional reports is sparse, but there are nonetheless indications that Brandeis's religion was another marker of his status as outside the legal establishment. That Peabody references the nominee's Judaism as an index of his untrustworthiness is not accidental.

Brandeis's religion was further "evidence" of his status as an outsider, as someone different and unusual. Given the structuring of the debate over the nomination as a "trial," this evidence was mentioned alongside commentary about the nominee's overall reputation and indexed powerful stereotypes designed to sow doubt and suspicion about Brandeis's fit on the High Court. Just as Brandeis the progressive was an outsider, so, too, was Brandeis the Jew on the fringe of mainstream American life, according to this construction of his religious heritage. Jewishness thus served as a further indication of Brandeis's lack of fitness, in character and temperament, for the Supreme Court.

The Soul of the Court

There are several explanations for the eventual confirmation of Louis D. Brandeis to the Supreme Court. One is that Woodrow Wilson engaged the controversy directly in a letter to Senator Charles Culberson, chair of the Judiciary Committee, in May 1916. Wilson wholeheartedly supported his nominee, arguing that of all the individuals he knew at the bar in the United States, Brandeis was "exceptionally qualified" because of his "impartial, impersonal, orderly, and constructive mind."[86] Another explanation points to Wilson's and Brandeis's direct persuasion of key senators. Brandeis met personally with Senators Hoke Smith of Georgia and James Reed of Missouri, both critical members of the Judiciary Committee, and both men were favorably persuaded by their meetings with the nominee.[87] President Wilson made a stop in the hometown of North Carolina senator Lee Overman and lavishly praised the senator in a speech. Soon thereafter, Overman became an ardent Brandeis champion.[88] Ultimately, on June 1, 1916, Louis D. Brandeis was confirmed by the Senate by a vote of 47-22, with twenty-seven senators not voting.[89] With this vote, the Senate reached its verdict about the suitability of placing Louis Brandeis on the Supreme Court. In so doing, it ended what one historical commentator called "the bitterest nomination controversy in the history of the Court."[90]

The implications and consequences of this nomination controversy for U.S. politics and law are significant. First, from a historical perspective, the Brandeis confirmation reveals many of the tensions present in the Progressive Era of the early twentieth century. Because of his well-known progressive activism, Brandeis's nomination to the Supreme Court put into ideological play "social justice" as a commitment for American jurisprudence. As the United Shoe case revealed, the commitment to "social justice" was tested and examined through the actions of the nominee, through his efforts to achieve reform and his attacks on corporate power. His actions in that case functioned, depending upon one's point of view, either to validate the antimonopolism of progressivism or to demonstrate how reform was only achieved through dishonesty and a lack of principle. From either perspective, judgments about progressivism and reform were fused with judgments about Brandeis and his conduct.

Of course, the contrasts that the partisans in the case drew between progressives and reactionaries served to polarize the debate. The layers and complexities of the Progressive Era and the variety of its reforms are simplified in this controversy. But that very simplification is instructive. The clear demarcation of those opposed to Brandeis and his supporters is largely a function of the forensic nature of these deliberations. That same clarity worked well in a mass media environment dominated by partisan media outlets with starkly defined political motives. Because Brandeis was constructed as a defendant facing specific indictments of his character and ethics, and because those indictments were so clearly related to his reform efforts, the differentiation between his supporters as progressives and his opponents as reactionaries served both parties well.

Second, the Brandeis struggle altered significantly the nature of Supreme Court confirmation debates. Not only were such debates readily politicized, they were now open to public scrutiny and examination. The news media took an active and persistent interest in the outcome of the confirmation process. As a result, the Supreme Court was renewed as a site of political and ideological struggle, much as it had been during the period leading up to the Civil War.

The Brandeis confirmation debate manifested a different framework for Supreme Court nominations that, in essence, placed the nominee on trial, forcing him or her to justify past actions and overall worthiness for a seat on the Court. Supreme Court nominations had always been politicized,[91] but the "forensic" nature of the Brandeis struggle instantiated a system that shifted the focus of nomination debates to the character of the nominee as manifested in past actions and in judicial philosophy. The ensuing twentieth-century conflicts over the nominations of Harlan Fiske Stone, Charles Evans Hughes, John J. Parker, Abe Fortas, Clement F. Haynsworth Jr., G. Harrold Carswell, Robert Bork, and Clarence Thomas indicate just how significant the Brandeis hearings and debates were for the nature of this important constitutional process. Indeed, this controversy was frequently referenced in the debate over Richard Nixon's nomination of Clement Haynsworth in 1969, with Haynsworth's supporters arguing that their nominee would be cleared of his ethical problems in the same way Brandeis was cleared fifty-three years earlier.[92]

The Brandeis controversy also began a process of Supreme Court confirmations wherein the nominee came to be associated with—came to embody—particular legal and ideological positions. Brandeis was the public embodiment of progressivism and reform; the struggle over his confirmation was therefore profoundly important on this ideological level. That Brandeis was a "radical" and that he was Jewish only worked to heighten the relevance of his nomination to the Supreme Court. Future nominees would come to embody different ideological commitments, including "civil rights," "property rights," and "judicial restraint." This process of ideological embodiment has magnified the Supreme Court confirmation process and intensified its importance for the U.S. political system.

The *New York Times* was not alone in 1916 when it argued that the Supreme Court was "of prime necessity a conservative body . . . since it is the great regulator of the machinery of Government."[93] The Brandeis nomination challenged that view, making him the incarnation of legal progressivism and forcing ideological dispute as to the nature and range of the law in America. This confirmation struggle, surely, was "a fight for the soul of the Supreme Court, [and] a deep-cutting controversy about its role in American life."[94] Perhaps that is what all confirmation controversies should be about. Such debates should engage important public concerns, they should challenge ideological orthodoxies. Not only should such debates assess the "soul of the Supreme Court" and its role in the community, they should also focus attention on the nature and quality of the nominee. The Brandeis nomination set the stage for the Senate's continued engagement with these questions and this process over the span of the twentieth century. His eventual confirmation assured that the principles of reform and "social justice" would be expressed, if only in dissent, as part of the constitutional law of the United States for many years to come.

3

From Property Rights to Human Rights

The Hughes and Parker Nominations of 1930

[T]he history of civilization shows that those who acquire great amounts of property are owned by their property; that they take on the very characteristics of the property they own . . . they grind down the rights of weaker human beings by force of law through the decisions that are written by judges who place property rights above human rights.

Senator Clarence C. Dill, *Congressional Record*

So I have said that in America human rights, personal rights—the rights to life, to liberty, and to property—are the rights which we must guard.

Senator Samuel Shortridge, *Congressional Record*

By 1932, Herbert Hoover finally got it right. Facing a perilous reelection fight and an economic depression that was crippling both the nation and his political future, Hoover still managed to, and without controversy, successfully appoint a justice to the Supreme Court. And his nominee was even a Jewish, Democratic jurist from New York. Benjamin Cardozo was universally acclaimed as one of the most eminent jurists in the United States, and Hoover was pressed by members of the Senate and the legal community to forward his name for the Court. When the president did so, the Senate unanimously and by voice vote confirmed Cardozo. The confirmation process took about ten seconds.[1]

The Cardozo nomination stands in stark contrast to Hoover's struggles just two years earlier to put two of his nominees on the Supreme Court. On February 3, 1930, two simultaneous announcements were made by the White House. Chief Justice William Howard Taft was resigning because of poor health, and President Hoover was nominating Charles Evans Hughes as Taft's successor. Just a month later, in response to the unexpected death of Justice Edward Sanford, Hoover nominated John J. Parker of North Carolina to the vacated seat.

Both these nominations were highly controversial, and they both speak to the ideological shifts in American law during the early Depression years of the 1930s. The Hughes and Parker nominations also demonstrate the evolving and highly politicized nature of the Supreme Court confirmation process, complete with adversarial hearings, contentious floor debates, and heated commentary in the nation's media. The Parker nomination, moreover, saw the rise of regularized and organized interest group opposition to a Supreme Court nominee, signaling yet another development in the process.[2] Ultimately, both of Hoover's nominations in 1930 continued the twentieth-century trajectory of politicized and adversarial debate about Supreme Court nominations that was put into place just fourteen years earlier during the Brandeis struggle.

In those fourteen years, between the Brandeis confirmation battle and the Hoover appointments of 1930, U.S. law emanating from the Supreme Court changed dramatically. The Supreme Court restrained itself in the first two decades of the century, rarely overturning reform legislation or overruling the will of legislatures.[3] In the 1920s that restraint disappeared when, in the words of Laurence Tribe, the Supreme Court validated and upheld the rights of Americans to be "overworked, underpaid, or unemployed."[4] Through a series of rulings, the Court "shackled almost every effort at social reform and virtually destroyed the movement for social legislation."[5]

An array of cases from the Court struck down state and federal reform efforts as violating the due process clause of the Fourteenth Amendment. In *Coppage v. Kansas*,[6] for instance, the majority of justices declared prohibitions of yellow-dog contracts unconstitutional restrictions of the right of contract.[7] Though the Court had sustained the regulation of working hours in *Muller v. Oregon*[8] and *Bunting v. Oregon*,[9] it did not allow for the regulation of wages for women in the District of Columbia.[10] Two separate cases, *Hammer v. Dagenhart*[11] and *Bailey v. Drexel Furniture Co.*,[12] invalidated legislative attempts to regulate child labor. Still other cases nullified legislative action seeking to regulate business entry (*Adams v. Tanner*[13] and *Liggett Co. v. Baldridge*[14]) and prices (*Williams v. Standard Oil Co.*[15]). In short, the Supreme Court in the 1920s "could be counted on to save the businessmen from the folly of legislators, [who were] egged on by demagogues expounding human rights at the expense of property rights."[16] While the Court only nullified twenty-five laws from 1790 to 1900, Ernest Sutherland Bates reveals, nineteen legislative reform efforts were declared unconstitutional by the Court from 1920 to 1930.[17]

Given the increased activism of the Supreme Court, presidential nominations to the Court since the Brandeis fight were surprisingly uncontroversial. President Warren Harding's appointments of William Howard Taft as chief justice and George Sutherland as an associate justice were confirmed by the Senate the day they were announced. The Senate also easily approved Harding's nomination of Edward Sanford. Only the nomination of Pierce Butler generated some controversy, and he was eventually confirmed by a vote of 61-8.[18] Calvin Coolidge's nomination of his attorney general, Harlan Fiske Stone, as an associate justice in 1925 encountered opposition, based largely on Stone's active pursuit of legal action against a sitting member of the Senate, Burton Wheeler of Montana. For the first time in history, a nominee appeared before the Senate Judiciary Committee when Stone went to Capitol Hill to address the concerns raised against him. Appearances by nominees before the Senate would become a routine part of the confirmation process; in 1925, Stone's testimony was remarkable, and he was finally confirmed by a vote of 71-6 on February 5.[19]

The relative serenity of Supreme Court confirmations ended in 1930. Hoover's nominations of Hughes and Parker, and the confirmation debates they elicited, publicly enacted, in highly charged ways, another ideological shift in American law. Both nominees became the ideological embodiment of "property rights," and both were portrayed as opponents of the assurance of "human rights." Hughes was eventually confirmed, while Parker was rejected, but the debates over their nominations and their character as potential Supreme Court justices are rich with ideological meaning. These rhetorical interactions publicly contributed to the expansion of the social commitment to "human rights," while they simultaneously narrowed the warrant of "property rights" in U.S. political culture. These debates thus expressed significant redemarcations in American law concerning the constitutional guarantees of rights and equality. In short, they manifested the rhetorical and ideological vicissitudes under way in the early 1930s as prevailing conceptions of justice underwent marked changes in both emphasis and meaning within the American constitutional framework.

The Hughes Nomination

Few individuals in 1930 possessed as impressive a résumé of public service as Charles Evans Hughes. He was, for six years, an associate justice of the Supreme Court, resigning in 1916 to run for the presidency as the Republican Party's nominee, barely losing to the incumbent, Woodrow Wilson. A former governor of New York, Hughes served as secretary of state in the Harding administration and was sixty-eight years old at the time of his nomination by President Hoover.[20]

Hughes was, by all accounts, reluctant to accept Hoover's nomination. His biographer, Merlo Pusey, records that the nominee did not seek the appointment to the Court, nor did he relish the loss of freedom that accompanied such a position.[21] Hughes's own notes indicate that his main concern was the possible debate over his nomination. Highlighting the fact that he was deeply involved in Republican Party politics and was "very active in my law practice," he agreed to accept the nomination only if Hoover could guarantee that it would not "evoke any contest over confirmation."[22] Hoover was confident there would be no opposition in the Senate.

Arguably, the only previous chief justice designate to elicit more opposition than Hoover's nomination of Hughes was Roger Taney, nominated to lead the Supreme Court by President Andrew Jackson in 1836.[23] The initial reaction to Hughes's nomination was positive, but it soon became apparent that there was serious opposition in the Senate from Democrats and progressive Republicans. Within a week, senators were giving speeches in opposition to Hughes's selection, and there were calls for Judiciary Committee hearings. Though such hearings never occurred, the floor debate in the Senate bespeaks many of the ideological tensions brought forth by this nomination; tensions that would resurface in full force during the Parker confirmation struggle. The prevailing economic and social circumstances in the country in the 1930s made such tensions particularly salient, as the stock market collapse of 1929 had dispelled "the aura surrounding American business."[24]

The opposition to Hughes emerged only a week after his nomination, even though most agreed that confirmation was imminent. On February 10, Senator George Norris of Nebraska, a progressive Republican and chair of the Judiciary Committee, acquired the floor to report favorably on the nomination, as directed by his committee. Upon fulfilling his obligation from committee, Senator Norris then spoke in harsh and pointed opposition to Hughes's confirmation. His speech made two specific arguments that formed the foundation of attacks on Hughes in the Senate.

First, Norris charged that the nominee's resignation from the Court in 1916 to seek the presidency made this nomination to the same Court inappropriate. The senator maintained that this particular instance "certainly establishes a precedent which tends to lower the standards of the Supreme Court tribunal—a precedent which in the future may result in the weakening of that great court and the lowering of its standards down to the level of the political machine."[25] Norris argued that such a precedent would be followed by future justices and that Hughes also used his prestige as a former justice of the Supreme Court to his advantage in his law practice.

Second, Norris put forth his progressive view that Hughes represented corporations and wealthy clients in his private practice and that such work closely aligned the nominee with these interests. From Norris's perspective, the power of wealth was considerable and dangerous, and Hughes was the legal embodiment of such wealth. As the senator evinced, "Perhaps it is not far amiss to say that no man in public life so exemplifies the influence of powerful combinations in the political and financial world as does Mr. Hughes." Norris went on to claim that wealthy individuals were attracted to Hughes as counsel because of his former position on the Supreme Court, reinforcing his first concern about the nominee's earlier resignation from the Court. Ultimately, Norris argued that Hughes's viewpoint was "clouded" and that "he looks through glasses contaminated by the influence of monopoly as it seeks to get favors by means which are denied to the common, ordinary citizen."[26]

Interestingly, Norris's construction of the nominee is the flip side of the arguments put forth in opposition to Louis Brandeis in 1916. Then, the nominee was a dangerous radical who threatened entrenched and powerful business interests. Brandeis's progressivism, moreover, was deceitful in its application and dangerous in its results. Hughes, conversely, embodied the exact opposite—he was a man who epitomized capital and who was unconcerned about the plight of the downtrodden. This embodiment framed the debate about Hughes's nomination, and it references how the politics of the era influenced Supreme Court nominations and their disposition in the Senate.

Norris's speech cued a series of oppositional floor statements against
Hughes's appointment. On February 11, the indomitable Senator William
Borah of Idaho rose first to state his views concerning the nomination. In a
powerful expression of the ideological struggle represented by this nomination, Borah condemned Hughes for his relentless representation of corporate wealth. According to Borah, the nominee held the "extreme view"
that "exalts property rights above all other rights . . . [and] which believes
that the Government, and all that the Government represents, may be reduced down at last to the rights of property." Asserting that no more profound issue faced the nation than the battle between the rights of property
and the rights of individuals, Borah asked the Senate to consider the following: "When during the last 16 years has corporate wealth had a contest
with the public, when these vast interests claimed advantages which the
public rejected, that Mr. Hughes has not appeared for organized wealth
and against the public?"[27] The next day, Senator Clarence Dill rose to continue the attack upon the nomination. He maintained, as did Borah, that
Hughes was a tool of corporate clients and that the nominee believed in
the ascendance of property rights over human rights. Hughes, the Washington Democrat argued, was "the *embodiment* of culture, good fortune,
and worldly success," who "believes in the doctrine of property rights as
superior to human rights under the law which he has so ably advocated."[28]
Dill's remarks elicited considerable coverage in the *Washington Star*—a
page-one story that detailed the entirety of the senator's remarks. The *Star*
highlighted Dill's warning that "if the members of the Supreme Court do
not watch their step in handing down opinions on economic questions the
people of the country will find a way to change the Constitution and upset
the judiciary itself."[29]

As the debate continued, there was considerable agreement about the
ability and stature of the nominee. But by conceding Hughes's expertise,
his opponents skillfully were able to embody the principle of property
rights with his character. The remarks of Texas senator Tom Connally are
typical in this regard. The senator admitted that Hughes was an individual
of "personal character" and "personal integrity" yet still charged that because of his views concerning property rights, Hughes was "more dangerous to the rights of the people than would be a weaker and less able
man."[30] Hughes's great ability even magnified his dangerous ideology for
his opponents. As Republican John Blaine of Wisconsin forcefully concluded: "whenever evil influence, whenever corrupting influence, whenever corporate influence, whenever the blighting influences of

combinations and monopolies have sought counsel and leadership, we find that their paths have all converged in the office of Mr. Hughes."[31]

Themes from the floor debate about Hughes appear in the media coverage of this nomination. Because it occurred in such a relatively short period of time, however, the debate attracted only a modicum of media coverage. Most of the commentary was in hindsight and focused on the intensity of the Senate debate. The *Nation* editorialized that the nomination was "a bad appointment," in part because of the nominee's "worship of property rights, and, afterwards, his readiness to take retainers from any great corporation, any master of privilege."[32] Calling the debate the "greatest peace-time controversy over the Supreme Court in history," William Murphy Jr. read the opposition to Hughes as a reflection of his embodiment of a federalism that "seeks to enfold property rights and privileges in a protecting mantle of law expounded by a Court far removed from and impervious to popular sentiment."[33] The *New York Times* remarked that the battle between property rights and human rights was really a regional conflict, with the farm states and the agricultural South pitted against the industrial heartland where senators "declared for Property and against human rights."[34] The political nature of the Hughes confirmation was also noted by Floridian C. E. Chillingworth in a letter to the *New York Times* when he praised his senators who "quite properly ignored all political considerations and voted to confirm the appointment of Justice Hughes."[35] Even three weeks after Hughes's confirmation, Caleb S. Miller felt that it was necessary to defend the new chief justice in a letter to the *Washington Star*, noting that Hughes "was the antithesis of the corporation lawyer, as he attacked mercilessly and utterly routed some of the largest and most influential corporations in the country, if not the world."[36]

The support for Hughes during the Senate floor debate was tepid, probably because his confirmation was a largely foregone conclusion. Most statements of support simply recited Hughes's impressive credentials. Senator Robert Wagner's comments are illustrative: "Mr. Hughes needs no defender. As to the question of his fitness to hold this great office it seems to me that his high character, the esteem in which the public holds him, and his past record of public service, completely answer the question."[37] Massachusetts Republican Frederick Gillett maintained that Hughes's corporate client list evidenced the nominee's "great intellectual acumen, breadth of view, power of argument, and a painstaking, unflagging industry."[38]

Hughes's defenders did address, tentatively, the issue of "property rights" and the reordering of U.S. law (and the Supreme Court) advocated by the opposition. Samuel Shortridge, a California Republican, suggested that "there is no such thing as a 'property' right as a right apart from a person; property has no rights. Men and women have rights to that which we call property."[39] The most extensive defense of the nominee was delivered by Illinois Republican Otis Glenn, who directly challenged the embodiment of "property rights" with the person of Charles Evans Hughes. "The story of the life of Mr. Hughes," Glenn proclaimed, "reveals his sympathy on the side of the downtrodden and the oppressed."[40] The senator proceeded to cite several legal cases and political events where Hughes represented the interests of the poor and the disenfranchised. Not only was Hughes the champion of the oppressed, according to Glenn, but he also represented the United States, where "no other nation in the world is advancing so rapidly in humanitarian measures for the protection of all human rights and liberties and freedom."[41]

This view of Hughes was echoed in the *Washington Star* profile written by Silas Hardy Strawn, a former president of the American Bar Association. Strawn's account specifically noted that Hughes "was no pampered son of the idle rich" and offered that Hughes's father was a Baptist immigrant from Wales while his mother was a schoolteacher. From this biography, Strawn concluded, "it was almost inevitable that Charles Evans Hughes would find his interest in the serious matters of life." Strawn also quotes labor sources from New York who praised Hughes after his term as governor as "the greatest friend of labor laws that ever occupied the governor's chair in Albany."[42] For those who supported the nomination, Hughes characterized public service, honor, and integrity and was uniquely qualified to be chief justice of the United States.

On February 13, Charles Evans Hughes was confirmed by a vote of 52-26, with eighteen senators not voting.[43] He served as chief justice for eleven years. The outcome of his confirmation debate, though, is less important than its demarcation of the tensions between "property rights" and "human rights" as ideological commitments for U.S. law and politics. Though he may have been too harshly judged by his opponents,[44] Hughes nevertheless came to embody "property rights" and all that that concept stood for in the progressive rhetorics of early Depression-era America. "Justice," at this time, was evolving as a touchstone of American communal identity, at once the shield that protected business and capital from the intrusion of government as well as the weapon that would guarantee the rights of individuals from tyranny and oppression. While it is the case that the quick nomination and the brief Senate debate attracted little public attention in the mass media, the Hughes nomination still enacted important shifts in the American conception of law, shifts that would resurface with even more consequence just a few weeks later with President Hoover's nomination of John J. Parker.

The Parker Nomination

Herbert Hoover adhered to the belief, maintains historian Francis O'Brien, that "Supreme Court appointments should not be made on grounds of political expediency."[45] Political expediency, though, is perhaps the only explanation for Hoover's appointment of John J. Parker to the Supreme Court in March 1930. Hoover hoped to "dramatize Parker as the symbol of all he desired in the new elite leadership for the South," according to Donald Lisio, and the appointment was meant to mobilize and reward southern Republican political efforts.[46] Furthermore, despite the fight over the Hughes nomination, President Hoover did not appear sensitive to the political reality that "his judicial appointments were not going to be taken lightly."[47] As the Hughes debate revealed, though, the Senate that would consider Parker's nomination was a highly charged and pointedly partisan political environment.

John J. Parker was a relatively young forty-four when he was nominated for the Supreme Court. A graduate of the University of North Carolina, Parker entered politics soon after his graduation, running as a Republican for the House of Representatives in 1910 and for attorney general in 1916. Most notably, Parker led the Republican campaign in North Carolina in 1920, running for governor and garnering 230,000 votes, a significant tally for a non-Democrat in North Carolina. During the Harding administration, Parker served as a special assistant to the attorney general of the United States, and in 1925 he was appointed by President Calvin Coolidge to the Circuit Court of Appeals for the Fourth Circuit.[48] His appointment was confirmed unanimously by the Senate.

Opposing Parker

Parker's nomination to the Supreme Court was announced by the White House on Friday, March 21, 1930. Only four days elapsed before representatives of the American Federation of Labor (AFL) challenged its propriety and "asked members of the Senate Judiciary Committee to investigate his [Parker's] participation in the decision upholding 'yellow dog' contracts."[49] Once again, the changing nature of Supreme Court confirmations is

apparent. The use of hearings as a means of vetting or investigating a nominee's record and philosophy was still somewhat unusual—the Brandeis
hearings had occurred just fourteen years prior to Parker's. Nonetheless,
the evolving confirmation process utilized hearings as a means of determining the fitness of the nominee, reflecting the tendency to invoke more
forensic parameters in this constitutionally deliberative process.

In 1927, Parker authored an opinion of the Fourth Circuit Court of Appeals in *International Organization, United Mine Workers of America, et al. v. Red
Jacket Consolidated Coal and Coke Co.*,[50] in which he upheld the practice of requiring employees—in this case, miners—to sign a contract pledging that
they would not join a union as a condition of their employment—so-called
yellow-dog contracts. Parker concluded in the *Red Jacket* case that such
contracts were constitutional, basing his decision on the Supreme Court's
ruling in *Hitchman Coal and Coke Co. v. Mitchell.*[51] Parker reasoned that
"there can be no doubt of the right of defendants [the United Mine Work-
ers] to use all lawful propaganda to increase their membership." However,
he continued, "this right must be exercised with due regard to the rights of
complainants."[52] The *Red Jacket* case reflected Parker's attempts to balance
"the competing interests of labor and management within the rigid confines of the labor law current at the time."[53] The AFL, though, did not recognize Parker's balancing and assailed him for upholding yellow-dog
contracts.[54]

In its opposition to Parker, the AFL articulated a vision of American law
that rejected claims to "property rights" frequently validated by the
Supreme Court with repeated reference to the due process clause of the
Fourteenth Amendment. AFL president William Green presented labor's
concerns in his appearance before the Senate subcommittee holding hearings on Parker's nomination. The initial premise of labor's opposition to
Parker concerned the power of the Supreme Court as its decisions "vitally
affect the well-being and happiness of millions of working men, their
wives and their families."[55] Green's statement warned that the confirmation of Parker would strengthen the power of "reaction" on the Supreme
Court and that it would be unwise and against the "common welfare" to
"strengthen the reactionary side of the Supreme Court, by adding another
to that powerful influence."[56]

Parker was of a reactionary orientation, Green suggested, because of his
willingness to uphold the legality of a yellow-dog contract. Green informed
the subcommittee that Parker "reduced the workers employed by these
numerous coal companies represented in the Red Jacket Consolidated Coal

and Coke Co. case to a condition approximating industrial servitude." Green continued that to seat Parker on the Supreme Court is "not in accord with the highest and best interest of the masses of the people and of the perpetuation of our form of government." Ultimately, Green concluded, Parker would simply add to the reactionary wing of the Supreme Court, a wing that "seems to put property rights above human rights."[57]

Green's opposition to Parker is powerful for its ideological shaping of the debate over the nomination. Green attacked Parker on two fronts. First, Parker had already exacted much harm on the "masses" with his decisions on the Fourth Circuit Court of Appeals, particularly the *Red Jacket* decision. More important, Green suggested, adding Parker to the Supreme Court would permit him to continue to threaten the "common welfare," as Parker would solidify the reactionary wing of the Court. This two-pronged assault allowed Green to define the nomination as a threat to "human rights."

Organized labor's opposition to Parker expanded the ideological meaning of "human rights" as a measure of the justice meted out by the Supreme Court and the lower courts. Attacking Parker elevated the cause of social justice. The construction of the nominee as the embodiment of "property rights" made such rights the source of harm and injury to the "masses" and to the "common welfare." The Supreme Court, according to labor's calculus, must be changed to reflect the growing importance of "human rights." Parker's nomination, they successfully maintained, was a barrier to such change and a threat to the very nature of American government. The rejection of the Parker nomination signaled, partially at least, the influence of this shift in the constitution of U.S. law and politics.

The power of labor's ideological construction of the Parker nomination is also found in its echoes from the Senate floor debate. Parker's opponents were quick to introduce into the debate newspaper editorials, letters, and telegrams that emphasized his alleged "reactionary" politics. A letter from John L. Lewis, president of the United Mine Workers, asserted that Parker "delivered 50,000 free Americans into indentured servitude" with the *Red Jacket* ruling.[58] A letter from William Green dated April 29, 1930 (almost a month after his testimony before the Judiciary subcommittee), reaffirmed labor's opposition to Parker and maintained that labor was obligated to "oppose men who lack a proper appreciation of human rights, human values, and human relationships in industry."[59]

Moreover, in their speeches concerning the nomination, opponents frequently employed labor's arguments in their justification for rejecting

Parker. Senator Norris of Nebraska, for example, stridently proclaimed: "Property rights! That is the contest that has gone on ever since the world became civilized. In every battle that has been fought, in the various steps we have taken from barbarism, it was a contest between human beings and dollars, and it is going on yet."[60] Idaho senator William Borah continued the assault when he maintained that "we [opponents of Parker] are insisting that here is a great problem involving human rights, a question of whether we shall *embody* into the jurisprudence of this country a principle which we believe to be at enmity with the welfare of not only the great working classes but with the public good."[61]

Parker's champions were largely ineffective in responding to those opposing the nomination. Parker's primary defense was that, as a lower court judge, he was bound to follow the Supreme Court; because of the Court's ruling in the *Hitchman* case, Parker had a duty to precedent and thus upheld the yellow-dog contract as constitutional. Much of the Senate floor debate concerned specific questions of legal interpretation and the duty of lower court judges to follow the rulings of the Supreme Court. The floor debate also addressed the particulars of the Supreme Court's holdings regarding yellow-dog contracts. Adding to Parker's defense was North Carolina senator Lee Overman, who maintained that "Judge Parker loves the plain people; he has worked for them; his practice has been among them; and he has never represented any of the great corporations."[62]

Both during the debate and after the final vote, the nation's media outlets were generally critical of the nomination, for a variety of reasons. Calling the yellow-dog contract the "most reactionary practice of the American courts," the *New Republic* chastised President Hoover for ignoring the warnings of the Hughes nomination.[63] The *Nation* opposed the nomination because it viewed it as "purely political" and "political and sectional,"[64] and the *Outlook and Independent* noted that the appointment "was born, it developed, and it died in politics."[65] The *New York Times* maintained that the nominee's "personal bearing" has some effect on the outcome, as he "showed himself too anxious, too small-minded."[66]

There is some sense as well that the struggles and ideological tensions of the Parker nomination were experienced by the larger public. James P. Roe, for example, wrote the editor of the *New York Times* to remark that "it will not advance the cause of justice, nor will it enhance respect for the law as interpreted by the courts if any organized body, such as the American Federation of Labor, can effectively attack court decisions and the judges who render them in accordance with lawful procedure by an appeal to class prejudice and resort to political pressure and threats."[67] Roe was writing in response to a letter submitted to the *Times* by William Green of the AFL. Another Parker supporter, Herbert W. Gediman, wrote to the *Washington Star* in defense of Parker's labor decisions, concluding that "Judge Parker is in reality a stalwart defender of labor unions in the proper enjoyment of their legal rights."[68] And W. R. Siegart queried in a letter to the *New York Times*: "Should a man be selected for this high office because of his judicial fitness or because of his ability to get voters for those who ratify the appointment?"[69]

The justifications for the nomination and the defense of Parker's *Red Jacket* decision did not, and could not, succeed. Parker's nomination represented, to those struggling with the Depression's onset in 1930, an important ideological moment. Its ideological relevance emerged from the tension between "property rights" and "human rights" already circulating in the symbolic environment and dramatically represented by the nomination. Parker's ruling in the *Red Jacket* case synecdochically represented that tension, giving opponents of "property rights" an opportunity to challenge the ideological boundaries of U.S. law. To claim simply that the judge was forced to follow "the law" as propounded by the Supreme Court was a response that ignored the ideological narrowing of "property rights" by Parker's opponents. As constructed by both labor and Senate progressives, American law and American justice were too often ordered by the commitment to "property rights" and did not adequately accommodate "human rights."

Human Rights and the NAACP

In his testimony before the Judiciary subcommittee, AFL president William Green argued that the *Hitchman* decision "was the Dred Scott decision to labor."[70] This comparison worked to fuse symbolically the two forces opposing the Parker nomination: organized labor and the NAACP. Such a fusion is important, for just as labor's opposition to Parker was premised on an expansion of "human rights" through the limitation of "property rights," the NAACP's opposition called for a further expansion of "human rights" to more fully involve African Americans.

The attack on Parker by the NAACP, and its role in defeating the nomination, enabled the organization "to become a leading force for the political, economic, and social equality of all Americans."[71] Moreover, it added another dimension to the reordering of commitments to "property rights"

and "human rights" within the larger rubric of American justice by involving concerns for racial justice.

The NAACP's involvement in the hearings also demonstrated the expanding role of interest groups in the Supreme Court confirmation process.
Individuals with particular interests had exerted influence in nominations
for years, but the presence and power of organized "interest groups" in the
Parker hearings were significant developments that would proliferate for
the remainder of the twentieth century. Only once before had organized
interest groups (organizations devoted to particular causes or political
agendas) been so actively involved in a Supreme Court confirmation struggle.[72] Following the Parker hearings, groups like organized labor and the
NAACP regularly, as a matter of group identity, would contribute to the debates over Supreme Court appointments. Their involvement is yet another
marker of the ideological significance of this process for U.S. law and political culture. In addition, interest group involvement also reflects the more
intensely adversarial nature of Supreme Court nominations and their symbolic construction as "trials."

Of greater ideological significance is the fact that the NAACP, as a group
dedicated to the advancement of rights for African Americans, was so involved in fighting against Parker's confirmation. For much of the period
leading to 1930, U.S. law regarding African Americans and the preservation of equal civil liberties for this group of citizens was largely a search for
ways to implement the separate but equal doctrine articulated in *Plessy v.
Ferguson* in 1896.[73] As Celeste Condit and John Lucaites reveal, the
Supreme Court did not fully support either white supremacy or egalitari-
anism, and "in practice this meant that the Court would do whatever it
could to preserve the Separate But Equal compromise."[74] While the Court
was striving to preserve segregation, Herbert Hoover's passive conception
of the federal government "guaranteed that his would be an administration
that made little change on race and equality."[75] Yet Hoover had created a
political "southern strategy" premised on "lily-whitism," or the exclusion
of African Americans from political power and influence, especially within
Republican Party organizations in the South.[76] The nomination of Judge
Parker appeared to be an attempt to further this southern strategy, and the
Outlook and Independent noted at the time that Parker "is the first justice appointed since 1860 from the fourth circuit, comprising Maryland, West Virginia, Virginia, North and South Carolina."[77]

Even though Hoover was committed to his southern strategy, his nomination of Parker surprised prominent African American leaders, and

especially the NAACP. The association, to 1930, was making significant gains in the courts, including a 1927 Supreme Court decision that struck down Texas's all-white primary system.[78] Moreover, the NAACP was also waging a crusade against lynching, an effort frustrated by congressional inaction.[79] When Hoover nominated Parker, the NAACP scrutinized the nominee's history and judicial record, even as the organization's leaders were fairly certain of his eventual confirmation.[80]

The NAACP's investigation uncovered what would eventually prove to be the most damaging evidence against Parker's nomination aside from the *Red Jacket* decision. The NAACP branch in Greensboro, North Carolina, discovered a quotation made during Parker's 1920 gubernatorial campaign. Responding to Democratic arguments that he wanted to extend the franchise to African Americans, Parker argued that

> the Negro as a class does not desire to enter politics. The Republican party of North Carolina does not desire him to do so. We recognize the fact that he has not yet reached that stage in his development when he can share the burdens and responsibilities of government . . . The participation of the Negro in politics is a source of evil and danger to both races and is not desired by the wise men in either race or by the Republican party of North Carolina.[81]

Upon discovering this quotation, the NAACP telegraphed Parker to ascertain the accuracy of the quotation and to solicit a response as to the nominee's current opinions. Parker refused to respond to the NAACP's telegram, though he did receive it, and after waiting two days the NAACP made public its opposition to the nominee in telegrams to thirty-five senators and to all of its branches nationwide.[82]

Through a series of press releases and in testimony before the Judiciary subcommittee, the NAACP presented its case against Parker. In a press release prior to the subcommittee hearings, the association argued that Parker was "unfit to pass on cases coming before the Supreme Court under these Amendments [Fourteenth and Fifteenth], affecting the civil rights of Negroes."[83] The People's Legislative Service of the NAACP echoed the concerns of labor as it charged that Parker's confirmation would "increase rather than lessen the grounds of just criticism of the Court by that large body of Americans spiritually akin to Jefferson and Lincoln who believe that human rights are superior to property rights." This particular press release expressed the rationale for the association's assault on Parker. His nomination threatened the expansion of "human rights" to African

Americans, the NAACP argued. As it concluded, "From the liberal viewpoint, the Supreme Court is now loaded to the limit with judicial representatives of *things* rather than *human flesh and blood.*"[84] Following the
subcommittee hearings, the NAACP mounted a considerable public effort,
urging its chapters to organize letter-writing campaigns to specific senators
and keeping the press informed of its efforts and its successes.[85]

The opposition to Parker from the NAACP was met with some hostility.
Despite their invocation of the Dred Scott decision, organized labor hoped
that no connection be made between their opposition to Parker and the
NAACP's efforts. Walter White, then secretary of the association, recorded in
his autobiography that he encountered a high level of antipathy when he
testified before the Judiciary subcommittee, specifically from Senators Borah
and Overman.[86] In the face of this hostility, White testified that Parker had
engaged in a "shameless flouting of the fourteenth and fifteenth amendments to the Federal Constitution." He further maintained that Parker had
indicated a "willingness to support some laws and to disregard others when
political expediency dictates." The transcript of the hearing reveals that
White did face hostile, even patronizing, questioning from Senators Borah
and Overman, but he maintained the central focus of his opposition to
Parker, that the nominee "is not of the caliber which loyal, intelligent Americans have the right to expect of Justices of the Nation's highest court."[87]

The subcommittee hearing, as with much of the debate concerning
Parker's nomination, focused mostly on the *Red Jacket* decision and Parker's
hostility to labor. Nonetheless, the Senate floor debate addressed the
NAACP's concerns. An important moment in the debate came with the introduction of Parker's defense to the charges he faced. North Carolina senator Overman read into the record a letter from Parker where he
indignantly argued:

> [W]hile I made it clear that my party was not seeking to organize the col-
> ored people of the State as a class, I at no time advocated denying them the
> right to participate in the election in cases where they were qualified to do
> so, nor did I advocate denying them any other of their rights under the Con-
> stitution and laws of the United States. Any charge or intimation that I ap-
> pealed to race prejudice is most unjust.[88]

Parker's champions in the Senate defended his conduct and offered as evidence the support given him by leading African Americans in North Carolina and his vote tally among African Americans in the 1920
gubernatorial election. In a somewhat pathetic attempt to answer the

NAACP's concerns, Senator Overman pleaded that "a man ought not be held responsible for what he said in a political speech."[89]

Senators feared the racial issues that emerged from the nomination fight and their possible political ramifications. That fear resulted in attacks on the leaders of the NAACP, who were identified as socialists, communists, agitators, and radical revolutionaries on the Senate floor.[90] Nonetheless, the NAACP mounted a fierce public campaign to defeat the nomination. As Walter White recounted, every branch of the NAACP in northern and border states was telegraphed following his testimony before the subcommittee. Mass meetings were arranged, White reports, and they were "addressed by various officers of the national office of the Association, [while] newspaper editors were kept supplied with the facts as the campaign developed."[91]

In what would be a prophetic editorial, the *New York Times* noted as well that "if Judge Parker is to be rejected because he has offended Negro voters, then it will appear as if the Senate had established a rule that no man from the Southern States . . . could ever be confirmed . . . for the Parker view is almost universal in the South."[92] Lucius Butts, in a letter to the *New York Times*, urged the newspaper and its readers to be "alarmed at the prospective accumulation of constitutional nullification directed against the Negro, and not advocate an increment thereof by such allegories as citation of the notoriously dormant Fourteenth and Fifteenth Amendments."[93]

The NAACP's efforts against the Parker nomination were extremely successful at generating media coverage in the African American press. Baltimore's *Afro-American* is a good example. A weekly newspaper, the *Afro-American* ran front-page stories on the nomination for four straight weeks in April 1930, as well as publishing several editorials, letters to the editor, and reviews of editorial opinions from other newspapers. On April 5, the paper headlined its story "NAACP Joins Labor in Asking Senate to Reject Parker, He's Lily-White."[94] A week later, the *Afro-American* published letters from the president of the North Carolina College for Negroes, J. E. Shepard, and from Norman Thomas, the noted Socialist leader. Shepard noted that he supported Parker, and "if I did not believe Judge Parker was absolutely fair and impartial, I would not write this letter on his behalf."[95] Thomas, conversely, fused labor's concerns with the NAACP's, noting that "Judge Parker of North Carolina has already declared himself on the side of property rights *uber alles* by enjoining the United Mine Workers from trying to organize certain West Virginia miners who had been forced to sign a yellow dog contract" as he concluded that Parker's racial oratory "disqualifies him to pass fairly on racial issues."[96] By April 19, the *Afro-American* asserted that the "Country Is Aroused Over Carolina Jurist" and reported on efforts by NAACP chapters nationwide to defeat Parker. The paper quoted the Baltimore A.M.E. Preachers' Meeting resolution: "We say to you that there is a widespread dissatisfaction over this appointment, not only among the Negroes of Maryland but all over the country. It is now common belief that the President knew before hand of Judge Parker's attitude toward Negroes and that tendering of the nomination to Judge Parker is being interpreted as a direct slap in the face of 15,000,000 Negroes."[97]

As the final vote on the nomination neared, the *Afro-American* published opinions from around the country. The *Philadelphia Record*'s editorial was featured: "The nomination of Judge Parker acquires special importance from the fact that if he is confirmed Republicans will have openly condoned the nullification of the 15th Amendment." The *Cleveland Gazette* labeled Parker's African American supporters "Uncle Toms," and the *Chicago Bee* argued, "We must seek another man whose mind is free from racial and religious prejudices."[98] In its own editorial, the *Afro-American* quoted the bishop W. A. Fountain's lament that "Hoover has turned us over to the Ku Klux Klan in the South," and the newspaper concluded that Parker is a nominee who "opposes the right of the Negro to vote and is willing to have the U.S. constitution nullified on this point."[99]

In symbolic conjunction with labor's concerns, the racial dimensions of this nomination battle reinforced Parker's "reactionary" positions, placing him outside the constructed parameters of American law as defined by the senators in their considerations. Parker came to symbolize an older, reactionary time, where the law protected U.S. business interests at the expense of labor and excluded whole groups of citizens from civic participation.

The Ideological Consequences of the 1930 Supreme Court Battles

On May 7, 1930, the U.S. Senate rejected President Hoover's nomination of John J. Parker to the Supreme Court. The vote was thirty-nine senators in favor of the nomination, forty-one senators opposed.[100] In the period from 1894 to 1969, Parker's rejection was the only instance when the Senate refused its consent to a presidential nominee for the Supreme Court.

Faced with the onset of the Depression, the American polity was reassessing its ideological foundations and the commitments at its core. The Hughes nomination foreshadowed the symbolic role of the judiciary in the ideological conflict under way, and the Parker nomination brought that conflict to its apex. Parker's confirmation debate publicly enacted the rhetorical shifts occurring in the prevailing importance and relevance of "property rights" and "human rights" for the American community and for U.S. law.

"Property rights," as an ideological touchstone of economic expansion and constitutional guarantees of substantive due process, was a commitment under rhetorical siege. For decades (as the Brandeis and Hughes nominations made clear), muckrakers, progressives, and revolutionaries questioned the validity of judicial concerns for property rights and the consequences of social adherence to the principles of unfettered economic expansion. Such an interpretation of constitutional law, they charged, denied the centrality of social justice within the U.S. legal framework and positioned the courts as a super-legislature thwarting the public will. Hughes's work in private practice and Parker's ruling in the *Red Jacket* decision offered the voices of social progressivism opportunities to denounce the utility and propriety of the ideological commitment to property rights and to assail the "reactionary" nature of the Supreme Court. The "mainstream" of American law had shifted away from the commitment to property rights, in the arguments of Hughes and Parker's opponents, and Parker was even judged as outside of that "mainstream."

While "property rights" declined in ideological significance, "human rights" emerged as a replacement. The arguments of both labor and the NAACP expressed this shift well. Because of Parker's opposition to unrestricted unionization and his stated hostility toward African American participation in government, the nominee did not embody the evolving nature of justice within the constantly changing formation of American law that manifested a commitment to human rights above property and capital.

The Senate's rejection of Parker may have also paved the way for the eventual progressive decisions of the Supreme Court in the area of civil rights. Many commentators on this nomination conclude in hindsight that Parker was not a racist. Martin Fausold, for instance, reveals that Parker's decisions on the Fourth Circuit "manifested the reverse," proving that he was not a racist.[101] Calvin Massey maintains that Parker "was one of the earliest southern judicial advocates of desegregation."[102] However, a more critical assessment of his judicial record reveals that his alleged support of desegregation was illusory and politically motivated. As Kenneth Goings suggests, Parker believed that, even though rejected in 1930, he would one day be appointed again to the Supreme Court, and he supported efforts by friends and associates to place his name in nomination. In addition, Parker maintained close correspondences with every president from Hoover to Eisenhower.[103] It was only after Eisenhower bypassed Parker in favor of Earl Warren that the North Carolinian realized he would not be nominated for the Supreme Court. Goings argues that following the Warren nomination, Parker's decisions in civil rights cases reflected his true opinion that "race mixing was not to be condoned or encouraged."[104] Moreover, following the *Brown v. Board of Education*[105] decision, Parker "emerged in the vanguard of southern obstructionists whose post-Brown rulings had 'frustrating effects' upon the Supreme Court's decision."[106]

In addition, the participation of the NAACP in the Parker nomination fight publicly performed the commitment to human rights by demonstrating the emerging power of the association, and of African Americans in general, to influence U.S. political life. As such, the ideological meaning of human rights expanded, and the confirmation process for Supreme Court justices was inexorably changed. J. E. Spingarn, the NAACP leader in the early twentieth century, is quoted as saying that the Parker controversy "was the most impressive demonstration yet witnessed of black Americans' united political strength."[107] W. E. B. DuBois called the nomination's defeat "the greatest single triumph of Negro voters" to that time.[108] Not only did the NAACP's involvement in the Parker rejection demonstrate the growing importance of diverse interest groups in the Supreme Court confirmation process, it also signaled the political viability of African American concerns and the constitutional legitimacy of this group of citizens. Indeed, the simple presence of the NAACP in the debate illustrated the ideological shift in U.S. law toward broader conceptions of human rights and civil liberties.

Finally, the Hughes and Parker confirmation battles altered the Supreme Court confirmation process, heightening once again the ideological importance of this process for U.S. law and politics. It represented the ability of this rhetorical ritual both to reflect and shape the ideological meaning of justice in American life. Because of the highly politicized nature of both battles, Supreme Court confirmations entered into the political realm with greater importance, continuing a twentieth-century development begun with the Brandeis nomination of 1916. Soon, Supreme Court nominees would be compelled to appear in person before congressional committees and subcommittees. Interest groups, as in the Parker fight, would multiply in number and increase their influence over the composition of the Supreme Court. Ultimately, ideological commitments, from "property rights" to "human rights," from "civil liberty" to "privacy," would continue to be tested, configured, and shaped by this process.

4

The Character of Civil Rights

The Thurgood Marshall Nomination

[Thurgood Marshall] is worthy of the honor of being the first of his race to occupy a seat on the highest court of the land . . . Mr. Marshall, by dint of his brilliant accomplishments, has earned the appointment on merit alone.

Representative Robert N. C. Nix, *Congressional Record*

Judge Marshall is by practice and philosophy a constitutional iconoclast, and his elevation to the Supreme Court at this juncture of our history would make it virtually certain that for years to come, if not forever, the American people will be ruled by the arbitrary notions of Supreme Court Justices rather than by the precepts of the Constitution.

Senator Sam Ervin, *Congressional Record*

According to Thurgood Marshall, his nomination to the Supreme Court happened very quickly and came as a bit of a surprise. Whisked to the White House unexpectedly on June 13, 1967, Marshall met with President Johnson who told him, "You know something, Thurgood, I'm going to put you on the Supreme Court." They then went before the press, where LBJ concluded in his introduction of Marshall that the nominee "has already earned his place in history, but I think it will be greatly enhanced by his service on the Court." Johnson ended his introduction with the rather bold statement: "I believe [the appointment of Marshall] is the right thing to do, the right time to do it, the right man and the right place. I trust that his nomination will be promptly considered by the Senate."[1]

Upon their return to the Oval Office, Marshall then asked the president's permission to call his wife with the news. Johnson grabbed the telephone away from his solicitor general and said to Cissy Marshall, "Cissy—Lyndon Johnson. I've just put your husband on the Supreme Court." Cissy Marshall's reply signaled the momentous quality of this nomination: "I'm sure glad I'm sitting down," she told the president.[2]

Marshall was selected by Johnson to replace Associate Justice Tom Clark, who resigned from the Court when LBJ appointed Ramsay Clark, the justice's son, to the post of attorney general. LBJ's description of Marshall as "the right man" for the time and place of 1967 America emphasized the role of Marshall's race in his nomination to the Supreme Court.[3] Michael Davis and Hunter Clark assert that Marshall's race made all the difference to Johnson and that LBJ saw the appointment as "a way to revive his flagging social agenda for the Great Society."[4] A member of the Court at the time of Marshall's appointment, William O. Douglas, was even more pointed. He argued that "Marshall was named simply because he was black . . . [and the] public needed a competent black on the Court for symbolic reasons."[5]

Johnson's comments also foreshadowed the ideological tension that the supporters of the nomination faced in their justifications for Marshall's confirmation. At the same time, Marshall's ethnicity figured powerfully in the rhetoric of his opponents as they sought to reconfigure the nominee and his relationship to civil rights. In so doing, the opposition to Marshall's elevation to the Supreme Court offered a redemarcation of civil rights that associated this commitment with crime, communism, and a liberal judicial activism leading to the potential downfall of the Republic. In many ways, then, the nomination of Thurgood Marshall was a meaningful moment in the definition of civil rights as that commitment of U.S. law was in dispute in the heady days of the late 1960s. It revealed, in the words of *Washington Post* columnist Roscoe Drummond, "the tremendous change in race relations in the last half-century and especially the last decade."[6]

In the thirty-seven years between the rejection of Judge Parker and the battle over Lyndon Johnson's nomination of Thurgood Marshall, the constitutional and ideological terrain of the United States changed dramatically. This was particularly true in the area of civil rights. This period saw the erosion and ultimate end of legal segregation and the beginnings of the full integration of African Americans into the fabric of American politics and culture. In terms of the politics and processes of Supreme Court confirmations, the importance of civil rights that was only emergent in the

Parker nomination debates came to full fruition in the discourses surrounding Johnson's nomination of Thurgood Marshall.

Most of the nominees put forth by Presidents Franklin Roosevelt, Truman, Eisenhower, and Kennedy were confirmed with relatively little controversy or difficulty. There were some notable exceptions. FDR's nomination of Hugo Black, an ardent New Dealer, created a flurry of controversy coming as it did so soon after the defeat of the president's "court-packing" plan, a plan that Black supported while in the U.S. Senate. Once on the Court, Black's membership in the Ku Klux Klan added to the concerns about his appointment and were only quelled after his unprecedented nationwide radio address of October 1, 1937.[7] Some concern was expressed about the alleged "Communist" leanings of Felix Frankfurter upon his appointment by FDR[8] and of William Brennan upon his appointment by President Eisenhower.[9] Eisenhower's nomination of Earl Warren as chief justice encountered some petty political maneuvering by Judiciary Committee chair William Langer.[10] But for thirty-seven years, the confirmation of Supreme Court justices was a fairly uncomplicated process even as the nation struggled with economic depression, war, and assuring the civil rights of all of its citizens.

The conflicts over civil rights, particularly, were filled with tension and violence. Just six years after President Harry S. Truman integrated the armed forces, the Supreme Court ruled in 1954, in *Brown v. Board of Education*, that segregation was unconstitutional, overturning almost seventy years of U.S. law and social policy. Hailed in retrospect as the most important High Court decision of the twentieth century,[11] *Brown* and subsequent laws and cases vitally reconstructed the ideological nature of the American community.[12] This reconstruction meant that future generations would have "integrated public Equality as a legal foundation of national life."[13]

The history of the *Brown* decision is well known and has been documented elsewhere.[14] Its legal and educational consequences are also clear.[15] Ideologically, *Brown* worked to mark another moment of the centrality of civil rights for the American community. With its declaration that "separate but equal" was an unconstitutional doctrine and the unanimity of the decision, *Brown* recast civil rights and the place of African Americans in American life. It was a moment made all the more remarkable by the efforts of a group of African American legal professionals to convince the Supreme Court (an institution that seemed to many "the epitome of the white man's world")[16] of their views.

At the center of that effort was Thurgood Marshall. Marshall's role in the *Brown* decision is seen now, in hindsight, romantically and hagiographically—he was the primary architect of the *Brown* decision, our collective memory relays, who brought down the structures of school segregation. For much of his professional life, Marshall had fought diligently for civil rights, and his identification with this effort was complete by 1954. He repeatedly sought federal intervention on behalf of African Americans facing lynching, segregation, and disenfranchisement and was roundly condemned for his work. Often, his efforts were met with hostility by communities around the country, where he was branded a Communist and an agitator.[17]

By 1954, and in the aftermath of the *Brown* decision, Marshall's efforts were, as Juan Williams notes, "widely praised" in both the black and white press, which characterized the lawyer "as the reasoned, smart leader of the nation's efforts to defeat racism."[18] He appeared on the cover of *Time* magazine even as he personified the tensions simmering in the civil rights community between those who acceded to the Supreme Court's "all deliberate speed" language and those who sought a more aggressive approach to segregationist attempts at resistance to *Brown*.[19] Indeed, Marshall was, for many, the face of *Brown* and the embodiment of both its promise and its problems. Thirteen years later, a president from the Texas hill country would nominate that same lawyer to become the first African American on the Supreme Court.

The confirmation debate concerning Thurgood Marshall's nomination explored the evolving commitment to civil rights as an organizing principle of U.S. jurisprudence and constitutional democracy. It was, at bottom, an event that invited a public judgment about the nature of civil rights for the American community. In the process, Marshall came to embody this commitment in the rhetorics that supported and opposed his elevation to the Supreme Court. Once again, the Supreme Court confirmation process reflected the evolving personalization of legal ideology and discourse in U.S. political culture. The result was that Marshall's ideological embodiment articulated an understanding of civil rights as a building block for the U.S. community, an understanding that was highly polarized and reflective of the tensions at work in U.S. politics in 1967.

Glorifying Civil Rights

Todd Gitlin describes 1967 as the beginning of four years that were "a cyclone in a wind tunnel."[20] The war in Vietnam was escalating, as was anxiety about the war in the United States. It was also the year, according to David Zarefsky, when the "rhetorical crisis of the War on Poverty came to a head," with significant political changes in Washington and throughout the nation.[21] Put simply, 1967 was a tumultuous year of intense change. On June 13 of that year, Lyndon Johnson introduced Thurgood Marshall as his Supreme Court nominee.[22] This introduction commenced a confirmation debate that Stephen Carter describes, somewhat myopically, as the "most vicious" in American history.[23]

The fact that Marshall was an African American was, for many of his supporters, a symbol of the success of civil rights and a barometer of the progress made in the United States as a result of civil rights legislation and judicial action. Marshall represented the success of civil rights both as a chief legal architect of this commitment and as a beneficiary of the American commitments to "equality" and "opportunity" that define civil rights. Marshall's supporters, though, also denied the role of his race in the appointment, repeatedly stressing the judge's merits as a lawyer and jurist. These discourses express, then, the inherent tension in the U.S. political usages of civil rights. Civil rights is simultaneously predicated upon demarcations of difference and celebrations of similarity,[24] and as Marshall's supporters justified his confirmation to the Supreme Court, they sought to negotiate the discursive ambiguity represented by his appointment and his personification of civil rights.

On the day of the nomination, Robert Kennedy, then a senator from New York, proclaimed in the Senate that for "Negro Americans, Thurgood Marshall is a symbol of their struggle for justice, for equal rights before the law."[25] Senator Philip Hart of Michigan spoke in support of the nomination, arguing that "because Thurgood Marshall is a Negro, because he has been associated with the cause of civil rights . . . Mr. Marshall's appointment has taken on added symbolic significance." He continued that the nomination "means that the American Negro is part of American society and not outside of it."[26] Democrat Wayne Morse of Oregon pronounced, on the floor of the Senate, that Marshall's nomination reveals America's "growing maturity as a people and as a nation,"[27] while Michigan senator Robert Griffin declared the nomination "living proof that every person in this country can go as far as his talents and qualifications warrant."[28]

One of the more peculiar—and, in hindsight, condescending—statements in support of Marshall's elevation to the Supreme Court was issued by Jacob Javits, Republican senator from New York. Javits saw the nomination as an educational opportunity:

This is a most appropriate time for an object lesson to a great people who are in such deep travail in our country—the Negro people. It is a time when object lessons are most desirable. These object lessons cannot be synthetically created. However, when God and nature and the process of public policy has [sic] produced a situation in which there is an extraordinary breakthrough and object lesson of this kind, we certainly have a right to speak of it and to be thankful that there exists in the United States a Negro who deserves to be a Justice of the U.S. Supreme Court.[29]

Not only may white Americans be proud of their benevolence in allowing an African American to sit on the Supreme Court, Javits suggested, but African Americans must see Marshall as a lesson for the possibilities of advancement with dedication and perseverance. Javits's remarks expressed the tensions present in liberal constructions of civil rights. These rights, in this formulation, are something given, or granted, to oppressed groups or individuals rather than something inherent to the constitutional framework of the community or derived from some "natural," extraconstitutional source. This construction, of course, creates the patronizing orientation of Javits's remarks and the troubling ideological entailment that civil rights are not inherent in the larger constitutional framework of the United States.

Indeed, all of the proclamations in support of Marshall's nomination that highlight his symbolism as an African American ratified the linkage of civil rights with "opportunity" and progress through "equality." As Senate minority whip Thomas Kuchel of California urged, the Marshall appointment represents "the American dream, a dream which says that every man, regardless of race, color, or creed, may achieve the goals he seeks in a free society."[30] Thus Marshall simultaneously reflected the difference of race that is at the heart of civil rights and the similarity of individual effort rewarded by civil rights within the American egalitarian ideology of opportunity and progress.

While Marshall's advocates crafted an interpretation of his nomination as a validation of civil rights, they were also quick to deny that Marshall's race was the reason for his appointment. Despite the fact that his appointment was "noteworthy" precisely because of his race, Representative William Ryan of New York claimed in the House that Marshall's race "should not be a relevant consideration."[31] "The fact that he is a Negro," claimed Senator Griffin, "should not affect our decision,"[32] while Senator Morse claimed that "Mr. Marshall was not nominated to the Court because he is a Negro."[33] Senator Edward Kennedy noted at the confirmation hearings before the Senate Judiciary Committee that "Judge Marshall is before us today because he is an outstanding lawyer, judge, and Solicitor General, not because he is a Negro; but we cannot ignore the fact of his race."[34]

Kennedy's comment expressed the dilemma faced by Marshall's supporters seeking to justify his nomination. As they worked to represent Marshall as a symbol of African American achievement and the successes of civil rights, they also fought awkwardly to deny his ethnicity's relevance to his nomination. Civil rights rhetorically depends upon the presence and amplification of difference. In the nation's development of the ideology of civil rights, the idea is bound inextricably with the uneasy tension between people of European descent and those of African descent who occupy and function within the same community. This history constructs civil rights as the granting of opportunity and "rights" to those previously excluded from the political and social systems by virtue of their difference. As such, Marshall's supporters noted his uniqueness and his resonance as an African American in order to validate the achievement of civil rights.

Civil rights are also, though, demarcated by the commitment to "equality." If civil rights are achieved, the discourse suggests, then members of the community are equal and are judged not by reference to difference but by merit, qualification, and achievement. In this precarious ideological formation, civil rights exist to provide opportunity to those who lack it (based primarily on the color of their skin) and then to assure that the differences that motivated change in the majority culture are ignored in favor of "equality" (based primarily on the content of character) before the law and society. Thurgood Marshall, as an individual nominated to the Supreme Court in such a culture, should not be judged, these rhetorics maintained, or assessed for his heritage—a mark of difference—but for his qualifications measured in terms of legal merit and achievement.

As an embodiment of civil rights, then, Marshall represented the conflicts that confronted, and that continue to confront, a U.S. political culture struggling to locate its ideological identity. Those voices in this rhetorical struggle that adhere to and utilize conceptions of civil rights faced tensions that exist today over such issues as affirmative action, welfare policy, and gay and lesbian rights. The anxiety created by the simultaneous celebration of difference and its sublimation in the rhetoric of civil rights is at the root of concerns over how the culture deals with those denied opportunity, those kept from the equality of the polity. Thurgood Marshall represented both of the dimensions of civil rights at work in U.S. culture—he was the embodiment of both the embrace of difference and the attempt to ignore it as a factor in personal achievement that defined civil rights and that continue to demarcate how the U.S. polity grapples with this commitment.

Other voices in the Marshall nomination, however, toiled to redemarcate civil rights both to oppose Marshall's elevation to the Supreme Court and to frustrate efforts to provide opportunity and equality to all citizens. Their attempts to define Marshall as an "activist" and an "iconoclast" work also to define civil rights as outside of America's heritage and as dangerous to the American community's future.

Vilifying Civil Rights

Most of the prognosticators assessing Marshall's nomination in 1967 predicted swift and certain confirmation by the U.S. Senate. Interestingly, the news coverage of the nomination was minimal, perhaps in part because of the assumption that confirmation was certain.[35] Yet the opposition to his confirmation was vehement. Faced with certain defeat, members of the House and Senate still vigorously opposed Marshall's nomination. His opponents were typically from the South, and they utilized his nomination to attack perceived activism on the Supreme Court and what they interpreted as gross misinterpretations of the Constitution by that Court.

Two days after the public announcement of Marshall's nomination, a first-term representative from the Sixth District of Louisiana, John Rarick, put forth the initial attack on the nomination in a speech on the House floor. Rarick's remarks defined in the starkest terms the interpretation of the nomination offered by its opponents. He began by noting that, facing racial riots, civil disorder, and increased crime, "the American people are now forced to tolerate more salt in their despairing wounds by suffering one of the originators and activists of the problem that now plagues America . . . [who] upset 180 years of law and order in the nonlegal decision known as Brown against the Board of Education, by the use of intentionally misrepresented facts and suppressed truths."[36] He continued, arguing that the "poor persecuted, occupied Southland" is forced to accept the insult of having "the agent who was used to foment the trouble now publicly lauded for his race-mixing work and because of it, not in spite of it, appointed to the Supreme Court." Rarick concluded by charging Marshall with prejudice and bigotry against white southerners.[37]

These remarks presaged the southern strategy in opposition to Marshall's nomination. The first rhetorical move of the opposition was to associate Marshall with civil rights law—not a very difficult task. During the confirmation hearings before the Judiciary Committee, for instance, Michael Jaffe, representing the Liberty Lobby's opposition to the nominee,[38] argued that Marshall's legal career has been devoted exclusively to civil rights law, and that such a concentration "may also be responsible for his failure to obtain a working knowledge of other areas of the law."[39] There was also some attempt to raise questions about Marshall's expertise regarding civil rights law and legal history. In a lengthy series of questions, Senator Strom Thurmond of South Carolina tested Marshall's knowledge of the most arcane and minute details of the passage and ratification debates concerning the Thirteenth, Fourteenth, and Fifteenth amendments. One such question was, "Turning to the provision of the 13th Amendment forbidding involuntary servitude, are you familiar with any pre-1860 cases which interpreted this language?"[40] Thurmond interpreted Marshall's inability to respond accurately to these questions as a sign of his lack of expertise in civil rights law. As the senator noted in the Senate floor debate, "I think it is a fair observation to say that the nominee displayed a surprising, for him, lack of knowledge of the area in which he is almost daily depicted as the outstanding scholar."[41]

Ultimately, attacking the supposed narrowness of Marshall's legal expertise functioned to marginalize the nominee and question his abilities to perform the work required of him at the Supreme Court. Senator Spessard Holland, Democrat of Florida, maintained in the Senate floor debate that Marshall's emphasis on civil rights leaves him "in no position to exercise balanced and impartial judgment on a point of law involving . . . civil rights."[42] Of course, this line of argument diminished Marshall's qualifications, manifesting a stereotypical perception not only of African Americans but also of civil rights lawyers. Marshall's commitment to civil rights law was well known, but the establishment of that commitment created the foundation for the next stage of his opponent's arguments.

Opposition senators relied primarily on an association between civil rights and crime in order to argue for the rejection of the Marshall nomination. They defined Marshall as a "liberal judicial activist" who would only further, in the interests of civil rights, the agenda of the Warren Court and contribute, therefore, to the crime epidemic sweeping the United States. In many ways, this characterization of Marshall reflected the tensions at work in the legal and political community over judicial interpretation. Responding to concerns about judicial activism, legal scholars and commentators posited that judicial interpretation should be guided by neutral principles—as Alexander Bickel wrote in 1962, of "the rule of the neutral principles as foreclosing *ad hoc* constitutional judgments which express merely the judge's transient feeling of what is fair, convenient, or congenial in the particular circumstances of a litigation." For Bickel, a neutral principle is "an intellectually coherent statement of the reason for a result which in like cases will produce a like result, whether or not it is immediately agreeable or expedient."[43] Marshall was the embodiment of judicial activism, guided by relativism rather than principle, judging according to personal whim and folly rather than constitutional directive. In the political context of the confirmation hearings, judicial activism was translated into a concern for crime and the dangerous consequences, for some, of unbridled judicial review.

The often hostile and belittling questions Marshall faced in the Senate Judiciary Committee, for instance, frequently concerned decisions of the Warren Court that extended rights to those facing criminal prosecution. An exchange between Arkansas Democratic senator John McClellan and the nominee illustrates this strategy:

Senator McClellan. Do you think it [crime] is reaching proportions where we will have a reign of lawlessness and chaos?

Judge Marshall. I would say that I have great faith in the ability of our country to meet any emergency, and I—

Senator McClellan. I am not asking what the country can meet, Mr. Solicitor. I am trying to determine your attitude or sense, realization, of the danger confronting this country with respect to this enemy of our security.

Judge Marshall. I think it is a great danger. I also think it is a sufficient danger to require every arm of the Government to do everything that is *constitutionally permissible* to stop the increase, and indeed to cut it down.[44]

When pressed to discuss specific rights—the Miranda ruling or the right to counsel—Marshall replied that cases pending before the Supreme Court concerning such issues required that he refrain from comment. Marshall's noncommittal responses provoked a frustrated reply from Senator Sam Ervin of North Carolina. "I will tell you, Judge," Ervin stated, "if you are not going to answer a question about anything which might possibly come before the Supreme Court some time in the future, I cannot ask you a single question about anything that is relevant to this inquiry." Marshall replied, "I say with all due respect, Senator, that is the only way it has been done before."[45]

Marshall's answers here foreshadowed an emerging strategy by administrations and their nominees to the Supreme Court. Marshall refused to answer questions about cases that he thought might appear before the Supreme Court, citing the precedent of previous nomination hearings. As a part of the confirmation process, this tactic worked to the nominee's obvious advantage and was used to its fullest extent by such future nominees as David Souter and Clarence Thomas. Those nominees who would engage senators on questions about controversial and potential cases before the Court found themselves often in difficult positions, as in the case of Robert Bork. On another level, such answers undermined implicitly the portrayal of Marshall as a judicial activist by demonstrating his unwillingness to immediately reveal his judicial predispositions. Marshall's invocation of this "precedent" thus is a significant moment in the evolution of the Supreme Court confirmation process.

Even with his "evasive" answers, Marshall was still portrayed as an activist judge who would extend the meaning of the Constitution well beyond the intent of the framers. During his lengthy speech in opposition to the nomination, Senator Ervin contended that:

> Judge Marshall is by practice and philosophy a legal and judicial activist, and if he is elevated to the Supreme Court, he will join other activist Justices in rendering decisions which will substantially impair, if not destroy, the rights of Americans for years to come to the Government of the United States and the several States conducted in accordance with the Constitution.[46]

Senator Holland labeled the nominee "a constitutional ultra liberal and an activist" who would apply his own "social philosophy" to his judicial decision-making.[47] The activism that Marshall represented had serious consequences, according to Mississippi senator James Eastland, who charged that the Supreme Court "is invariably found on the side which would expand the rights of criminal suspects and which would diminish the powers of Federal, State, and local law-enforcement agencies to deal with the ever-mounting crime wave."[48]

The linkages between civil rights, "judicial activism," and the increase in criminal activity emerged quite clearly from the opposition to the Marshall nomination. According to these attacks, Marshall exemplified civil rights through his public life and his judicial philosophy, even to the exclusion of other legal areas and concerns. Such a focus leads to a judicial philosophy that is "activist" and "liberal," resulting in constitutional interpretations based in subjective "social philosophy" with no grounding in the meaning or intent of the original document. The consequence, such discourses conclude, is a Supreme Court (with Marshall as a new justice on that Court) that will only add to and worsen the "epidemic" of crime. Moreover, the associations that such linkages suggest were powerful. To a society in 1967 where, in that year alone, eighty-three people were killed and over 3,000 injured by racially based disturbances and riots, and where the federal courts were asserting their supremacy concerning desegregation and civil rights in general,[49] the association of activism, civil rights, and crime resonated powerfully. As one study demonstrates, "Democratic senators from states with large (but largely un-enfranchised) African American populations, where racial politics were traditionally divisive and the 'Negro bloc' vote feared, voted against Marshall for both ideological and demographic reasons."[50] As Louis Kohlmeier maintains, southern senators "succeeded in sowing the implication that black militancy was somehow connected with the Warren Court's decisions."[51]

Ideologically, the connection between civil rights and crime played upon powerful stereotypes about African Americans, sowing further doubts about Marshall's capacity to be a justice of the Supreme Court. To link the two rhetorically was skillful, capitalizing on the widely circulated images of African Americans rioting in the streets, committing crimes, and generally upsetting the law and order of the community. In this depiction, Marshall embodied not only the beneficial side of civil rights but also the racially charged prejudices that linked African Americans and crime together in the popular imaginary.

The final strategy by opponents to Marshall's confirmation to the Supreme Court invoked a familiar specter ever present in American politics—communism. This was a common strategy used by opponents of civil rights generally and specifically against Marshall prior to his nomination. As Michael J. Klarman notes, "NAACP leaders such as Thurgood Marshall were not as doggedly anticommunist as the professional redhunters would have liked."[52] Marshall faced charges of Communist sympathy at various places around the country—in Arkansas, where he worked on behalf of school integration, Marshall and local organizer Daisy Bates "were among the NAACP leaders singled out for their allegedly subversive connections."[53] When Marshall was nominated to the Court, West Virginia senator Robert Byrd wrote to the FBI's J. Edgar Hoover requesting FBI checks on Marshall's Communist ties.[54]

Not only did Marshall's opponents question his associations, but they also suggested a connection between Marshall's "Communist" leanings and his decision-making regarding civil rights. Marshall's associations were questioned in the Judiciary Committee hearings, when the Liberty Lobby's Michael Jaffe maintained that "Mr. Marshall's associations with groups of questionable loyalty is clearly relevant to his fitness to serve as a Justice of the Supreme Court."[55] Senator Everett Dirksen, the Senate minority leader in 1967, recalled that while the opposition to Marshall was not particularly threatening to the nomination, "they [his opponents] resented somewhat his continuing identity as a defense counsel for some of these organizations with which he was associated."[56]

The nominee's alleged "communist" associations worked in conjunction with a more specific allegation concerning Marshall's citation of a "Communist" author in a decision he wrote while on the Second Circuit Court of Appeals. In the hearings before the Judiciary Committee, Senator Eastland pressed Marshall on the nominee's citation of Herbert Aptheker in the case of *New York v. Galamison*,[57] though the senator claimed that he "didn't . . . want to leave the impression that [Marshall had] ever been a Communist or anything like that."[58] Marshall denied knowing that Aptheker was a Communist and claimed that had he known of Aptheker's politics, he would not have cited him. Eastland pursued the attack on the floor of the Senate. "How anyone could even casually read this book," Eastland argued, "and fail to see [its obvious adherence to communism] is difficult to understand." The Mississippi Democrat noted that the "various introductory material written by Mr. Aptheker clearly revealed the Communist slant of the book. For instance, in discussing the role of the Negro during the Spanish-American War, that war is referred to as a 'war of imperialism.'"[59]

Eastland's suggestion was clear—either Marshall was incompetent in his accidental citation of a known "Communist," or he knew, as surely he must have known, of Aptheker's politics and cited him anyway. Moreover, the implication of this line of opposition to Marshall is powerful. The conclusion that Marshall is incompetent in his citation of Aptheker reinforced the conception of Marshall as solely concerned with civil rights to the exclusion of even the most rudimentary decision-crafting skills as a judge. However, if Marshall did know Aptheker's politics, then civil rights are implicated with the works of a known "Communist" and are justified by reference to "subversive" works.

As if associating civil rights, and Marshall, with crime was not enough, opponents of the nomination played the ultimate cold war card by marginalizing civil rights through an association with communism. This depiction functioned to keep civil rights outside of the legal and political mainstream. The result was insignificant to the outcome of the nomination debate but ideologically important for what it expressed about the tensions over civil rights in the late 1960s.

The opposition to Thurgood Marshall's elevation to the Supreme Court sought to define the nominee as a dangerous, activist, subversive individual who might possibly damage the nation irreparably through an erosion of constitutionally protected rights. In so doing, Marshall's detractors offered a redemarcation of civil rights as an ideological warrant of U.S. politics and law. Because of Marshall's incarnation of civil rights, the attacks on his confirmation worked to circumscribe this commitment as one leading to increased crime and lawlessness and undermining constitutional democracy. While the attacks were directed at Marshall, they were also significant as expressions of the cultural and political fears attendant to the rise of civil rights in U.S. law. Those same fears did not disappear when Marshall assumed his seat at the Supreme Court.

Indeed, the ideological themes and meanings that emerged from the Marshall debate find expression in the Nixon presidential campaigns of 1968 and 1972 attacking the Warren Court. As will be evident in chapter 5, these themes are implicated in the confirmation struggles waged by the Nixon administration as it sought to place Clement Haynsworth and G. Harrold Carswell on the Supreme Court. Much of the rhetoric aimed at Thurgood Marshall achieved further expression in Nixon's quest for "law and order" and his desire to see a renewed "strict constructionist" interpretation of the Constitution. Even now, these concerns about civil rights and the entailments of this ideological commitment are present in contemporary discourses that malign, for example, affirmative action programs and extensions of civil rights to gay men and lesbians. Indeed, the Marshall hearings expressed and foreshadowed the intense struggling about the meaning of civil rights characteristic of much of American public discourse for the last twenty-five years.

Marshall's Shining Hour

On August 30, 1967, the Senate confirmed Thurgood Marshall's appointment to the Supreme Court by a vote of 69-11, with twenty senators not voting.[60] Senate majority leader Mike Mansfield remarked on the Senate floor immediately following the vote that "this is a shining hour" and that "we have come a long, long way toward equal access to the Constitution's promise."[61] Marshall would serve on the Court for twenty-four years, becoming to some "perhaps the most admired human being ever to sit on the Supreme Court" and remaining to others an intractable iconoclast.[62] The power of the Marshall legacy was illustrated quite clearly when President Bill Clinton introduced Ruth Bader Ginsburg as his nominee to the Supreme Court, claiming that she was to women's rights what Marshall was to civil rights. Upon Marshall's retirement from the Court in 1991, President George Bush nominated Judge Clarence Thomas to the vacated seat. Thurgood Marshall died in 1993.

The confirmation debate concerning Thurgood Marshall's nomination to the Supreme Court is instructive of not only the ideological meaning of civil rights in the American political language but also of how this community's ideology is constructed in public texts that express it. Rhetorical analyst Michael Calvin McGee argues that American culture is fragmented, evidenced by the development of a "presumption of cultural heterogeneity" and the "'psychologizing' of literally every social-political institution."[63] In an important sense, this fragmentation results, at least in part, from the characterological orientation of American political institutions. It is hardly surprising to find the discourse about that government "psychologized" as citizens attempt to ascertain the character and trustworthiness of those they select/elect to leadership. Indeed, as I have argued in this book, the Constitution requires such a focus in its commands and structure.

When the tension among and between the commitments that form the American community are understood by their representation in the particular characters of public life, the fragmentation of contemporary culture increases. The Marshall confirmation debate expresses such a fragmentation. By embodying civil rights in the person of Thurgood Marshall, both advocates and opponents of his elevation to the Supreme Court exacerbated the tensions and ambiguities present in the larger cultural meanings of this commitment. So intense was the struggle that President Johnson even credited the appointment of Marshall to the Supreme Court as the primary reason for his political downfall in 1968—ahead of the Vietnam War.[64] Thurgood Marshall's nomination to the Court was, not surprisingly, a crucible in which the simmering tensions about civil rights were reheated. The different cultural meanings of civil rights were organized by reference to Marshall himself.

The focus on character and personality may also yield an increasingly democratized community, as audiences are invited to select and adapt competing ideological discourses into their own conception of the American community. As McGee notes, "text construction is now something done more by the consumers than by the producers of discourse."[65] If McGee is correct, and I believe that he is, then audiences consuming the Marshall debates were asked to construct a text of the character of Thurgood Marshall and to use that text to give meaning to civil rights as a commitment in American society. They could see Marshall as a heroic figure, fighting to extend civil rights to all Americans regardless of their race and working to end a system of segregation that had polarized the nation. They were given the option of understanding, through Marshall's embodiment, the power of civil rights to create change and to promote opportunity.

Marshall's embodiment of civil rights is evident in an examination of even a small sampling of news and commentary about his appointment. As it proclaimed Marshall a "trail-blazer in civil rights," Baltimore's *Afro-American* newspaper editorialized that Marshall was the "one man mostly responsible for that historical decree [*Brown v. Board of Education*] . . . who unleashed a brilliantly slashing, and relentless attack on the institution of slavery and all of its ramifications, including school segregation."[66] The newspaper also commented on the irony of Marshall's appointment as only the second Marylander since Roger Taney to sit on the Supreme Court.[67] *Afro-American* reader John H. Wrighten wrote to the paper's editor to argue that Marshall's appointment "shows that America is trying to fulfill those things written in the Declaration of Independence and the Constitution," even as he cautioned that readers "not become too jubilant over this appointment, because there is still much to be done to fulfill the American dream of justice, freedom, and equality for all."[68]

But these same audiences were also given the option of seeing Marshall as an iconoclast, as someone who posed a dangerous threat to constitutional governance. The debate about Marshall allowed audiences to construct him as someone unqualified for the Supreme Court, as someone who would increase the level of crime in America, as someone who was affiliated with the most hated of American enemies in 1967—Communists. Moreover, those audiences could construct their understanding of civil rights through this particular prism of Marshall's history and come to the conclusion that civil rights, as constructed, was a dangerous commitment for the American community.

The broader public commentary about Marshall's nomination in the press was more muted than even some of the statements from the floor of Congress, but such commentary often attacked or minimized the significance of the appointment for understanding civil rights. *Washington Post* columnist Joseph Kraft remarked that Marshall was appointed "on the out-moded principle of ethnic representation, and for years to come his seat on the Court will probably be a Negro seat." The outcome, for Kraft, was not good for the Court, which, in his view, "has seemed to be ruled not so much by the internal logic of cases as by a desire to reach results in line with a simple good guys versus bad guys morality."[69] *Post* columnist William S. White concluded that "the point is not the color of Marshall's skin, which is irrelevant, but the cast of Marshall's mind," and called the nominee an "undeniably zealous liberal advocate" who was not appropriate for the "aseptic impartiality" of the Supreme Court.[70] *Washington Star* reader J. F. Steinberg argued that Marshall's nomination was only made to "reinsure the fading Negro support for the next presidential election" and that Marshall would join other justices who "decide cases on their own concept of morality . . . rather than legal bases." And W. A. Power Jr. wrote to the *Star's* editor to lament the "effective brain-washing perpetrated upon Americans by almost every means of national communication," with the result that there were not more strenuous objections to the Marshall appointment.[71]

The potential for vastly varied text constructions in this case, and in most such cases, enhances the circulation and cultural discourse about both the characters in question and their political relevance. This is important for the political culture, because it politicizes the law, allowing members of the community to realize that the decisions made by the nine individuals on the Supreme Court have impact and power. Such text construction is also important for the popular understanding that how we order our collective political culture is often tied inextricably with the individuals we ask to lead that culture, whether as president or as justice of the Supreme Court. Such was the case with Thurgood Marshall, Lyndon Johnson, and the meaning of civil rights in 1967.

In just a few short years, the American ideological landscape would shift again as the demarcation of civil rights continued with the nominations of two southerners to the Supreme Court by President Richard Nixon. Once again, the ideological embodiment of competing conceptions of "justice" would invite further public scrutiny of individuals selected to arbitrate that "justice" at the highest level.

5

Nixon's Southern Strategy and the Supreme Court

The Haynsworth and Carswell Nominations

I understand the bitter feeling of millions of Americans who live in the South about the act of regional discrimination that took place in the Senate yesterday. They have my assurance that the day will come when men like Judges Carswell and Haynsworth can and will sit on the High Court.

President Richard M. Nixon, *Public Papers of the Presidents of the United States: Richard Nixon, 1970*

[T]here are a lot of mediocre judges and people and lawyers. They are entitled to a little representation, aren't they, and a little chance? We can't have all Brandeises and Frankfurters and Cardozos and stuff like that there.

Senator Roman Hruska, quoted in Harris, *Decision*

Two years is a long time in politics, especially when one of those years is 1968. In the short time between Marshall's confirmation in 1967 and the rejected nominations of Clement F. Haynsworth Jr. and G. Harrold Carswell in 1969 and 1970, respectively, much had changed in the ideological and political landscape of the United States. Those changes were significant, ranging from the increasingly uncomfortable presence of American troops in Vietnam to the widespread civil unrest in the urban centers and on college campuses throughout the nation. These two years witnessed, among many other events, the assassinations of Martin Luther King Jr. and Robert Kennedy, the clash of Mayor Richard Daley and protesters in Chicago, and the election of Richard M. Nixon.

The U.S. Supreme Court was at the center of much of this social and political upheaval. The "sweeping permissiveness" of the Supreme Court, according to Theodore White, created a time "when the clash of [America's] two great cultures, the old and the new, was to burst in the political arena to fill the air with an entirely new rhetoric."[1] The Court had, in the final years of the chief justiceship of Earl Warren, issued a series of rulings that reformulated the establishment clause of the First Amendment, dramatically extended rights to those accused of criminal activity, and continued the judicial crusade for the achievement of civil rights.[2] In the 1962 case of *Engel v. Vitale*,[3] the Court deemed unconstitutional state-sponsored prayers in public school classrooms, and it declared compulsory Bible readings similarly unconstitutional a year later in *Abington School District v. Schempp*.[4] The Warren Court required police officers to inform those arrested of their constitutional rights in *Miranda v. Arizona*,[5] required that all accused persons be given legal counsel in *Gideon v. Wainwright*,[6] and construed the Fourth Amendment as prohibiting the admission of illegally seized evidence in a criminal trial in *Mapp v. Ohio*.[7] It was, of course, the Warren Court that outlawed school desegregation in *Brown*. The Warren Court also upheld the principle of "one person-one vote" in *Baker v. Carr*[8] and *Reynolds v. Sims*[9] and upheld controversial passages of the 1965 Voting Rights Act as constitutional in *South Carolina v. Katzenbach*.[10] With each case, the Court offered a new, ideologically loaded interpretation of the relationships and power dynamics of the American community, in the process often expanding legal and political meanings of "equality" and "civil rights."

As such, the Court was of great political importance in the waning days of the Johnson administration. Chief Justice Warren, sensing correctly that Richard Nixon would be elected and concerned about his own advanced age, resigned in 1968 with the hope that Johnson would appoint his successor.[11] LBJ turned to his political ally and adviser, Associate Justice Abe Fortas, as his nominee to succeed Warren. To replace Fortas, Johnson put forth Homer Thornberry, his long-time Texas confederate and a judge on the Fifth Circuit of the U.S. Court of Appeals. For a variety of reasons political and ethical, Fortas's nomination was assailed and ultimately withdrawn by the White House.[12] Johnson was unable to replace Warren, and Abe Fortas resigned in disgrace from the Supreme Court in 1969, leaving a newly inaugurated President Nixon with one guaranteed opening and the likely opportunity of appointing the successor to Earl Warren.[13]

Nixon used the Warren Court and its "permissive" rulings as a powerful campaign tool in 1968. The Republican candidate held the Supreme Court responsible for much of the social upheaval of the 1960s.[14] Nixon even reflected on this view in his memoirs: "I felt that some Supreme Court Justices were too often using their interpretation of the law to remake American society to their own social, political, and ideological precepts."[15] Along with his pledge to bring an "honorable end to the war in Vietnam," Nixon promised to restore "law and order" to an America rife with crime and turmoil. In a not-so-veiled indictment of the Warren Court, Nixon told the delegates at the 1968 Republican convention in Miami to "recognize that some of our courts in their decisions have gone too far in weakening the peace forces as against the criminal forces in this country." Nixon then offered his own reconstruction of the evolving commitment to civil rights: "Let those who have the responsibility to enforce our laws and our judges who have the responsibility to interpret them, be dedicated to the great principles of civil rights. But let them also recognize that the first civil right of every American is to be free from domestic violence. And that right must be guaranteed in this country."[16] Nixon promised throughout the campaign to appoint judges and Supreme Court justices who would be "strict constructionists," who would interpret the law rather than make the law.[17]

Nixon's rhetorical antipathy toward the Warren Court had meaningful political consequences, particularly as his attacks worked to advance his southern electoral strategy. Harry Dent, Nixon's adviser on southern political tactics, remarked that the GOP candidate's 1968 pledge to appoint more conservatives to the Court was one of his "most appealing points."[18] There was a "deep-seated resentment in the land, especially in the South, against decisions for civil rights and civil liberties by the Supreme Court," and Nixon capitalized on that resentment.[19] Indeed, as Nixon expressed in an unguarded moment in the 1968 campaign, praising a campaign commercial: "It's all about law and order and the damn Negro–Puerto Rican groups out there."[20]

Nixon, of course, did appoint Warren's successor: Warren Burger. Burger would serve for almost twenty years as chief justice. His nomination elicited only three negative votes in the Senate and commanded just one day of hearings before the Judiciary Committee.[21]

Nixon's attempts to fill Justice Fortas's seat were not nearly as successful as the Burger nomination. His selection of two southern "strict-constructionists" brought his southern strategy to fruition. As Keith Whittington writes, "Nixon's goals in choosing Justices were as much political as ideological, and even his ideological concern with selecting 'strict constructionists' for the Court was oriented toward the themes of his 'law and order' campaign."[22] Clement F. Haynsworth Jr. and G. Harrold Carswell, furthermore, were opposite sides of the civil rights coin from Thurgood Marshall, and the debates about their nominations to the Court expressed the extent to which the ideological terrain would permit constraints on the fullest extension of civil rights to all Americans. In his crusade to curb the "excesses" of the Warren Court and to garner even more southern support, Nixon nominated one judge, Haynsworth, with a spotty record on civil rights and with alleged ethical improprieties in his background. When that nomination was rejected by the Senate, Nixon elevated a little known and barely respected appellate judge, Carswell, who by all accounts was "mediocre" at best and downright racist at worst. With these nominations, Nixon was issuing his challenge to the evolving construction of civil rights and to the perceived and rhetorically constructed constitutional interpretations of the Warren Court. The Senate's rejection of both nominees for political, ethical, and ideological reasons signaled an evolution in the communal understanding of civil rights and of justice. Both men embodied jurisprudential positions at odds with the developing sense of these commitments that upheld civil rights and equality as cornerstones of U.S. jurisprudence. Though many Americans resisted much that the Warren Court accomplished, the community seemed unwilling to drastically retreat from the progress brought about by that Court. As such, the rejections of Haynsworth and Carswell solidified even further the ideological power of *Brown*, of civil rights, and of equality as central components to the American understanding of justice.

The Haynsworth Rejection

Even his name sounded Confederate: Clement Furman Haynsworth Jr. In many ways, Haynsworth, "an Anglo-Saxon Republican from South Carolina," embodied what Deputy Attorney General Richard Kleindienst called "past grievances" and a time that was ideologically and politically bygone.[23] A graduate of Furman University (a school founded by his great-great-grandfather) and Harvard Law School, Haynsworth was chief judge of the controversial Fourth Circuit Court of Appeals when he was nominated for the Supreme Court. The hearings and the debate surrounding this nomination would express many of the fissures present in the U.S. polity in 1969, leading ultimately to the first outright rejection of a Supreme Court nominee by the U.S. Senate since 1930.

The Haynsworth nomination symbolically resembled the previous nomination controversies of Louis Brandeis and John J. Parker. While comparisons have often been made between the Haynsworth debate of 1969 and the Parker fight of 1930,[24] the added dimension of ethical charges leveled against Haynsworth recalls the Brandeis struggle of 1916. Not only was Haynsworth unacceptable to labor and the civil rights community, but his personal integrity was questioned as well. As such, the processes that characterized those earlier nomination fights—the rhetorical structuring of the hearings according to a trial metaphor and the heavy involvement of the increasingly powerful labor and civil rights movements—reappeared in the Haynsworth debate of 1969.

Haynsworth as the Standpat Jurist

By August 1969, civil rights leaders and lobbyists were quite concerned about the new Nixon administration. One example of the administration's incremental approach to civil rights occurred when it sent government lawyers into court to argue for further delays in implementing Mississippi's desegregation orders. This attempt to forestall integration transpired at the same time the president sent the Haynsworth nomination to the Senate.[25] All indications were that the Nixon administration was going to block or slow affirmative progress toward the civil rights goals that were becoming entrenched as a part of American life. Haynsworth came to represent the Nixon administration's approach to civil rights, as he was constructed as a jurist who was slow to realize and implement the promise of civil rights.

Much of the evidence for this characterization of Haynsworth was drawn from his opinions as a judge on the Fourth Circuit Court of Appeals. Despite protests from his defenders, those looking for evidence of a standpat, incremental southern record from Haynsworth only had to consult his legacy from the Fourth Circuit. In the 1962 case of *Dilliard v. School Board of Charlottesville*,[26] for example, the judge dissented from the majority when they struck down a plan requiring African Americans to request a school transfer in order to achieve desegregation. Haynsworth resurrected arguments from opponents of the *Brown* decision when he argued that children would be traumatized if forced to move from their all-black school. When

Prince Edward County, Virginia, sought to close its public schools rather than achieve integration, Haynsworth upheld the school district's decision as constitutional in *Griffin v. Board of Supervisors of Prince Edward County*,[27] an opinion that was overturned by the Supreme Court in a unanimous ruling. The nominee's opponents emphasized both cases. Baltimore's *Afro-American* featured a cartoon of President Nixon pointing to a chalkboard where the judge's decisions were detailed: "1. Wanted to delay opening Prince Edward County schools for state action. 2. Wanted to keep ineffective freedom of choice plan."[28] Two weeks later, *Afro-American* columnist Roy Wilkins highlighted both cases and argued, "It is a tragedy of unusual dimensions for the nation that President Nixon has nominated this man for a post where he will have a voice in shaping the destiny of the black minority for at least two decades."[29] And these were only two of the most notorious cases in a string of decisions from Haynsworth that offered evidence of his position on civil rights for those who opposed his elevation to the Supreme Court.

Questions about Haynsworth's civil rights record on the appellate court surfaced almost immediately following his nomination. *U.S. News and World Report*, for example, reported that the opposition to Haynsworth "focused on [his] labor and civil rights rulings," even as it predicted certain confirmation.[30] Labor and civil rights groups requested the opportunity to testify before the Judiciary Committee and began mobilizing for the debate over the nomination. Senators from both parties and from all sections of the country began to marshal their arguments regarding the nominee. As Stephen Ambrose recounts, "the southerners were pleased to have one of their own named to the Court; the northerners anticipated with glee what they could do to this southern gentleman in the confirmation hearings."[31]

Haynsworth's supporters tried at the very outset of his confirmation hearings to obviate any consideration of his "judicial philosophy." Such a preemptive strategy expressed an emerging trend in Supreme Court confirmations—the rhetorical construction of nominees as bland, mainstream jurists devoid of controversial views. Toward this end, Nebraska senator Roman Hruska maintained in a prepared statement that, as with the Marshall nomination, "Whether the nominee is liberal or conservative should not concern this Committee. . . . Political questions should play no part in our decision."[32] During the questioning of the nominee, Senator John McClellan, a Democrat from Arkansas, remarked that in his reading of Haynsworth's opinions, he was unable "to detect that they show a trend of a philosophy that is biased or prejudiced in any direction with respect to civil rights cases or labor cases."[33] When questioned by Michigan's Philip Hart, the nominee even testified that he personally agreed with Chief Justice Warren's view that "'separate but equal' wasn't equal and wasn't constitutional."[34] In addition, Haynsworth's Senate supporters would frequently highlight the cases where the judge upheld civil rights positions.[35]

Witnesses also testified in support of Haynsworth's civil rights record. Lawrence Walsh, chair of the American Bar Association's (ABA) Committee on the Federal Judiciary, noted that he had spoken with several district judges knowledgeable about civil rights, and "they spoke in the highest terms of Judge Haynsworth."[36] One witness given considerable attention by the committee was John Bolt Culbertson, president of the Greenville County Bar Association in South Carolina. Describing himself as "active in the field of civil rights" and an NAACP sympathizer, Culbertson was unabashedly supportive of Haynsworth. He maintained that the nominee was "absolutely honest" with "impeccable integrity." He further suggested that Haynsworth was supported by the South Carolina NAACP and that "there is not a single Negro that I know of connected with the civil rights movement, the respectable civil rights movement, that I know of, that has indicated any desire to come up here and attack Judge Haynsworth. Now, I think that is significant."[37]

Ultimately, the Judiciary Committee's majority report maintained that Haynsworth's civil rights record did not disqualify him for the Supreme Court, arguing that a full review of that record offered a complete portrait of the nominee. The majority found "that he has frequently voted in favor of persons claiming deprivations of their federally protected rights."[38] They also cited the case of John J. Parker, where "the Senate made a mistake when it refused to consent to the nomination"[39] because of charges that Parker was antilabor and opposed to civil rights. The majority of the Judiciary Committee maintained that "Judge Haynsworth is extraordinarily well qualified for the post to which he has been nominated."[40]

The judge's defenders put forth the image of him as a moderate on civil rights in the floor debate that addressed the nomination. Senator Hruska concluded that Haynsworth was consistent with the Warren Court and argued that he "will continue to work fairly and pragmatically to insure that all Americans receive their civil rights."[41] Senator Howard Baker of Tennessee concluded that "the fact that Judge Haynsworth has adhered to the [Supreme] Court's pronouncements should end the inquiry."[42] Hruska later entered into the *Congressional Record* a lengthy statement by G. W. Foster, a Wisconsin law professor and "liberal Democrat" who maintained that

Haynsworth was "an intelligent, open-minded man with a practical knack for seeking workable answers to hard questions."[43]

While Haynsworth's champions tried to blunt the attack on his civil rights record, considerable effort was put forth by the nominee's opponents to cast him in a segregationist light. This effort fused Haynsworth's southern persona with a segregationist jurisprudence to embody him as the quintessence of standpat anti-integrationism. For instance, William Ryan, a representative from New York, called the nomination a "litmus test" for a nation in "deep controversy and division" over the "direction and speed with which the fundamental American promise of equality and equal rights for all of our citizens is being fulfilled." Representative Ryan went on to conclude that Haynsworth's appointment to the Supreme Court would result in the "further retrenchment on the fundamental law of our land."[44] Stephen Schlossberg, the general counsel for the United Automobile, Aerospace and Agricultural Implement Workers of America, argued to the committee that Haynsworth maintained close associations with "socially backward, irresponsible, and reactionary economic interests in the South" and that he "is essentially anticivil rights and that his decisions support segregation."[45] Representing the International Union of Electrical Radio and Machine Workers, Irving Abramson offered a similar conclusion when he presented a series of cases to demonstrate that the nominee held a "segregationist point of view."[46]

The testimony of Clarence Mitchell and Joseph Rauh of the Leadership Conference on Civil Rights was particularly brutal. Mitchell began by praising the Supreme Court as "the symbol of protection" for African Americans, asserting that Haynsworth's nomination "is a deadly blow to the image of the U.S. Supreme Court." The nominee represented a judicial philosophy, according to Mitchell, that was tantamount to legalized racism. Strict constructionism, Mitchell told the committee, "produced the spurious separate but equal doctrine" and "means granting their [African Americans] constitutional rights with an eye dropper at a time when these rights should be flowing like a river in a thirsty land."[47] Rauh argued that Haynsworth was a "segregationist" who "appears always to be running away from *Brown*."[48]

Both Rauh and Mitchell parried difficult questions from the committee. At one point, they were presented with a letter defending Haynsworth's civil rights record that cited twelve of his "integrationist" decisions. Rauh concluded that these were meaningless cases that "could not have gone any other way [and] that were unanimous."[49] Mitchell revealed that

Haynsworth maintained a membership in a Richmond, Virginia, country club that was "one of the longstanding symbols of racial segregation" and that continued to practice segregation, even against African American members of the Virginia State Legislature.[50] Their concerns about Haynsworth were validated by Princeton political scientist Gary Orfield, who testified that though there was an impression of Haynsworth as a civil rights moderate, his opinions reflected "a very conservative member of a very conservative court."[51]

Haynsworth's detractors took their case to the Senate floor as well, steadfastly suggesting that the nominee was outdated in his views toward civil rights and that he actively sought to preserve his antiquated view of civil rights law. New York's Jacob Javits, for instance, called Haynsworth's civil rights views "consistently out of date," and he lamented that the nominee "has been consistently in error, systemically and relentlessly opposed to implementation of the Supreme Court's 1954 desegregation decision and consistently sympathetic to every new device for delay for desegregation."[52] New Jersey's senior senator, Clifford Case, determined that "Judge Haynsworth has shown a persistent reluctance to accept, and considerable legal ingenuity to avoid, the Supreme Court's unanimous holdings in the *Brown* case."[53] Both Javits and Case were Republicans, moreover, indicating just how significant Haynsworth's civil rights record was for those deciding his fate.

The competing positions concerning Haynsworth and his suitability for the Court reflected the persistent battle in 1969 America over the meaning of civil rights for the community. As with many of the ideological controversies of the twentieth century, this one primarily concerned race. Proponents cast Haynsworth as well within the mainstream on questions of civil rights, as an integrationist who reflected and supported the law of the land. Opponents constructed the nominee as a standpat segregationist who championed the prevailing southern obstructionism to integration. As such, Haynsworth became a site of struggle, a focus of tension about what civil rights means and how best to achieve full civil rights for all Americans. Eugene G. Eisner, for instance, wrote to the *New York Times* that the Haynsworth nomination was a payoff to South Carolina's Strom Thurmond to reward him for Nixon's southern support—"President Nixon is indeed paying a heavy debt to Senator Thurmond for the support he received in the 1968 Presidential election," Eisner wrote.[54] Attacking Haynsworth's opponents, David C. Carrad wrote to the *Times* that criticism of the judge centered on his "social philosophy," and he concluded that "I do not think that Judge Haynsworth would make a good head of the O.E.O. [Office of Equal Opportunity]; but then Roy Wilkins is not my idea of a good Justice of the Supreme Court."[55] Frank Askin, a law professor from Rutgers, in his letter to the *New York Times* concluded that the nomination was "tragic" because Nixon selected for the Supreme Court "a man so closely associated with the racial views of the old South."[56] In short, Haynsworth embodied the competing positions that characterized so much of the public controversy about civil rights, equality, segregation, and integration—indeed, all of the questions defining race in twentieth-century American discourse.

A Southern Gentleman

Haynsworth's civil rights record, as a source of conflict over his nomination, was of interest to the news media, though such coverage typically simplified the issue. Much of the coverage only explained that labor and civil rights groups opposed the nomination. *U.S. News and World Report* announced that "two powerful political groups played the key roles in the rejection of . . . [Haynsworth]: labor unions and civil-rights activists."[57] The magazine's editor wondered if such groups would "continue to dictate who shall be permitted to sit on the Supreme Court of the United States."[58] As *Newsweek* speculated about Fortas's replacement, it dubbed Haynsworth's record on civil rights "impeccably moderate."[59] Later, as the controversy over the nomination developed, the same magazine noted that one of the most fascinating aspects of the nomination was how "labor and civil-rights leaders forged their alliance against the conservative nominee."[60]

Several media outlets were openly and editorially critical of Haynsworth's civil rights record. The *Nation* maintained that "for Negroes, and therefore for all of us, the selection of Haynsworth . . . can prove to have unfortunate consequences."[61] The *New Republic* highlighted Haynsworth's mediocrity in the area of civil rights law, noting that two recent "important" Supreme Court decisions in this area were reversals of Haynsworth decisions. *Commonweal* remarked that "ideologically . . . Haynsworth is back around 1922."[62] Indeed, this judgment of Haynsworth as anachronistic pervades much of the coverage of his nomination.

The most intriguing aspect of the news media coverage of this nomination, though, is the manner in which Haynsworth was portrayed as a southerner. Such portrayals, of course, were not directly critical of his civil rights jurisprudence, but they reinforced an image of the judge that implicitly constructed him as a standpat jurist unwilling to work toward the fulfillment of civil rights for African Americans. In short, through such depictions, Haynsworth came to incarnate a stereotypical "southern" attitude toward civil rights. This portrayal reinforced the anti-Haynsworth rhetoric regarding the nominee's lack of true commitment to civil rights and equality for all Americans.

Several of the profiles of Haynsworth emphasized his southernness as if it were a marker of important difference.[63] *Time* noted that the judge journeys home every day for lunch and to "tend his camellias" and it labeled him the product of "Southern gentility." The profile also noted that Haynsworth's "relationships outside his own class—and race—have been few and distant."[64] Another profile in *Time* proclaimed Haynsworth "the stereotype of a courtly Southern judge."[65] Other news sources were concerned that the nomination was a "payoff" to Nixon's southern supporters. *Newsweek* concluded that Nixon sought a southerner who was "Dixified enough" to give backers like Strom Thurmond a "symbolic victory."[66] The *New Republic* editorialized that the nomination was a "payoff to the White South . . . for the support it gave Mr. Nixon last year and may be asked to give him again in 1972."[67]

The news media also featured photographs of Haynsworth that emphasized his southernness and courtly gentility. *Newsweek* displayed one photograph of the judge in a white suit, jauntily leaning against a chair in a conference room.[68] *Time* also showed Haynsworth in a white suit admiring a flower (undoubtedly a camellia) with his wife, Dorothy.[69] *Newsweek* featured a photograph of the judge in his greenhouse,[70] while *Time* included a picture of the nominee and his wife, who is holding a parasol to shield the sun.[71] These images of gardening, white suits, camellias, and stereotyped southern femininity signify a southern worldview or ideology that the Haynsworths embodied. They worked in tandem with the more direct commentary that suggested this nominee was not part of the mainstream of American law, especially concerning civil rights for Americans of African descent.

Clement Haynsworth was constructed during the debate over his nomination as a symbol of the South and of southern standpatism on questions of racial integration. James Simon argues that the nominee's southernness factored into and may have been the deciding element in his nomination— Nixon appointed Haynsworth largely for this reason.[72] Haynsworth's southernness, though, was also his undoing. The fact that Haynsworth came from South Carolina was supposed to work as a marker of his strict constructionism and of a more representative Supreme Court. Instead, he came to embody a segregationist, southern outlook toward civil rights and the extension of equality to all Americans. Haynsworth was the standpat jurist, the obstructionist, a representative of a time and place long gone and forgotten for most of the U.S. polity. Coupled with other areas of concern, Haynsworth's detractors successfully put forth an image of the judge as outside of the broad parameters of American jurisprudence—an image that was amplified in the media and that proved highly damaging to his nomination.

The Appearance of Impropriety

Haynsworth might well have been confirmed for the Supreme Court if the only charges he faced were that he was conservative on labor and civil rights issues. But when he confronted charges that he was unethical, that he had violated judicial codes of conduct, the pressures that ultimately led to his rejection truly began to build.

The ethics charges that Haynsworth faced and that occupied so much of the attention devoted to his nomination are difficult to assess in terms of their impact. On one level, they were only significant because of the criticism leveled at Justice Abe Fortas. The charges that ultimately drove Fortas from the Court established new standards for ethical propriety and accountability, standards Haynsworth was unable to meet. Fortas's nomination also established a new level of scrutiny that was not present even in the intensity of the Brandeis and Parker nominations. This new threshold would come to define many nominations—to the Court or the cabinet, for example—for the remainder of the century. The nomination process, following Fortas, would never be the same, and Haynsworth was the first to face this intense examination.[73]

The essential charge against Haynsworth was that he failed to recognize the appearance of impropriety in several of his business dealings. Haynsworth was a wealthy man with a considerable investment portfolio, and there were instances in his history when, as a judge, he ruled on cases that involved his business interests.[74] Two of these instances were especially notable.

In the first instance, Judge Haynsworth participated in the case of *Darlington Manufacturing Company v. National Labor Relations Board*,[75] in which the Fourth Circuit Court of Appeals held that the closing of a textile plant to prevent the unionization of its workers did not violate existing labor law. Although the ruling itself was used by labor unions as evidence of Haynsworth's hostility to the labor movement,[76] the ethical relevance of the case stemmed from Haynsworth's investments in a company called Carolina Vend-A-Matic. This company did considerable business with the

Deering Milliken Company, of which Darlington Manufacturing was a subsidiary. Haynsworth was a vice president of Carolina Vend-A-Matic (and his wife was secretary of the board of directors) when the *Darlington* case appeared before him.

Two ethical questions emerged from Haynsworth's involvement with Carolina Vend-A-Matic and the *Darlington* case. The first concerned Haynsworth's ethical responsibilities to disqualify himself from a case in which he held substantial interest. As he had decided to maintain his business dealings with Carolina Vend-A-Matic, there were some who argued that the ethics code required that he disqualify himself from the case. Still others noted that the issue of disqualification should never have arisen, because the ethics code advises judges to divest themselves of investments that might pose a conflict of interest in their official duties. As Iowa Republican Jack Miller said on the floor of the Senate, Haynsworth needed to follow the code of ethics "so that not only would there be no conflict of interest, but there would be no connection with Carolina Vend-A-Matic that would arouse the suspicion that he was biased in his judgment."[77]

Haynsworth's supporters, though, held that it was his duty to sit on the case. As Senator Strom Thurmond noted in his statement to the Judiciary Committee, "The judge's duty to sit on a case is equal to the duty not to sit." With his trademark simplicity that obscured nuance, Thurmond went on to assert, hypothetically, "No Senator would refuse to vote on income tax reform because he paid income tax, and no judge would expect to excuse himself from a telephone case because he had a telephone in his home and office."[78]

In the hearings concerning the nomination, expert testimony was solicited on the precise question of Haynsworth's responsibility to disqualify himself in the *Darlington* case. That testimony was offered by John P. Frank, a well-known authority on legal and judicial ethics. Frank concluded that "it would not have been proper disqualification practice for Judge Haynsworth to have disqualified himself in that case. . . . There was no legal ground for disqualification."[79] Haynsworth himself maintained in his testimony to the Judiciary Committee that he did not inform the parties to the case of his financial stake in Carolina Vend-A-Matic because "I did not regard myself as having any financial interest in the outcome, and I still do not."[80]

The other notable ethical dimension to the *Darlington* matter was an apparent contradiction in Haynsworth's testimony before a Judiciary Committee subcommittee in June 1969, when he maintained that upon his

elevation to the federal bench, he "resigned from all such business associations . . . directorships, and things of that sort."[81] Of course, this was an
untrue statement given his position with Carolina Vend-A-Matic (and his
involvement with the Main-Oak Corporation). As Senator Birch Bayh, a
Democrat from Indiana and a leader of the anti-Haynsworth effort in the
Senate, pointed out to the judge in the hearings, "[I]t is most unfortunate
that we have had this inconsistency which tends to cloud the whole picture."[82] The nominee rather lamely tried to defend his comments, noting
that when they were given, in June 1969, he had resigned, but acknowl-
edging that his statement was mistaken "to the extent that I said that I resigned from them all when I first went on the bench" in 1957.[83]

This lapse in memory, and perhaps in judgment, was a source of considerable discussion and criticism during the debates surrounding this nomination. As Idaho Republican Len Jordan maintained on the Senate floor:

> It is hard to believe that Judge Haynsworth could have forgotten in June the
> weekly board meetings, the fees he received, and the duties he performed as
> director of this unusually successful business which had been more lucrative
> for him than his judge's salary. By this discrepancy in his testimony, Judge
> Haynsworth set up, in my opinion, his own credibility gap.[84]

Senator Bayh concluded that Haynsworth's comments demonstrated an
"amazing lack of candor" and that all of the nominee's business dealings
were not "acceptable conduct for a nominee to the Supreme Court."[85]
Caught clearly in a misrepresentation, Haynsworth and his supporters offered little or no defense to these charges.

Haynsworth faced another ethical challenge because of his conduct in
the case of *Brunswick Corp. v. Long*,[86] in which the Fourth Circuit Court of
Appeals affirmed a district court ruling concerning the sale and rental of
bowling equipment. The details of the case are less important than Judge
Haynsworth's actions during the disposition of the case. The case itself was
heard by the judges of the Fourth Circuit on November 10, 1967. After the
judges hearing the case decided in favor Brunswick, and while the opinion
was being drafted, Haynsworth met with his stockbroker, who advised him
to purchase stock in the Brunswick Corporation. The judge followed the
advice and bought 1,000 shares of stock. This meeting occurred in December 1967, and the opinion in the case was not filed until February 1968.[87]

When the facts of this particular case were revealed by the anti-
Haynsworth forces, the judge returned to the Judiciary Committee to explain his actions. He briefly sketched out the details of the case as he

remembered them and concluded, "I do not think under the circumstances that under the statute, I did not think then, I do not think now, that what I did in the decisional process in that case was done while I had any interest whatever in the case or in its outcome."[88] His defenders were even more pointed. Democrat Robert Byrd of West Virginia maintained on the Senate floor that "these cases afford no legitimate reason for voting against the confirmation of the nominee."[89]

Even with his denials, Haynsworth's opponents saw evidence in both the *Darlington* and *Brunswick* cases of ethically suspect behavior. As Senator Bayh remarked during the floor debate, "Though I believe Judge Haynsworth to be honest, he has not shown the proper sensitivity to ethical problems which have arisen during his career. Indeed that career has been blemished by a pattern of insensitivity to the judicial precepts concerning the appearance of impropriety."[90] Both Senator Bayh and Senator Millard Tydings (D-MD) of the Judiciary Committee put forth detailed accounts of Haynsworth's ethical travails in the report about the nomination. Tydings argued that the judge's "past actions and present approach to the principles of judicial conduct have cast a shadow over his ethical sensitivities."[91] Meanwhile, Montana Democrat Lee Metcalf concluded in his statement to the Senate that Haynsworth "has not met the high standards of judicial ethics the Senate set as the first prerequisite for a potential Supreme Court Justice" and that his Judiciary Committee testimony was "shot through with ambiguity, evasion, and misrepresentations."[92]

Haynsworth's supporters were quick to defend the nominee's ethics. Republican Roman Hruska asserted on the Senate floor, "We are dealing with an honorable man, who has a high reputation for integrity, and therefore his statements [to the Judiciary Committee] should be taken as the truth in this regard."[93] Haynsworth's chief Senate supporter, Kentucky Republican Marlow Cook, referenced the 1916 Brandeis confirmation debate in his advocacy of Haynsworth's nomination. Noting that Brandeis was opposed primarily for his jurisprudential viewpoints, Cook maintained that just as the Brandeis hearings disproved the ethical charges against that nominee, so, too, the Haynsworth hearings "failed to substantiate any violation of the prevailing standards of conduct." Cook proceeded to predict that Haynsworth's career on the Supreme Court would be "just as dignified and distinguished" as was Brandeis's.[94] Senator Robert Byrd also highlighted the comparisons between Brandeis and Haynsworth. Brandeis was opposed because he was Jewish, Byrd maintained, and Haynsworth is opposed because "he is a white, conservative, southerner."[95]

The ethical concerns raised in response to the Haynsworth nomination attracted the attention of the nation's news media. Early in the nomination process, *Time* revealed that the "most damaging" allegations against Haynsworth were those related to his business dealings.[96] Just two weeks later, the same magazine noted that Haynsworth had been connected to Bobby Baker, a Democratic Senate aide convicted of tax evasion and larceny in 1967. *Time* concluded that the association with Baker "is enough to frighten most politicians."[97] *Newsweek* highlighted the long "shadow" cast by the Fortas nomination, noting that Haynsworth's alleged ethical improprieties would not typically be enough to halt the nomination.[98] In its cover story assessing the failed nomination following the Senate vote, *Newsweek* concluded that Haynsworth was the "most tragic victim" of the process, because the "high ethical standards" that he faced would never have been applied "except in reaction to the Fortas affair."[99]

There was frequent editorial outrage that President Nixon would appoint someone to the Supreme Court with such slim ethical credentials. The *New Republic*, for example, dubbed Haynsworth "an honest man, but a limited one . . . [who] will do the ethical thing as soon as someone tells him what it is."[100] The magazine also featured the comments of Alexander M. Bickel, who argued that the "issue is not his honesty, but his ethical sensitivity," when he urged the Senate to consider this issue in its deliberations.[101] Consistent in its opposition, the *Nation* attacked the ABA's Committee on the Federal Judiciary for approving the Haynsworth nomination. Editorialist Patrick Owens concluded that "Haynsworth violated the ABA's own code of judicial ethics when he sat on cases involving corporations in which he owned stock."[102]

Rejecting Haynsworth

Correctly sensing that his nomination of Haynsworth was in trouble, President Nixon convened an "informal meeting" with members of the news media to answer the charges made against the judge. Calling the ethical attacks against Haynsworth "a vicious character assassination," Nixon proceeded to favorably cite the testimony of John Frank in support of the nomination and to rebut the specific ethics charges individually.[103] The president then claimed it was improper to reject a nominee because of that nominee's philosophical outlook. Nixon cited the remarks of some senators during the Marshall hearings that rejected judicial philosophy as a confirmation criteria, concluding that "if Judge Haynsworth's philosophy leans to the conservative side, in my view that recommends him to me." Citing the

Parker and Brandeis nominations as precedent, the president concluded that "it is not proper to turn down a man because he is a southerner, because he is a Jew, because he is a Negro, or because of his philosophy."[104]

Nixon's comments, of course, were unsuccessful. Just before the floor vote on the nomination, Senator Roman Hruska pleaded with his colleagues: "Where do we go from here, if there is a rejection of the nominee? It will amount to a rejection of the president's plan to make appointments to the Supreme Court which will restore balance. . . . [T]here is every reason why we should confirm the nomination."[105] Despite such lamentations, the Senate rejected the Haynsworth nomination 45–55, with many Republicans deserting their newly elected president and voting to reject. Senator Mark Hatfield, an Oregon Republican who voted nay on the nomination, expressed his frustration immediately following the vote: "This nomination will not reestablish the trust and respect that is needed so gravely today for our Nation's Highest Court. For the sake of the Court, I opposed it."[106]

Nixon was, predictably, upset by the Senate's rejection of Haynsworth, especially since he had every reason to expect a "halo" effect for his nominee so soon after the 1968 elections and his inauguration in January.[107] Maintaining that Haynsworth's "integrity is unimpeachable, his ability unquestioned," the president promised to nominate another individual using the same criteria he employed with the Haynsworth choice. Nixon also suggested that the "majority of people in the Nation regret" the Senate's rejection.[108] Nixon's anger about the rejection is reported by Evans and Novak, who indicate that in the privacy of the White House, "Nixon inveighed against the liberal press which had built the opposition to Haynsworth, against organized labor for its vendetta against the judge, and most of all against those Republican senators who had betrayed their President."[109]

The reasons for the rejection of Clement Haynsworth are complicated and varied. Some explain the rejection by referencing the arrogance of the Nixon administration, especially in the wake of the successful Burger confirmation.[110] In an exhaustive study of the Nixon papers, Dean Kotlowski maintains that the defeat of Haynsworth resulted from "ad hoc" decision-making and a failure to "establish clear lines of staff authority and a strategy for dealing with Congress."[111] Others blamed the Senate. Senators sought, these observers claim, to limit presidential power and to hold Nixon's nominees to the Court to impossibly high standards because of the Fortas incident.[112] One contemporary commentator maintained that the Fortas and Haynsworth debates reflected growing conflict over the role of the Supreme Court in American life.[113] William Safire asserts that

Haynsworth was undone by his speech impediment—stuttering—which meant "he could not properly defend himself in the court of public opinion."[114]

All of these factors were undoubtedly relevant to the rejection of Haynsworth by the Senate. Yet they seem unsatisfying by themselves. The rejection of Clement Haynsworth was a complicated ideological event that enacted an important aspect of American definitions of justice—the survival and maintenance of civil rights as a fundamental foundation of justice in this community. Haynsworth was constructed and constructed himself as a judge who was conservative, who believed in incrementalism, and who represented a time and place that existed long ago and far away for most Americans. Add to that the failure of Haynsworth and the administration to adapt to the new form of the Supreme Court nomination process, where individual conduct and ethical propriety were carefully scrutinized, and there was little chance of confirmation.

Richard Vatz and Theodore Windt conclude that "neither political issues nor judicial decisions truly influenced the final rejection" and that it was the "ethos" of the nominee that was the determining factor.[115] Of course, such a judgment is limited in its definition of ethos as separate from politics or jurisprudence. Haynsworth came to embody an ideological approach to the law that was highly political. His character as a nominee was defined by the president who appointed him, by the descriptions of him as conservative or moderate on civil rights concerns, by the depictions of his "southernness," and by the ethical charges that he confronted. The rejection of Haynsworth, then, reflected the politics of his times. It was an act by the Senate that established high standards of ethical behavior and one that (re)introduced judicial philosophy into the deliberations over "advice and consent." The judgments regarding judicial philosophy, particularly in the area of civil rights, partially defined this controversy and this nominee, and his rejection represented another step in the evolution of American conceptions of civil rights and justice as cornerstones of the community's political and legal identity.

The Carswell Rejection

Following the rejection of Clement Haynsworth, Richard Nixon committed a serious miscalculation—he nominated G. Harrold Carswell to the Supreme Court. Dubbed as "one of the most ill-advised public acts of the early Nixon Presidency,"[116] the Carswell nomination was hurried to the Senate and probably resulted from several converging factors. Nixon wanted another southerner but needed a nominee who lacked any financial or ethical entanglements, and Carswell qualified on these criteria. The president received assurances that a nominee without ethical problems would be confirmed. And because of his pique about Haynsworth, Nixon's other motives for nominating Carswell might have included insulting both the Supreme Court and the Senate by putting forth such a blatantly unqualified individual.[117] Furthermore, the fact that the White House was caught unprepared by confirmation revelations about Carswell and opposition to this nomination indicates its hastiness.[118]

Clement Haynsworth and G. Harrold Carswell were alike in only one respect—they were both conservative, southern federal judges. Apart from this, the two men were very different. Haynsworth epitomized southern gentility, with his camellias, white suits, and refined manner. Carswell was a "good old boy" who was fond of hunting. Haynsworth attended Harvard Law School, while Carswell's legal training occurred at Mercer University in Macon, Georgia. Haynsworth came from the refined circles of South Carolina society, where he had long-standing family connections; Carswell was a transplanted Georgian in Tallahassee, Florida. While Haynsworth's record on civil rights was slightly obstructionistic, Carswell's approach to civil rights was highly recalcitrant. This final difference was significant, and Carswell's ultimate rejection by the U.S. Senate, once again, reaffirmed the community's unwillingness to risk its civil rights and to place those rights at the mercy of a Supreme Court justice with mediocre credentials and an open hostility to the equality of all Americans.

The Segregationist Jurist

Soon after the White House submitted his name, it was revealed that Carswell gave a speech in 1948 upholding the principles of white supremacy and ongoing segregation. While campaigning for the Georgia state legislature, before an audience of American Legionnaires, Carswell said:

> I am a Southerner by ancestry, birth, training, inclination, belief, and practice. I believe that segregation of the races is proper and the only practical and correct way of life in our states. I have always so believed, and I shall always so act. I shall be the last to submit to any attempt on the part of anyone to break down and to weaken this firmly established policy of our people. . . . I yield to no man as a fellow-candidate, or as a fellow-citizen, in

the firm, vigorous belief in the principles of white supremacy, and I shall always be so governed.[119]

This statement is compelling on several levels. First, it firmly identifies Carswell as a southerner and links his beliefs in white supremacy and segregation with his southernness. The southernness of the nominee would later be significant (as it was for Haynsworth) in the coverage of the confirmation debate by the mass media and in the actual debate over the nomination. The statement also projects into the future, asserting that Carswell not only believed in white supremacy and segregation in 1948 but that he would "always be so governed." Finally, the tone of the statement is unequivocal, mitigating somewhat Carswell's repudiations in 1970 of these sentiments. The beliefs of the speaker in 1948 were "firm" and "vigorous" to the extent that Carswell would "yield to no man" in his convictions. All of these factors worked against Carswell's eventual negation of this speech when he was nominated to the Supreme Court, paving the way for attacks on his commitment to civil rights as an important dimension of American jurisprudence and the construction of him as the embodiment of segregation.

The power of the 1948 speech was revealed quite clearly in the hearings before the Senate Judiciary Committee, which commenced in late January and continued into early February, 1970. After revealing the ABA's assessment of Carswell as "qualified" for the Supreme Court, the committee members immediately turned to the question of his statements in 1948 and the repudiation of those sentiments. Edward Gurney, the junior senator from Florida, told the committee that Carswell's rejection of the 1948 speech "shows forthrightness, candor, integrity, and strength of character."[120] Gurney's statement was followed by the testimony of the nominee. When asked by Senator Roman Hruska to comment on the 1948 speech, Carswell rather sternly replied that "those words themselves are obnoxious and abhorrent to me. I am not a racist. I have no notions, secretive, open, or otherwise, of racial superiority."[121]

Despite these strong words, Carswell's opponents on the committee would not let the matter drop. Michigan Democrat Philip Hart entered into the record of the hearings the statement itself and asked the judge to reflect on his beliefs at the time he made the speech. Carswell maintained that the speech "came to me like something out of the *disembodied* past, almost."[122] Hart pressed the point, asking if Carswell believed the statement when he first delivered it in 1948, and Carswell was forced to admit that he did hold those beliefs. The process clearly affected Carswell. Just a few moments later, facing Senator Edward Kennedy's questions, the nominee was practically incoherent. Asked to comment on the frustration of "young people," Carswell began discussing the problems facing the nation. He concluded:

> These are vast problems, tremendous problems. Again, my statement to you of recognition of these problems in no way, I think, and certainly I don't want it to be so interpreted, that this has gotten into any area of affecting the judicial process. This is the grist mill from which cases arise. This is perhaps the oven where the bread is first cooked.[123]

The rambling statement, filled as it is with mixed metaphors and odd imagery, indicates just how significant the pressure of the hearings was for Carswell.

Another element of Carswell's racial attitudes emerged early in the hearings when the nominee was questioned about his involvement with a segregated country club in Tallahassee. The Supreme Court had ruled that the private incorporation of public clubs for the purpose of circumventing desegregation was unconstitutional, and Carswell played some role in such a club following the Court's ruling. In his questioning of the nominee, Indiana senator Birch Bayh remarked, "[I]t concerns me, very frankly, for you incidentally to be involved at the time you were district attorney in the incorporation of a club at least some the members of which have made public allegations that the purpose of this was to avoid the integration order which had been previously set down by the Supreme Court of the United States."[124] The nominee was forced to admit his involvement with the club, as an incorporator, but he denied knowing the subterfugal purpose of the incorporation documents.

Carswell's record on civil rights thus dominated the hearings concerning his nomination, and once again a Supreme Court nomination became a focal point of public discussion about this critical principle. The third day of the hearings, for example, featured testimony from civil rights activists and academics about the nominee's commitment to various forms of civil rights law. Hawaiian representative Patsy Mink testified that Carswell's nomination "constitutes an affront to the women of America."[125] Mink was followed by Betty Friedan, then president of the National Organization for Women (NOW), who maintained that the committee needed "to understand the dangerous insensitivity of Judge Carswell to sex discrimination." Friedan further noted that "human rights are indivisible and I and those for whom I speak would oppose equally the appointment to the Supreme

Court in 1970 of a racist judge who has been totally blind to the humanity of black men and women since 1948 as to a sexist judge totally blind to the humanity of women in 1969."[126] These sentiments expressed rather starkly the connections present between the enduring problem of civil rights and race and the emerging concern with the civil rights of women.[127]

The committee heard testimony from several prominent academic and legal witnesses who also questioned the nominee's commitment to civil rights. Gary Orfield, a Princeton politics professor, concluded that Carswell's "chief qualification appears to be an abiding unwillingness to protect the constitutional rights of black Americans."[128] Union lawyer Stephen Schlossberg remarked that the Carswell nomination was "an insult . . . to the Senate of the United States, to the people of the United States, to the Negroes of the United States, and to the whites of the United States."[129] Leroy Clark, an NAACP Legal and Educational Defense Fund lawyer and law professor at New York University (NYU), unequivocally expressed the relevance of the Carswell nomination for civil rights. Clark told that committee that "Judge Carswell was the most hostile Federal District Court judge I have ever appeared before with respect to civil rights matters."[130]

The attacks that Carswell faced in the Senate Judiciary Committee were confirmed by an examination of his record, carefully reported in the national news media. Fred Graham penned a thorough examination of Carswell's record in the *New York Times*, concluding that the nominee's rulings often "had the result of allowing dilatory school officials to delay desegregation." Graham also cited a Yale study that showed Carswell's reversal rate to be 60 percent.[131] In some cases, Carswell's opinions ran "completely counter to the Supreme Court's mandate for genuine school desegregation."[132] Upholding the segregation of faculty, arguing that *Brown* only applied to students, Carswell was reversed by the appellate court in *Augustus v. Board of Public Instruction of Escambia County*. In that case, Carswell likened claims of segregated faculty to concerns by students about the leniency or strictness of teachers.[133] In *Due v. Tallahassee Theaters, Inc.*,[134] Carswell dismissed a case against a theater chain that alleged a conspiracy to deny African Americans equal access to movie theaters. His order to dismiss was unanimously overruled by the court of appeals. Another case, *Youngblood v. Board of Public Instruction of Bay County, Florida*,[135] found Judge Carswell supporting a "freedom of choice" plan that was designed to forestall forced integration of the schools through an elaborate and complicated plan that would make integration virtually impossible. Again, his ruling was overturned. Ultimately, in several cases over several years, Carswell routinely fought desegregation efforts and worked to prevent active integration of the public schools.

Segregationism Personified

The cumulative impression of this testimony was of Carswell as a southern judge with a racist past and a definite hostility toward civil rights in the present. This impression was also furthered by the news media's coverage of the hearings and the events surrounding the nomination. *Newsweek* highlighted a new discovery from Carswell's past—a 1966 deed signed by the judge and his wife that included a segregationist proviso. The deed contained language that restricted the sale of the property "to members of the Caucasian race," and *Newsweek* reported that Carswell's critics "demanded to know why a Federal judge was casually ignoring the Supreme Court ruling [that restricted such covenants]."[136] The *New Republic* opined that "neither racism nor the unrebutted appearance of racism belongs on the Supreme Court."[137] When the 1966 land deed was publicized, the same magazine concluded that "he was a federal judge, and those words about the Caucasian race should have leaped to his eye. Such a covenant is wrong as well as unenforceable under the law I am sworn to uphold, he should have said. Yet he signed. That is the record, and on it Harrold Carswell should not be confirmed."[138]

The focus on his civil rights difficulties worked alongside the news media's descriptions of Carswell as a southerner. As with Haynsworth, the southernness of Carswell demarcated his difference as it became a marker of what he stood for and his character. *Newsweek*'s profile of Judge Carswell described him as a "hustling, out-going, fairly roughhewn man of the kind known as 'a good old boy' in the South."[139] In another profile, the same periodical noted that Carswell came from "red-neck country" and that he had developed a sense of "courthouse trading and deer-camp masculinity." The judge, *Newsweek* revealed, was a member of the "plantation crowd" in Tallahassee, and it reported on a racist joke that Carswell told to an audience of Atlanta attorneys, some of whom were reportedly shocked. *Time* maintained that "Carswell's decisions have reflected his close ties to the society in which he lives."[140]

Despite the portrayal of Carswell's "southernness," the news media was also quick to highlight southern discontent with the nomination. *Time* noted, following the nomination's rejection, that "even many Southerners felt insulted that Nixon had chosen Carswell to represent them."[141] The

Nation editorialized that Carswell was an "embarrassment to the Old South," resulting in an "obvious lack of enthusiasm" for the nominee from southern senators.[142] Carswell was defined, by the news media and in the Judiciary Committee hearings, as someone outside of the mainstream, a nominee who was different in origins and in attitude. His stereotypical southernness determined his attitudes toward civil rights, so that the portrayals of the judge as a segregationist, a racist, were made consistent and validated by his origins as a "good old boy" from Florida and Georgia.

Lingering impressions of Carswell as an ideological agent, as a marker of southern segregationism, are found in the public reactions to his nomination and the ensuing controversy. A large group of Harvard law professors, writing to the *New York Times*, emphasized the ideological importance of the Carswell nomination: "No matter how ready we may be to accept and welcome the judge's recent statements, there seems an ineradicable symbolism in his appointment to the Supreme Court."[143] Another law school contingent, from the University of Pennsylvania, noted that Carswell's only qualifications for the Court "appear to be his Southern heritage and his lack of investment in the securities market."[144] Some citizens lamented the stereotypical vision of the South represented by Carswell—Benjamin Zwerling called the nominee a "sop" to southern prejudices and saw the Nixon administration's southern strategy, "which crudely uses the Supreme Court as one of its props," as a "monumental affront."[145] Writing as a "native of the South," Bernard L. Mitchell defended Carswell, noting that his statement about white supremacy "was probably the result of the inculcation in him by precept and example of the view he now repudiates" and emerges from prejudices that are "too-easily-learned."

Rejecting Carswell

The Judiciary Committee reported favorably on the nomination of Carswell to the Supreme Court, albeit with strongly worded dissenting views. The majority of the committee actively sought to portray Carswell in a positive light, especially given the accusations that the nominee was a segregationist and a racist. The majority noted that they could not possibly hold all nominees accountable for every utterance made and concluded that "both by his own statement, and by his public career spanning the years from 1953 to the present time, that he has long since abandoned the notions which he expressed in his 1948 speech."[146] They called Carswell's judicial record on civil rights one of "balance and even-handedness," and the fact that he did sometimes oppose civil rights for African Americans "neither indicates anti-Negro or anti–civil rights animus, nor does it furnish grounds to oppose his confirmation."[147]

The minority view in the Judiciary Committee report was quite harsh in its assessment of Carswell's attitudes toward civil rights. Senators Bayh, Hart, Kennedy, and Tydings submitted a joint statement that concluded: "Judge Carswell's record indicates that he is insensitive to human rights and has allowed his personal views and biases to invade the judicial process. His decisions and his courtroom demeanor have been openly hostile to blacks, the poor, and the unpopular."[148] In a separate statement of his individual views, Tydings remarked that "Judge Carswell was simply unable or unwilling to divorce his judicial functions from his personal prejudices. His hostility toward particular causes, lawyers and litigants was manifest not only in his decisions but in his demeanor in the courtroom."[149] After reviewing the testimony of many witnesses concerning Carswell's demeanor, Tydings concluded that such testimony "paints a picture of blatant hostility and aggressive unfairness that casts serious doubt upon Judge Carswell's judicial temperament to sit even on a federal District Court much less on the Supreme Court of the United States."[150]

Similar comments were issued by Carswell's opponents in the Senate floor debate. Indiana's Birch Bayh, for instance, maintained that Carswell was not a "strict constructionist," as he was portrayed. Bayh labeled Carswell a judicial "activist" who "has not adhered to a strict construction of the law of the land in civil and human rights cases, but has used his judicial office to advance his own personal racial and social philosophy."[151] New Jersey Republican Clifford Case concluded that the nomination was "a slap in the face to the black community of this country." Carswell's nomination, Case further argued, "represents a most unfortunate repudiation of those black moderate leaders who have been doing their best to help this country stay on an even keel."[152] Harold Hughes, an Iowa Democrat, maintained that the president nominated an individual in Carswell "who has repeatedly demonstrated blindness toward, if not outright disapproval of, the major developments in American society and in constitutional law over the past 22 years."[153] And in a particularly moving statement to the Senate, Massachusetts Republican Edward Brooke—the only African American member of the Senate—noted the difficulty in voting against a nominee for the Court. Brooke concluded that, after much soul-searching, he believed that the nominee in 1970 was "the same G. Harrold Carswell who spoke before an American Legion assembly in the State of Georgia in 1948."[154]

Ultimately, Carswell emerged from the debate surrounding his nomination as a recalcitrant concerning civil rights and as a potential racist. The 1948 speech, his role in the segregated country club, and the racial covenant all combined to put forth the character of an individual who was outside of the evolving mainstream of civil rights and equality as these commitments were incorporated into the laws and politics of the American community in 1970. These incidents and the nominee's "southernness," as communicated by the news media, made Carswell the ideological embodiment of an approach to civil rights that was generally unacceptable. Despite his advocates' best efforts, Carswell, like Haynsworth before him, was a judge without the "character" necessary to serve on the Supreme Court.

Carswell's Mediocrity

As the Carswell nomination progressed, the Nixon administration worked both to defend the nominee and to distance the president from him.[155] Just a week before the full Senate vote on Carswell, President Nixon publicly exchanged letters with Senator William Saxbe of Ohio. After a standard defense of Carswell, Nixon remarked that "what is centrally at issue in this nomination is the constitutional responsibility of the President to appoint members of the Court." Nixon concluded that "if the Senate attempts to substitute its judgment as to who should be appointed, the traditional constitutional balance is in jeopardy and the duty of the President under the Constitution impaired."[156] In part, this rhetorical shifting occurred because the administration realized it had made "a blunder of mammoth proportions" in nominating Carswell.[157] The reason for this conclusion was fairly simple—Carswell was clearly not qualified for the Supreme Court.

The news media were quick to highlight Carswell's mediocrity and his overall lack of qualifications for the Supreme Court. *Newsweek*, in the midst of the debate, reported on a Columbia University law school student study that revealed Carswell's unusually high reversal rate—59 percent, or "three times higher . . . than the national average."[158] Three weeks later, *Newsweek* dubbed Carswell a "lackluster judge from Tallahassee."[159] In an indictment of both of President Nixon's nominees, the *New Republic* concluded that neither Judges Haynsworth or Carswell were "noted for personal, professional or intellectual qualities that are out of the ordinary."[160] Even the normally sympathetic *U.S. News and World Report* quoted a lawyer who noted that Carswell was "not an outstanding judicial scholar, nor an innovator."[161] A rare defense of Carswell's qualifications in the news media appeared in a William F. Buckley column in *National Review*. Buckley maintained that the Supreme Court needed more mediocrity if mediocrity meant "that when you read the Constitution and the Constitution says two plus two equals four, . . . you therefore rule that two plus two equals four, rather than rule that it depends on whether you had an underprivileged educational background."[162]

Much of the Judiciary Committee hearings about the Carswell nomination addressed his positions on civil rights, but there was some mention of his overall qualifications as well. One of Carswell's most diligent detractors, Princeton's Gary Orfield, remarked that the judge was "obscure" and had "made no visible contribution to the development of the law."[163] The dean of the Duke University law school, William Van Alstyne, concluded that there was "nothing in the quality of the nominee's work to warrant any expectation whatever that he could serve with distinction on the Supreme Court of the United States."[164]

Yale's law school dean was particularly damning in his assessment of Carswell's qualifications. Louis Pollack told the committee, in a phrase widely quoted and repeated, that Carswell "presents more slender credentials than any nominee for the Supreme Court put forth in this century."[165] Similar charges of incompetency are found in the committee's report on the Carswell nomination. Senators Bayh, Hart, Kennedy, and Tydings maintained that the nominee is "at best, an undistinguished lawyer, a mediocre judge, and an unimpressive thinker." They cited the testimony of the law deans from Harvard and Yale and concluded that Carswell was "personally unqualified to sit on the Supreme Court."[166]

The defense of Carswell's qualifications was tepid, largely because of the weight of evidence against the nominee. Michigan senator Robert Griffin remarked following Carswell's testimony, "I believe the Nation could use a lot more of your kind of 'mediocrity'; obviously that is intended as a high compliment."[167] The Judiciary Committee's majority report referenced the "high esteem in which Judge Carswell is held by his colleagues." These senators also observed that the judge "personally impressed the committee by the reasonable, thoughtful, and articulate manner in which he responded to questions from the members of the committee."[168] Calling the attacks against Carswell "neo-McCarthyism," Arizona's Barry Goldwater maintained that the judge's testimony to the Judiciary Committee revealed "the brilliance, character, and qualities attached to greatness." Unbelievably, Goldwater told his colleagues that Carswell was "an exceptional man, deeply versed in the philosophy and practicality of the law."[169]

Senators found the cover they needed to oppose Carswell because of his judicial philosophy. The fact that so many eminent legal individuals reached the same conclusion about his overall lack of qualifications for the Supreme Court allowed senators to safely vote against the nominee on these grounds. As Vatz and Windt suggest, the issue of judicial competence "provided opponents a non-racial ground for opposing the appointment; it gave conservatives and Republicans a non-political reason for deserting the President."[170] Ultimately, the Carswell nomination was rejected by the Senate on April 8, 1970, by a vote of 45-51.

Nixon's Failed Nominees and the Future of Civil Rights

With his nominations of Judges Haynsworth and Carswell, Richard Nixon asked the U.S. community to affirm or deny his vision of a strict construc- tionist, conservative Supreme Court. In rejecting these men, the U.S. Sen- ate likewise rejected Nixon's judicial vision. Of course, it is easiest to blame these rejections on mismanagement by the White House, on Haynsworth's ethical difficulties or Carswell's incompetence, or on the arrogance of a complacent White House.[171] But, fundamentally, both men came to em- body a perspective toward civil rights as an American ideological commit- ment that was outside of the evolving jurisprudential mainstream. They both were, therefore, lacking in the "judicial temperament" necessary to sit on the Supreme Court.[172]

Nixon retorted with a northern nominee, Harry Blackmun from Min- nesota. In so doing, not only would the nominee appear different from Haynsworth and Carswell, but he would lack an established record on civil rights. As such, Nixon avoided the debate on civil rights that was the foun- dation of the Haynsworth and Carswell defeats.[173] There could be no charge that Blackmun lacked judicial temperament because of civil rights. Blackmun was constructed as clearly within the mainstream.

In addition, the Haynsworth and Carswell nominations reflected two important shifts in the nomination process. Coming off of the Fortas con- flict, both Haynsworth and Carswell were subjected to an intense level of scrutiny. Both nominations were plagued by revelations from the past that quite possibly would not have affected nominees prior to Fortas. Haynsworth's alleged ethical problems and Carswell's racist past were problems that had faced prior nominees (Brandeis and Black, for instance) who were confirmed for the Court. But by 1969–70, the process had changed and would never be the same again.

Importantly, the Haynsworth and Carswell nominations reflected the maturation of Supreme Court confirmations into fully political events. Despite the protestations of supporters for both men, they were subjected to a highly political process where their entire records, public utterances, and private behaviors were scrutinized. Other nominees had faced considerable examination, but the highly charged, partisan atmosphere facing Haynsworth and Carswell magnified the political quality of their confirmation debates and set the stage for future nomination struggles.

The other critical consequence of these nominations was their manifestation of the continued ideological scrutiny of civil rights in the Supreme Court confirmation process. Once again, as with the nominations of Hughes, Parker, and Marshall, the Supreme Court confirmation process was a significant site for the disputation of what civil rights means for the U.S. political culture. And as with the men who came before them, both Haynsworth and Carswell came to embody an anti–civil rights jurisprudence not so much for their judicial records but for their identities. Once again ideological embodiment rose to prominence in the mediated understanding of Supreme Court nominees. These men represented the South, from its most genteel and refined to its roughest and most racist. Like Brandeis's religion and Marshall's ethnicity, the judges' regional origins marked them as unusual. Their southernness combined with media portrayals that highlighted that difference and political and judicial records that revealed and proved that difference worked to make these men the very essence of the opposition to civil rights. In so doing, these nominations furthered the critical importance of identity to discussions of judicial temperament, judicial philosophy, and appropriateness for the United States Supreme Court.

6

"Bork's America"

Supreme Court Confirmations as Political Spectacle

America is a better and freer nation than Robert Bork thinks. Yet in the current delicate balance of the Supreme Court, his rigid ideology will tip the scales of justice against the kind of country America is and ought to be.

Senator Edward M. Kennedy, *Congressional Record*

Tactics and techniques of national political campaigns have been unleashed on the process of confirming judges. That is not simply disturbing, it is dangerous. Federal judges are not appointed to decide cases according to the latest opinion polls. They are appointed to decide cases impartially according to the law.

Judge Robert H. Bork, *Nightline*

To hear Robert Bork tell it, he was blindsided in 1987—blindsided by a Democratic Senate bent on his destruction, a politicized confirmation process spiraling out of control, an array of special interests waging political war against him, and a public deceived by the tactics of partisan spin doctors. As if his own defeat by the Senate was not enough, ever since the day of his rejection in October 1987, Robert Bork has spun a tale of woe and despair about the entire judicial confirmation process. Such a process, Bork still maintains years later, is dangerous for the law, for the judicial branch, and for U.S. democracy.[1]

Robert Bork's reading of his confirmation process for the Supreme Court is more reflective of his personal disappointment than of meaningful or actual decline in the process itself. Robert Bork was not the victim of a new or more dangerous politicized Supreme Court process. He was not blindsided by a political context that has run amok and continues to imperil the objectivity of the judiciary. Robert Bork was simply another player in a political process that has frequently been contentious and personal, where nominees for the Court have often been subjected to tremendous scrutiny.

What set the Bork confirmation process apart from previous confirmation debates was its broad scope and the way in which it riveted public attention and dominated national debate. Unlike any confirmation since the 1916 Brandeis hearings, the Bork hearings featured countless witnesses from a collection of special interest groups, all seeking to influence a small group of Senators of their view. The combined testimony of these witnesses, the nominee, and the questioning by Senators totaled thousands of pages in five bulky volumes. Hours of television coverage and reams of print journalism were devoted to covering the debate. In short, the Bork confirmation debate was a full-fledged political spectacle in ways that previous confirmation debates were not. Its role as a spectacle, and not its political nature, is what makes this confirmation process significant for the American community and for the evolving Supreme Court confirmation process.

Much had changed in America between the failed Nixon nominations of Clement F. Haynsworth Jr. and G. Harrold Carswell and Ronald Reagan's nomination of Robert H. Bork. The political and cultural upheavals of Vietnam and Watergate were over, and the failed presidencies of Gerald Ford and Jimmy Carter gave way to the sunny optimism and strident conservatism of Ronald Reagan. One thing that did not change, however, was the Republican focus on the Supreme Court for political advantage. Echoing Richard Nixon, Reagan promised judges and justices who would interpret the law rather than make the law. Like Nixon, Reagan's assault on the liberal judiciary of the 1960s resonated in the larger culture—as Michael Schaller reveals, "discontent with the direction of Supreme Court rulings had spread beyond the New Right."[2]

As the 1980 campaign unfolded, the issue of judicial appointments surfaced with some regularity and demonstrated the power of Reagan's political arguments against judicial activism and the fears by some of what his position on judicial nominations would mean. Just a few days before the election, Harvard law professor Raoul Berger wrote to the *Washington Post* to attack the constitutional interpretation rooted in the "gut" reactions of judges. "Under democratic principles," Berger opined, "that 'gut' reaction is no substitute for the will of the people."[3] The debate also appeared in competing letters just prior to the election in the *New York Times.* Supporting the Reagan approach was Harvard's Nathan Glazer, who concluded, "If the issue is between judges who vote their preferences over the Constitution and are committed to quotas, and judges willing to stick closer to the Constitution, leave abortion to the states and protect equal rights for individuals, I think there is little question where most Americans would stand." Conversely, Yale's Charles Black revealed that "the question is whether one wants a Supreme Court, and other Federal courts, heavily influenced or dominated by people . . . whose sense of social justice approximates that of the most reactionary judges now on the bench." Optimistically, Anne de Gregory wrote to the *Times* that all the fear about Reagan's potential to nominate Supreme Court justices should not ignore that "the Senate has the power to reject or accept the nominee."[4]

That the issue of judicial selection and nomination was salient in the 1980 campaign is reflected by competing advertisements that appeared in the *New York Times* just days before the election. One, sponsored by the Reagan Bush Committee, was billed as a statement by "leading members of the Bar." It accused President Carter of only appointing judges "who agree with him on a broad range of political questions," and argued that "we are confident that Ronald Reagan will nominate judges of the highest caliber, male and female, black and white—judges who understand that it is a Constitution, not a personal philosophy, they are sworn to expound and uphold."[5] Another ad, sponsored by Americans Concerned for the Judiciary, appealed for money and featured a picture of nine Supreme Court justices, each with Ronald Reagan's face. The ad maintained that "the effect of this GOP litmus test would destroy the independent federal judiciary as we know it."[6] These ads reveal the relative importance placed on this issue, the effectiveness of the years of Republican assaults on the "liberal" judiciary, and the ideological resonance of these concerns for the broader community.

Despite these political disputes, in the sixteen years between the Carswell defeat and the Bork nomination, the rulings of the Warren and Burger courts remained largely intact, expanding civil liberties and extending unenumerated rights to privacy and due process, even as they were excoriated by the emerging right wing of the Republican Party. Of course, the most notable ruling during this period was the 1973 case of *Roe v. Wade,* establishing a constitutional right of women to legally procure abortions. The fact that *Roe* would command considerable attention in Supreme Court confirmations subsequent to 1973 speaks to the power of the case and the enduring impact of abortion as a cultural and political issue in the American community.[7] Beyond *Roe*, another enduring case of the period was the 1978 ruling in *Regents of the University of California v. Bakke*,[8] overturning the use of racial quotas in university admissions but permitting the use of non-merit factors in the interests of diversity. It was *Roe*, though, that epitomized for conservatives, yet again, the tendency of the Supreme Court to find rights and processes in the Constitution that they believed were not there, demonstrating for the New Right how judges and justices impose their own values and beliefs when interpreting constitutional law.

Reagan's expression of the larger cultural discontent with the judiciary had several roots. On one level, the political Reagan understood the power of this rhetoric in solidifying and mobilizing the emerging religious right as a Republican base of support.[9] On another level, the ideological Reagan also opposed the sustained judicial activism that he perceived emanating from the Supreme Court.[10] Upon his inauguration in 1981, Ronald Reagan began to put into practice the jurisprudential philosophy that he espoused during his several campaigns for the presidency.

Supreme Court historian Tinsley Yarbrough concludes that no president except for Franklin Roosevelt "gave greater attention to the ideological leanings of his prospective nominees" than did Ronald Reagan.[11] In terms of the Supreme Court itself, Reagan appointed largely conservative justices—those individuals who shared the New Right's philosophy of returning constitutional interpretation to a time of "original intention," where judgments are formalistically based in the meaning of the Constitution as originally drafted and ratified, where preeminent hermeneutic value is accorded to the Constitution and thoughts of the founders, and where nonconstitutional decision-making devolved to elected legislatures.[12] This was especially true of his elevation of William Rehnquist to succeed Warren Burger as chief justice and the nomination of Antonin Scalia for Rehnquist's seat. Both men were staunchly conservative, believing that much of the jurisprudence emanating from the Court was wrongly decided and violated the basic tenets of "original intention." Moreover, despite their ideologies and the control of the Senate by Democrats, both nominees were confirmed, though Rehnquist faced some difficult questioning about personal and political matters from his past.[13]

The same can be said of Reagan's nomination of Sandra Day O'Connor. Remarkable as the first nomination of a woman for the Supreme Court, O'Connor's confirmation was also relatively trouble free.[14] As a result of his nominations, "Reagan was able to enhance the station of the conservative wing of the Court, not only by replacing moderates with conservatives, but by replacing an older conservative with a much younger ideologue."[15]

Each time a Supreme Court seat opened during the Reagan presidency, speculation centered on the administration's likely nomination of Robert Bork. Reagan had placed Bork on the District of Columbia Federal Circuit Court, and the judge was widely seen as one of the intellectual and judicial leaders of the conservative "original intention" movement.[16] Bork famously advocated the application of neutral principles in judicial decision-making—a jurisprudence that limited the results-orientation of judicial review and sought to restrict judges to finding neutral rules and guidelines and applying them to presented cases. In so doing, Bork either explicitly or implicitly critiqued some of the most notable Supreme Court decisions in recent memory—*Roe v. Wade, Griswold v. Connecticut, Brown v. Board of Education.* Quite simply, he was at the forefront of the conservative retrenchment of judicial review.[17] Thus, when Reagan nominated O'Connor in 1981, then elevated Rehnquist and nominated Scalia in 1986, most observers were surprised, and Bork himself was reportedly "crushed" at being passed over.[18] By 1987, the time had come. When Justice Lewis F. Powell announced his resignation from the Court on June 26, the Reagan administration turned to Robert H. Bork. In announcing Bork's nomination on July 1, the president said, "Judge Bork, widely regarded as the most prominent and intellectually powerful advocate of judicial restraint, shares my view that judges' personal preferences and values should not be part of their constitutional interpretations."[19]

The Bork nomination came during the waning years of the Reagan administration. Much of the sheen and goodwill that bathed Reagan during his first term and during the campaign of 1984 were gone.[20] By 1987, though still popular, Reagan was beset by problems—most notably the Iran-contra affair. Into this mix of partisanship and scandal, with the election campaign to select Reagan's successor in its early stages, the president dropped the bomb of the Bork nomination. Reagan's announcement immediately called forth reactions from the nation's liberal and civil rights communities and from partisans of every stripe. The fight over Robert Bork would be intense.

Days of extensive hearings, weeks of controversy, and months of heated debate defined the Bork nomination, and the historical and biographical details of this debate can be found elsewhere.[21] Rather than concentrate on the details of this nomination, I explore how the debate about Robert Bork expressed jurisprudential thinking in the 1980s and how his rejection as a Supreme Court nominee signaled, again, the boundaries of the mainstream of American law. Robert Bork was constructed in apocalyptic terms, as the embodiment of an unfeeling, reactionary jurisprudence that would destroy the very essence of America's commitment to individual rights and civil liberties. In this way, the confirmation debate over Robert Bork enacted an escalation in arguments about Supreme Court nominees, away from nominal concerns about the nominee as potential jurist and toward a focus on the dramatic, sometimes exaggerated, consequences of the nominee for U.S. law. The threat that Bork was said to pose to civil rights and privacy rights and the power of the discourse that personified Bork as such a threat speak to the role of this Supreme Court confirmation struggle to enact the nature of American jurisprudence for the larger polity. In addition, the stark rhetoric used to define Bork reflected the increasing intensity and expanding importance of the Supreme Court confirmation process in American politics. Thus, despite the best efforts of the Reagan administration and Bork's supporters, the construction of the nominee as a representative of extremist approaches to the law and the evolution of the debate into a political spectacle overwhelmed any attempts to paint him as a moderate and reasonable jurist. Furthermore, the disputational nature of the confirmation hearings themselves could not compete with the powerful and frightening prospect of what "Bork's America" would be like.[22] In the end, it was this enduring vision of legal apocalypse that kept Robert Bork off the Supreme Court, that defined again the contemporary nature of American law, and that altered the Supreme Court confirmation process in profound and powerful ways.

Constructing the Confirmation Spectacle

Political spectacles are cultural dramas that invite public attention by their sheer scope. As mediated political moments, such spectacles define U.S. political culture, from the spectacularization of election campaigns to the scandals that are sensationalized for public consumption by an eager, diligent, tabloid-driven press. American politics is thoroughly technologized by mass media, spreading the symbolic power of political spectacles to larger audiences in ways not found earlier.[23] Though not necessarily new, such spectacles have greater ideological and persuasive power by virtue of their circulation in the mass media. As such, the political spectacle is, in the words of Guy Debord, "a social relationship between people that is mediated by image," as well as a "self-portrait of power."[24]

Within the dynamics of political spectacles, individuals and interests are defined for their ideological resonance. Allies will be constructed as the epitome of virtue, policy goals will come to represent the ultimate end, and enemies will personify danger and despair.[25] Such characterizations are broadly drawn in the political spectacle because of its scope. Subtlety is sacrificed to the need for hyperbole that fuels the political spectacle and gives it reverberation in the larger political culture. Political enemies within a spectacle will thus work to "arouse passions, fears, and hopes, the more so because an enemy to some people is an ally or innocent victim to others."[26]

In electoral politics, exaggerated images of actors in political spectacles are common and have existed in the U.S. context since at least the days of Andrew "Old Hickory" Jackson and William Henry Harrison's "Tippecanoe and Tyler Too" campaign. Rarely, though, has such spectacularization intruded into the legal workings of the U.S. government, making the Bork nomination a unique moment in the evolution of U.S. legal culture. While Supreme Court nominations have long been politicized in powerful ways, as I have tried to demonstrate throughout this book, the Bork controversy was unique as political spectacle for its ability to command tremendous attention and for the extent to which partisan activists constructed the issues and the individuals involved.

Embodying Bork

Even before Ronald Reagan nominated Robert Bork to the Supreme Court, liberal activists and civil rights groups feared what Bork's appointment would mean for the cause of civil liberties in the United States. Reagan's appointees had already shifted the Supreme Court rightward on many of these concerns, and the anxiety that Bork would complete the shift, pushing the Court even further, was palpable. These individuals and groups feared, rightly or wrongly, that if he ascended to the Court, Bork would continue his "passionate, relentless, assault on virtually everything the Supreme Court had done in the latter half of the twentieth century to strengthen the equality of citizens before the law and the defense of individual rights against the power of the state."[27] Given these fears, it is not surprising that the opposition to Bork's nomination defined the appointment in stark terms.

Bork's opponents also discovered that there was precious little in the nominee's personal background to attack. His career and family life were fairly conventional and absent of scandal. Bork's first wife had died of cancer, so raising questions of personal impropriety might appear un-seemly, and such questions were not readily apparent at any rate.[28] Profes-sionally, Bork's career was largely devoid of scandal save for his firing of Independent Counsel Archibald Cox during the Watergate affair. In short, aside from his involvement in the "Saturday Night Massacre," when he fired Cox after others refused, Bork's opponents were forced to forge their arguments from his judicial and scholarly writings and not from his per-sonal background.

Bork's foes did not wait long to define this nomination struggle. Just minutes after the nomination was announced at the White House, Massa-chusetts senator Edward Kennedy took the Senate floor on July 1, 1987, to warn the nation about the dangers of "Bork's America." In doing so, Kennedy set a tone for the entire confirmation that would ensnare and ul-timately doom Bork's chances for confirmation.[29] Reminding his col-leagues of the nominee's role in the Watergate firing of Archibald Cox, Senator Kennedy offered a litany of the civil rights and liberties that Bork "opposed." He then intoned that "Bork's America"

> is a land in which women would be forced into back-alley abortions, blacks would sit at segregated lunch counters, rogue police could break down citi-zens' doors in midnight raids, schoolchildren could not be taught about evo-lution, writers and artists would be censored at the whim of government, and the doors of the Federal courts would be shut on the fingers of millions of citizens for whom the judiciary is often the only protector of the individ-ual rights that are the heart of our democracy.[30]

With this simple speech, delivered just moments after the announcement of Bork's nomination to the Court, Kennedy defined the enemy in power-ful, possibly exaggerated ways. Robert Bork was not simply a conservative jurist in Kennedy's rendition—he was an agent of a powerful and impend-ing legal apocalypse that must be opposed vigorously. By defining Bork in this manner, Kennedy drew the boundaries of this confirmation debate by elevating the stakes to levels of a political spectacle.

Apocalyptic rhetoric generally refers to religious discourse that portends a coming disaster or culmination to be followed by the revealed deliver-ance and salvation. In this way, notes Barry Brummett, such discourse "re-stores order through structures of time or history by revealing the present to be a pivotal moment in time, a moment in which history is reaching a state that will reveal and fulfill the underlying order and purpose in his-tory."[31] Not restricted to religious rhetoric, however, apocalyptic themes function powerfully in secular rhetoric as well, working as "preliminary to religious or political prescription," according to J. Michael Hogan.[32]

Kennedy's description of Robert Bork and the potential of his elevation to the Supreme Court tapped into the powerful tradition of apocalyptic rhetoric in U.S. political culture. This tradition is "more than a tradition of nihilistic doomsaying," argues Hogan; it is a means of inspiring action and assuring deliverance.[33] Kennedy's statement functioned in this way. The statement provided a vision of what would come in the absence of action and resolve. Order will be maintained only if Bork is rejected, Kennedy's statement suggested, and the dangers of the coming legal apocalypse, where rights are lost and prejudices prevail, will be avoided. The lines were clearly drawn with this statement, and a trajectory for the ensuing nomination debate was established. Bork's opponents would define him as dangerous, as a sign of an undesirable legal future. The nominee and his supporters would be forced to defend the appointment against the fears of the legal apocalypse that Kennedy warned would result from Bork's confirmation, a difficult task to be sure. In this way, as journalist Ethan Bronner remarked, Kennedy's speech was a "landmark for judicial nominations."[34]

Liberal interest groups and advocates took up Kennedy's apocalyptic themes in their assault on the Bork nomination. At a scope unprecedented in Supreme Court confirmation history, hundreds of interest groups, advocacy organizations, and other parties offered commentary on the nomination. Many groups not normally associated with judicial confirmation politics involved themselves in the Bork effort, including, among others, the American Nurses Association, the Epilepsy Foundation of America, and the Oil, Chemical, and Atomic Workers.[35] A large majority of these groups were in opposition to the nomination, and their advocacy was enhanced because of their organizational unity underneath the umbrella of the Leadership Conference on Civil Rights, which played a "pivotal role" in organizing the disparate groups.[36]

Virtually all of these groups argued for the apocalyptic dangers of Robert Bork's ascendancy to the Supreme Court. The American Civil Liberties Union warned, for instance, that Bork's "extreme judicial philosophy" would "radically reduce the role of the Supreme Court and seriously diminish the force of the Bill of Rights and the liberties it protects,"[37] arguing that Bork was a threat to religious freedom, sex discrimination laws, and an array of other rights held by U.S. citizens. The stakes were quite high with Bork's nomination, according to the National Women's Law Center, which maintained that the nominee threatened "women's role in the workplace, their access to educational opportunities, their health and reproductive rights, their status as citizens with full access to equal treatment by our government, and even their rights as parents."[38] In its report about Bork, People for the American Way worried that he would upset the balance of the Supreme Court, "turning back the clock on individual protections that Americans have relied on for decades." Bork's ascendancy to the Court, for this group, also "would limit the rights of American citizens to free expression and receive information."[39] The NAACP feared that Bork would upset the balance on the Supreme Court and that over "31 major lines of precedent" might be reversed if he were to replace Justice Powell.[40]

Constructing Robert Bork as an apocalyptic agent of legal digression and despair was a powerful strategy in the emerging political spectacle of the Bork confirmation. A political spectacle requires high stakes to maintain momentum and capture attention. The actors in such a spectacle must pose real threats or offer heroic efforts to preserve hope.[41] By tapping into the apocalyptic tradition of U.S. politics, Bork's adversaries argued that the nominee must be rejected for the preservation of a mainstream view of U.S. law and justice—a view that protected individual rights and personal liberties from government intrusion and that gave the actors in the spectacle the power to restore stability through actions to oppose the nominee. The stakes were so high, this rhetoric maintained, that collective action was necessary. Indeed, the embodiment of Robert Bork as an agent of legal apocalypse did much to elevate this confirmation debate to the level of political spectacle.

The apocalyptic vision of Robert Bork, articulated so powerfully by Senator Kennedy, spread quickly throughout the news media. Representatives of liberal interest groups and civil rights organizations, as well as members of the U.S. Senate, expressed similar concerns, albeit in less dramatic fashion than Kennedy. Indeed, in the first few weeks following the announcement of the nomination in July, the impression of Robert Bork as a dangerous legal retrogradation spread through the political culture, shaping the contours of the hearings and debate over the nomination that would commence in the fall.

A critical component of a political spectacle is the presence of competition—journalistic norms and practices highlight the presence of controversy and give greater coverage to those happenings that manifest such tension. From the very outset, the Bork nomination provided media outlets with just the level of competition necessary to motivate extensive coverage. ABC News was fairly typical. Its announcement of the nomination on *World News Tonight* emphasized the confidence of the White House that the nomination would prevail, along with numerous comments from senators opposing Bork. Though it did not feature Kennedy's floor speech, ABC quoted the Massachusetts senator arguing that President Reagan "should not be able to reach out from the muck of Irangate, reach into the muck of Watergate and impose his reactionary vision of the Constitution on the Supreme Court." ABC's profile of Bork by correspondent John Martin also featured Ralph Neas of the Leadership Conference on Civil Rights articulating the apocalyptic view: "Well established law on voting rights, affirmative action, on school desegregation, on women rights, could overnight be substantially eroded or overturned." In the same story, NOW president Eleanor Smeal worried that Judge Bork was "against *Roe v. Wade* which means he would reverse the legal right to abortion."[42] Later that same evening, ABC News's *Nightline* program played significant portions of Kennedy's floor speech about "Bork's America."[43]

The immediate reactions on television were amplified in subsequent print coverage of the nomination. While *U.S. News and World Report* concluded that much of Kennedy's speech, liberally quoted in the coverage of the nomination, was exaggerated, it suggested nonetheless that "there is no doubt Bork's elevation would set in motion far-reaching changes. The 14-year-old legalization of abortion seemed the most in jeopardy."[44] Contrasting the upcoming nomination struggle with the sedate commemoration of the Constitution's bicentennial, *Newsweek* proclaimed that "the spectacle has begun" and that "Bork's proposed elevation may set in motion a series of important reversals," particularly in the areas of criminal law, abortion, and affirmative action. The weekly also quoted Ralph Neas again saying, with remarkable consistency, "Well-established laws could overnight be substantially eroded or overturned."[45] Major newspapers, like the *New York Times* and the *Washington Post*, commented on Bork's conservatism and were preoccupied with the confirmation process and the role of judicial philosophy in the hearings.[46] Implicit in their commentary about the confirmation process, however, was the assumption that Bork would significantly shift the jurisprudence of the Supreme Court, justifying the scrutiny of the nominee's judicial philosophy by his opponents and adding legitimacy to their fears of the coming legal apocalypse were Bork to be confirmed.

By the time the hearings began in September, the parameters of the debate were in place, set largely by the initial decision by Bork's opponents to define the nominee as a significant danger to basic rights and liberties. In so doing, those arrayed against the administration positioned Bork as outside of the mainstream of American law. But their rhetoric went farther, posing that Robert Bork was actually a serious, potentially powerful threat to the very defining characteristics of U.S. law. Within the dynamics of the political spectacle, these appeals to an impending legal apocalypse should Bork be confirmed successfully magnified the competition, the tension already present in U.S. politics at the time. This rhetoric forced the administration and the nominee into a defensive position, having to justify that Robert Bork was not the dangerous, frightening jurist who would usher in a new America—"Bork's America."

Defending Bork

In his consternation about his treatment by the U.S. Senate, Robert Bork writes of Kennedy's speech on July 1, 1987:

> We were incredulous. Not one line of that tirade was true. It had simply never occurred to me that anybody could misrepresent my career and views as Kennedy did. Nor did it occur to me that anybody would believe such charges. . . . I should have known better. This was a calculated personal assault by a shrewd politician, an assault more violent than any against a judicial nominee in our country's history. As it turned out, Kennedy set the themes and the tone for the entire campaign.[47]

Putting aside Bork's hyperbole about the viciousness of the speech, this passage is interesting for its recognition of the "political" nature of the confirmation process. Bork acknowledges his own failure, and the failure of the Reagan administration, to see this event for what it was—an emerging political spectacle with powerful forces that defied history and conventional nomination protocols. Their failure to recognize the political nature of this compelling spectacle would be the undoing of Robert Bork's nomination to the Supreme Court.

The defense of Robert Bork was trapped by several different dynamics at work in the unfolding rhetorical trajectory of his nomination. By portraying the nominee as a dangerous legal activist who would seek to undo decades of constitutional law in the name of "original intent," Bork's opponents had successfully demarcated the parameters of this debate. While Bork's supporters would try to discuss the role of "judicial philosophy" in Senate confirmation debates, and while they frequently stressed the nominee's extraordinary qualifications, they were also forced to confront the legal apocalyptism that Kennedy and the liberal interest groups used to define Bork. Add to this disagreement between the White House and the Justice Department about the proper framing and handling of the confirmation, and the situation was rhetorically challenging for Bork and his cohorts.

On one level, Bork supporters agreed with the nominee's adversaries that there would be changes in Supreme Court doctrine as a result of the nomination. Featured on ABC's *World News Tonight* the evening of the nomination, Heritage Foundation scholar Bruce Fein basically agreed with Eleanor Smeal and suggested that "I think Judge Bork, given the fact that the recent abortion decisions have been five to four, would tip the balance the other way." This allowed correspondent John Martin to conclude, "both liberals and conservatives expect Robert Bork to complete a conservative takeover and make the new Court as conservative in its way as the Warren Court was liberal in its way."[48] This approach to the nominee reflected the Justice Department's approach to the nomination. To ignore Bork's potential as a conservative justice who would pursue the conservative agenda on the Court, the attorneys at Justice maintained, would be to obfuscate the administration's real reason for putting forth Bork at all—namely, to tip the balance of the Court.[49]

On another level, when responding to the interest groups' reports attacking Bork's record and judicial philosophy, the administration and its supporters in Congress argued that the nominee really was not as conservative, not as judicially reactionary, as he was portrayed. The White House responded to the initial attacks on Bork from the civil rights and liberal interest groups by arguing that Robert Bork was a moderate, in the mold of retiring Justice Lewis Powell. Early in the process, on July 16, the White House orchestrated an opinion column in the *New York Times* penned by Lloyd Cutler, a well-known Democrat who served as counsel to President Jimmy Carter. In the column, Cutler maintains that "Judge Bork is neither an ideologue nor an extreme right-winger, either in his judicial philosophy or in his personal position on current social issues." He suggests that Bork will be seen as "not far from the Justice whose chair he has been nominated to fill" and that Bork was not likely to create a decisive change in the "balance" of the Court.[50] In addition to the public campaign, the White House also prepared a briefing book for Bork advocates that advanced the same argument—Bork was a moderate judge not likely to upset the balance of the Supreme Court.

The White House also prepared a report outlining Bork's qualifications for the Supreme Court and constructing an image of the judge as a moderately conservative jurist who posed no danger to established constitutional doctrine. The report highlighted Bork's background as a legal scholar and judge, calling him "one of the most qualified individuals ever nominated to the Supreme Court," and it quoted liberally from Cutler's *New York Times* op-ed. In its effort to combat the apocalyptic images already articulated about Judge Bork, the report's authors maintained that he was firmly within the "mainstream of American jurisprudence" and that he "does not adhere to a rigid conception of 'original intent' that would require courts to apply the Constitution only to those matters which the Framers specifically foresaw." The report detailed Bork's positions on a variety of important constitutional matters and defended his role in the "Saturday Night Massacre" during Watergate.[51]

After the release of the various reports by liberal interest groups, the Reagan administration issued a response from the Justice Department with significant revisions from the White House. This report is also telling in its attempt to depict Bork as firmly within the mainstream of U.S. law. The jurisprudential theories advocated by Bork, according the Justice Department report, were "strongly supported by such eminent and mainstream jurists and scholars as Frankfurter, Black, Harlan, and Bickel." The administration's lawyers also were troubled by the tactics of opposing interest groups that, they maintained, took the nominee's decisions out of context, noting that "at least 86 percent of the decisions in which Judge Bork participated were unanimous" and that liberal interest groups were guilty of "inherent, gross distortions of his record." Robert Bork, these advocates argued, was generally supportive of claimants in civil liberties cases and respects "the law as a neutral set of rules, impartially applied to all people." To allay the worries about Bork's potential to overrule existing law, the Justice Department suggested that he "recognizes that even wrongly decided precedent ought not to be overturned without an extraordinarily searching examination of all possible effects of such a reversal."[52]

Three contrasting images of Robert Bork were thus articulated in the time period between the announcement of his nomination in July and the beginning of Judiciary Committee hearings in mid-September. The first image of Bork crafted a portrait of the nominee as an agent of legal doom, ushering in stark erosions of civil liberties and racial discrimination and utterly disrespectful of existing precedent and meaningful balance on the Supreme Court. I have labeled this rhetoric legal apocalypticism, wherein the nominee embodied a vision of the law outside of the mainstream of American jurisprudence. Coming as it did very early in the confirmation process, the apocalyptic image of Judge Bork established the parameters of the debate over his confirmation and contributed powerfully to the elevation of this process from simple confirmation to full-fledged political spectacle. "Bork's America" was a compelling and rhetorically skillful moment in defining the symbolic trajectory of the confirmation debate, setting the stage for all that would be forthcoming in this political spectacle.

In reply, the Reagan administration offered competing, indeed clashing, images of the nominee, reflecting its own internal disputes as to the management of Bork's confirmation. Bork was nominated, according to one dimension of the administration's rhetoric, precisely because he would bring change and a conservative ideological outlook to the Supreme Court and its decision-making. At the same time, largely in response to the apocalyptic vision of Bork offered by senators and interest groups, the administration also constructed Bork as firmly within the mainstream of U.S. law, arguing that he would not upset the balance on the Supreme Court and that he would not overturn existing legal precedents. Ultimately, neither construction of Bork worked to respond effectively to the apocalyptic fears articulated by the liberal interest groups. The inherently contradictory nature of these images of Bork meant that the nominee would be responsible, in the hearings before the Judiciary Committee, for conveying his own legal persona, for defining what approach to U.S. jurisprudence he embodied and would bring to the Supreme Court. At this task, Robert Bork would fail spectacularly.

The Spectacle's Summit

Fully two and one-half months passed between the announcement of Robert Bork's nomination to the Supreme Court and the beginning of hearings by the Senate Judiciary Committee to consider the nomination. In that time, the rhetorical trajectories and symbolic themes that would define this confirmation debate were firmly in place. The significance of this debate was elevated higher than previous Supreme Court confirmations, to the level of political spectacle. The anticipation of the interrogation of the nominee by the U.S. Senate intensified, making the hearings the pivotal moment in this confirmation debate. All of the parties involved recognized the importance of the hearings; they spent hours planning statements, assembling witnesses, even preparing the physical setting of the hearing room.[53] Nothing was unimportant, everything mattered, and the stakes were quite high in this evolving political spectacle.

As with much about the Bork nomination, the hearings themselves have been thoroughly discussed and digested in other sources. What makes them interesting for the purposes of this examination is how, as they unfolded, Robert Bork was wholly unable to dispel the lingering, compelling concern that he would somehow threaten fundamental understandings of constitutional rights and protected liberties. Everything Bork did, everything he said, the way he comported himself as a witness, all confirmed a developing impression about his understanding of the law as an intellectual game, a laboratory for the testing of theory—an impression that played quite easily into the legal apocalyptism articulated by Senator Kennedy and others.

The task facing Robert Bork and his advocates from the outset of the hearings was to dispel the image of Bork as a legal ogre—as a judge who would, if placed on the Supreme Court, bring back illegal abortions and racial segregation. Bork's supporters used the opening introductory statements at the hearings to position Bork, again, in the mainstream of U.S. jurisprudential thinking. Kansas Republican Robert Dole, seeking his party's nomination for president in 1988, argued that Bork was a man of "unquestionable ability and integrity."[54] Another prominent Republican, Missouri's John Danforth, maintained that Bork did not resemble an "unyielding ideologue," because such individuals "do not encourage dissent; they do not have a sense of humor; and they do not evolve in their own thinking."[55] All of the Republican senators openly supportive of Bork's nomination made similar points—the nominee was highly qualified, they all maintained, and he was not an extremist. Many of them also attacked the politicization of the confirmation process, forgetting their own complicity in the development of such a process.

If Bork's supporters all read from the same script, they were evenly matched by the consistency of his opponents' condemnations. Bork "believes women and blacks are second-class citizens under the Constitution," charged Senator Kennedy. "In Robert Bork's America, there is no room at the inn for blacks and no place in the Constitution for women."[56] Kennedy's apocalyptic vision of Robert Bork was echoed by Ohio Democrat Howard Metzenbaum. "Judge Bork," Metzenbaum claimed, "categorically rejects any constitutional right to privacy. He believes the Government has the right to regulate the family life and sex life of every American. . . . He would have upheld a law allowing the forced sterilization of convicts."[57]

Vermont's Patrick Leahy lamented Bork's extremism, arguing, "I doubt that any other nominee to the Supreme Court has ever come before this committee with a record of such unremitting and relentless opposition to the directions that the Court has taken on such a wide range of issues that touch on the basic freedoms of the American people." The nominee has generated, Leahy maintained, "a record of consistent and forceful opposition to the mainstream of modern constitutional jurisprudence."[58]

A primary fear for the Bork partisans was the defection of moderate Republicans and conservative Democrats, senators who would normally support qualified conservative nominees.[59] These senators resisted the "politicization" of the Supreme Court process and were not nearly as opposed to Reagan appointees as were more liberal senators like Kennedy and Metzenbaum. The initial remarks of some of these senators undoubtedly worried Bork's supporters. Pennsylvania Republican Arlen Specter, for example, fretted in his opening statement that Bork's writings "are at sharp variance with Justices from Oliver Wendell Holmes to William Rehnquist." For Specter, the important test was whether "you fit within the tradition of U.S. constitutional jurisprudence."[60] Professing an open mind, Specter's remarks indicated the penetration of the legal apocalypticism into this confirmation debate. Democratic senator Howell Heflin, a former judge from Alabama, noted in his opening statement that "if the evidence shows you [Bork] are intelligent, but an ideologue—a zealot—that you are principled but prejudiced, that you are competent but closed-minded, then there is considerable doubt as to whether you will be confirmed by the Senate."[61] Both of these moderate senators reflected the compelling image of Bork offered by the interest groups and liberal senators—they were worried about the impact of Robert Bork sitting on the Supreme Court. It would be up to Bork himself to dispel their doubts.

All Bork had to do was convince these senators, and by extension the larger public, that he was in the mainstream of U.S. law, that he was not the agent of legal apocalypticism but would protect fundamental rights and preserve core constitutional guarantees. Everyone agreed that he was qualified; everyone agreed that there were no, or limited, moral or ethical problems with his background. In dispute was his vision of the law, his sense of the importance of U.S. constitutional values and rights. These publicly televised hearings were his last, best chance to assure his place on the Supreme Court.

Bork began his appeal in his opening statement, indicating his adherence to the Constitution and articulating a belief in the importance of precedent. "It is one thing," Bork stated, "as a legal theorist to criticize the reasoning of a prior decision, even to criticize it severely, as I have done. It is another and more serious thing altogether for a judge to ignore or overturn a prior decision. That requires much careful thought." Not content to be defined, Bork claimed that his philosophy of judging "is neither liberal nor conservative" but one "which gives the Constitution a full and fair interpretation, but where the Constitution is silent, leaves the policy struggles to the Congress, the president, the legislatures and executives of the 50 states, and to the American people."[62] In his statement, Bork specifically highlighted those areas of most concern to his detractors—the fear that he was an originalist and the worry that he would overturn existing precedent.

Political spectacles are premised on conflict, on the presence of clashes, and the Bork hearings offered such conflict when the questioning of the nominee began in earnest after the opening statements. When given the chance to demonstrate his humanity and to indicate his sense of law and judicial philosophy, Bork failed to allay the fears of those who worried he would actively undermine constitutional liberties. In one notable exchange with Delaware Democrat and committee chair Joseph Biden, Bork powerfully reinforced the image of himself as a detached legal scholar. Biden asked Bork about the *Griswold v. Connecticut*[63] decision, where the state of Connecticut sought to bar the use of contraceptives. Bork criticized this decision as articulating an unprincipled right to privacy, and Biden pursued his opinions on the case in the hearings:

> *The Chairman*: Does a state legislative body, or any legislative body, have a right to pass a law telling a married couple, or anyone else, that behind— let's stick with the married couple for a minute—behind their bedroom door, telling them they can or cannot use birth control? Does the majority have the right to tell a couple that they cannot use birth control?
>
> *Judge Bork*: There is always a rationality standard in the law, Senator. I do not know what rationale the State would offer or what challenge the married couple would make, I have never decided the case. If it ever comes before me, I will have to decide it. All I have done was point out that the right of privacy, as defined or undefined by Justice Douglas, was a free-floating right that was not derived in a principled fashion from constitutional materials. That is all I have done.[64]

What is most remarkable about this exchange is Bork's inability to seize the opportunity given to him by Senator Biden—the opportunity to demonstrate his humanity, his understanding of the law's impact on people's lives. Bork failed to see the political meaning of his dialogue with Biden and the overall political consequences of his testimony before the Judiciary Committee. He seemed to view this event as a law school classroom, an opportunity to discuss with senators the nuances of constitutional legal theory. But political spectacles do not lend themselves to complex argument and theorizing—their messages must be clear and responsive. Bork's answers to Biden were neither.

The nominee had other chances to seize the moment and convince his audiences that he was a mainstream jurist. At one point, reading prepared questions from his staff, South Carolina Republican Strom Thurmond asked Bork, "It appears to me that much of the attack on you is based on selective citation and taking your statements out of context. Is there any particular area where this has occurred on which you would like to comment?" Bork was presented a huge opening here, a chance to correct the record and present a vision of his legal philosophy to contradict the one so firmly established in the public mind. Furthermore, this chance occurred at a pivotal moment in the hearings, right before a recess, in the late afternoon of the first day, at a perfect time to make the evening news. Instead of grabbing this opportunity, Judge Bork replied blandly, "I think I will get to comment on it as we go through these hearings. I do not think I have time to discuss all of them right now but thank you for the opportunity."[65]

Another telling moment occurred late in the testimony of the first day of the hearings. In a lengthy colloquy with Utah Republican Orrin Hatch, a Bork supporter, the nominee was asked about *Roe v. Wade*. Senator Hatch completed an exposition on the scholarly assault on *Roe*, securing Bork's agreement with an array of scholars who attacked the decision. Hatch then asked the nominee, "In your lengthy constitutional studies, is there any Supreme Court decision that has stirred more controversy or criticism amongst scholars and citizens than that particular case?" Of the hundreds of possible cases, from the entirety of Supreme Court history, Robert Bork selected perhaps the most revered and hallowed case of the last one hundred years: "I suppose the only candidate for that, Senator, would be *Brown v. Board of Education*."[66] Hatch tried to help Bork by suggesting the Dred Scott decision as a possibility, but the damage was done. Here again, Robert Bork did not recognize the nature of the political spectacle under way, opting to play the role of constitutional scholar in his answers to the committee.

The predominant theme of news media coverage of the Bork hearings' first day was the highly informative and detailed nature of the testimony.

This same coverage, however, reflected Judge Bork's inability to assuage doubts about his confirmation. The *Washington Post*, for example, concluded that while Bork was forthcoming in his views about various constitutional doctrines, he "seems, thus far, almost unaware of what is troubling his serious critics."[67] R. W. Apple Jr., in the *New York Times*, described Bork as "the deadly serious pedagogue, rigorous if informal in speech, making careful distinctions about the circumstances of cases and the reasoning that lay behind the decisions reached." In Apple's estimation, Bork's legalese contrasted badly with Biden's invocation of popular and enduring constitutional rights, and he warned that "Judge Bork may find it hard to enlist the popular following that the White House has hoped he would be able to do."[68] Peter Osterlund, writing in the *Christian Science Monitor*, forecast the problems for Bork as the hearings continued, noting that "what he says and how he says it may settle the minds of the senators who have not already decided how they will vote on the Bork nomination."[69] By this measure—indeed, by most measures—the first day of hearings had not gone well for the nominee.

Bork's second day of hearings did not enhance his image as a caring judge in the mainstream of U.S. law. As if his comment from the day before concerning *Brown* was not disconcerting enough, Bork proceeded to question the rationale of another desegregation case—*Bolling v. Sharpe*.[70] Coming on the heels of *Brown*, *Bolling v. Sharpe* held that the federal government was prohibited from racial discrimination on the basis of the "due process" language of the Fifth Amendment, just as the states were controlled by the similar language of the Fourteenth Amendment. When questioned by Senator Specter about the role of substantive due process in U.S. law, Judge Bork revealed that he was unable to accept the role of due process in *Bolling* and that "I have not thought of a rationale for it."[71] Dramatic largely for its symbolic value, this statement suggested that Bork was unable to find a constitutional basis for the end of segregation by the federal government. Realizing the consequences of this implication, Bork corrected himself after a break in the hearings, saying he would never dream of overruling *Bolling* and pronouncing segregation "not only unlawful but immoral."[72] But the damage was done.

The rest of Bork's testimony followed a similar pattern. Much of the questioning was redundant, with senators often covering the same cases, the same legal ground, over and over again. By the time Bork's testimony ended, after five days of questioning, more questions remained than were answered about his commitment to the mainstream of U.S. law. In the end, a powerful impression of Robert Bork resulted—an impression that would mean the end of his nomination. Over the span of his testimony, Bork had questioned the basis of decisions that upheld privacy, racial desegregation, equal rights for women, freedom of speech, and a range of other rights. Perhaps more troubling, Bork would often reverse himself, claiming to believe something that was totally contradicted by his published writings.[73] At other times, he would utter simply unbelievable statements, as when he claimed that women who were given a choice between forced sterilization and losing their jobs "were glad to have the choice . . . the company gave them."[74] Indeed, in his answers to the committee's questions, Bork missed his chance to humanize his positions and himself, to convince a skeptical public and a wavering Senate that he was not the agent of a legal apocalypse, a cold and unfeeling legal academician. At bottom, Bork the legal formalist, the academic thinker, the theoretical provocateur emerged in full force, and so did the opposition to his nomination.

The press coverage was not kind. Stuart Taylor, writing in the *New York Times*, paid particular attention to Bork's shifts in position, noting that the nominee's "surprising revisions of some controversial past positions now made his candor a major issue."[75] Saying that Bork emerged as a "warm, open, generous and sympathetic person" in the hearings, *Washington Post* columnist David Broder still observed that "when in the thrall of theory, he [Bork] has managed to ignore the harsh reality of the pain real people experience when the law ignores their pleas for justice."[76] *Newsweek* wrote that Bork was in trouble from the start of the hearings because of "his unusual theoretical remarks and his apparent willingness to upset settled law." Its coverage concluded that, in the hearings, "he tried to put those problems to rest, sometimes by essentially eating his words at the witness table," leading to questions about his candor.[77] Bork had his defenders in the press, but they were dwarfed by the detractors who either concluded he was disingenuous about his record or unfeeling in his jurisprudence. Others questioned the process, as with Gloria Borger's concern about the "apocalyptic tones typical of this debate" in *U.S. News and World Report.*[78]

After twelve days of hearings, including an unprecedented five days of testimony from the nominee himself and the commentary of scores of witnesses,[79] the hearings closed, and the committee voted to send the nomination to the full Senate with a negative recommendation. The previously undecided senators, both Democrats and Republicans, voted against Bork—Specter, Heflin, Byrd, and Arizona's Dennis DeConcini all cast negative votes against the nominee. The committee vote was 9–5, essentially dooming Bork's nomination and dealing the Reagan administration a significant defeat. As ABC's Peter Jennings noted in his broadcast of October 6, 1987, "Having emerged from his ordeal before the Senate Judiciary Committee a loser, winning confirmation to the Supreme Court in the full Senate will be like getting to the top of Mount Everest without oxygen."[80]

There was little anyone could do to forestall the inevitable. At the White House, the administration scripted a series of calls for the president to undecided senators. Reagan's scripts highlight the administration's focus on what they saw as the distortion of Bork's record. For instance, in his call to Mississippi Democrat John Stennis, Reagan was supposed to say, "What really disturbs me is that some of these interest groups are blatantly distorting the facts with regard to Judge Bork's record and literally turning this into a political campaign." The same argument was made to several other senators.[81] Ultimately, there was anger from the White House, frustration from Senate Republicans, and satisfaction from the hundreds of individuals and groups that opposed the nomination. And there was defiance from Robert Bork, who insisted on a vote by the full U.S. Senate. That vote would not matter—the result was a foregone conclusion. In the end, fifty-eight senators voted against Robert Bork, and his margin of defeat was the largest of any Supreme Court nominee in history.

Supreme Court Confirmations as Spectacle

Robert Bork's defeat by the U.S. Senate cannot be explained easily. Mistaken is the Borkian view that he was defeated because the confirmation process had, suddenly in his case, become a political event, where judicial philosophy was subject not to dispassionate analysis but political manipulation.[82] Many previous nominees to the Supreme Court, including some who were confirmed and some who were rejected, would undoubtedly think their philosophies were also unfairly scrutinized and distorted. Indeed, the history of the Supreme Court confirmation process is filled with instances of nominees who were rejected or vigorously questioned about their judicial philosophy. None of these men and women were given the vast amount of time and the endless chances in testimony, speeches, interviews, and countless other venues to define themselves and their views as was Robert Bork.

Mistaken also is the view that Bork's defeat was the collective voice of the American people, rising up to resist the right-wing takeover of U.S. law.[83] Many citizens did care deeply about the Bork appointment, on both sides, and many involved themselves by donating time and money, writing to senators, or expressing their views in other ways. But there was not a unified, collective disapproval of this man's elevation to the Supreme Court. Polling indicated that a majority of those polled opposed the nomination, but a sizable percentage supported it, and many of the polling questions were skewed in an anti-Bork direction. Some polls also pointed to the detachment of many citizens from the entire process—one poll revealed that only one-third of the sample even knew how many justices sat on the Supreme Court.[84]

The ads, the polling, the interest groups, the politics, the process's politicization—no single factor explains why Robert Bork was rejected by the U.S. Senate. Rather, as I have suggested, a confluence of factors contributed to this particular Supreme Court confirmation debate, factors that continue to teach us much about the nature of this process and the rhetorical articulation of U.S. law.

Robert Bork became, in this debate, the embodiment of an apocalyptic vision of U.S. law. That vision stripped rights away from citizens, was retrograde in its approach to racial equality and equal opportunity, and displayed little respect for existing legal precedents. Moreover, the extremism of this vision of Bork was possible because of the spectacularized nature of U.S. political culture. In a political system predicated on conflict, where competition is magnified to the extreme, such visions can take hold, can prevail on the popular consciousness. The individual in such a political spectacle is the repository for all of the competing images and characteristics. Bork became, thus, the vision of the legal apocalypse envisioned by his detractors and the agent of truth and quality as defined by his advocates. And he failed to manage either characterization successfully.

Forgetting that "truth" matters little in a political spectacle, Robert Bork missed limitless opportunities to dispel the fears of the legal apocalypse in "Bork's America." Instead, he seemed detached, remote, acting as if the law was an intellectual game to be played by only the most privileged. His "truth" was unfamiliar to citizens who did not grasp the complexities of "neutral principles" or "strict scrutiny." Citizens did understand that the government should not prohibit couples from using contraceptives, that the Supreme Court did a good thing when it desegregated public schools, that women should not be forced to choose between their employment and their right to have children. The political spectacle of the Bork confirmation converted the particularities of the law into straightforward political questions with immediate relevance for citizens and senators alike.

The process also converted Robert Bork. Just as it had for Louis Brandeis, John J. Parker, Charles Evans Hughes, Thurgood Marshall, Clement F. Haynsworth Jr., and G. Harrold Carswell, the Supreme Court confirmation process transformed Robert Bork from a legal theorist and judge into the embodiment of U.S. law and jurisprudential identity. More important than the rejection of Robert Bork, individually, was the public scrutiny of the legal theory he embodied. The result was a lively public discussion about many important matters of considerable impact on people's lives—matters that often were not discussed outside of the rather narrow confines of the legal establishment. As Michael Kinsley, then editor of the *New Republic*, remarked, "We've had a political debate that's about exactly what politics should be about. It's been about the meaning of original intent, the meaning of equal protection of the law, the role of the Senate, the role of the Supreme Court and the separation of powers." It was, Kinsley noted, "an extremely inspiring political debate."[85] Once again, as it had so many times in the twentieth century, the Supreme Court confirmation brought important legal subjects out of the shadows of America's courthouses and into the blazing sunlight of contentious, spectacular politics. The process and the polity are better for it.

7

The Future of Supreme Court Confirmations

Beyond Bork

The Senate's failure to act on my nominations, or even to give many of my nominees a hearing, represents the worst of partisan politics. Under the pretense of preventing so-called judicial activism, they've taken aim at the very independence our Founders sought to protect.

President Bill Clinton, *Public Papers of the Presidents of the United States: William J. Clinton*

We face a vacancy crisis in the federal courts, made worse by senators who block votes on qualified nominees. These delays endanger American justice. Vacant federal benches lead to crowded court dockets, overworked judges and longer waits for Americans who want their cases heard.

President George W. Bush, "President's Weekly Radio Address, February 22, 2003"

When it comes to judicial nominations, most recent presidents sound pretty much alike. Republicans and Democrats both complain from the White House of Senate intransigence, partisan politics, and the impending danger to the federal judiciary as a result of congressional unwillingness to approve nominees. Zealous in defense of their prerogative to shape the judiciary as they see fit, contemporary U.S. presidents rail against the inconvenience of having to secure the Senate's consent to their nominations as they tell a tale of a politicized confirmation process with dire consequences for the Republic.

Usually, presidential arguments degenerate quickly, from practical concerns about the lack of staffing in the federal courts to ad hominem and hyperbolic charges of partisanship and inequity. The Senate is not much better. Nominees are denied hearings or votes, and nominations are filibustered by senators opposed to the president. While a large percentage of presidential nominations are confirmed with relative ease, the high profile nature of controversial nominations means that the vitriol coming from both Capitol Hill and the White House is intense.[1] Moreover, such intense debate typically concerns the individual nominee as a representative, an embodiment, of a specific ideological position. As such, some nominees from a Democratic president are opposed for their liberal outlook and their personification of "judicial activism," while some Republican nominees are reflective of the dangerous, reactionary possibilities of "strict constructionism," especially involving civil rights and liberties. These constant complaints about the politicized, personalized confirmation process, offered so frequently by presidents and senators, ignore the complicity of both the White House and the Senate in creating and politicizing the process in the first place.

While these ongoing conflicts over judicial nominations are often inane and overblown, during the Bill Clinton and George W. Bush administrations the tensions regarding judicial nominations have intensified. A Republican Senate stalled or delayed dozens of President Clinton's nominees, while a Democratic Senate did the same to President Bush's appointments. So concerned about the process and its consequences for his nominees, President Bush announced a plan in October 2002 to ensure "timely consideration of judicial nominees" by the U.S. Senate. Among other provisions, the plan called for advanced notice of judicial retirements and an up-or-down vote on judicial nominees by the full Senate 180 days after their announcement.[2]

The contemporary anxieties about the judicial confirmation process are in large measure a response to the Supreme Court nominations of Robert Bork and Clarence Thomas. Both nominations occasioned tremendous controversy—both were political spectacles of the most extreme kind. The stakes in both cases were quite high and the partisan divide that characterizes U.S. politics exacerbated by their importance. Those nominations, though, have much to teach about this process, a process that is likely to be even more politicized and partisan in the future.

In this final chapter, I reflect on the current state of the Supreme Court nomination process as it has emerged from the twentieth century and specifically from the nominations of David Souter, Clarence Thomas, Ruth Bader Ginsburg, and Stephen Breyer. On the basis of that discussion, I speculate as to the potential benefits and likely problems that will result from an increasingly politicized Supreme Court confirmation process. Unlike most observers of this process, though, I believe that the U.S. polity has much to gain from politicized and controversial nomination debates and that unnecessary hand-wringing about the confirmation process is historically myopic and unjustifiably fatalistic.

Confirmability Pressures and the Supreme Court Nomination Process

A central outcome of the Bork nomination was an increased pressure on presidents to nominate candidates for the Supreme Court who will be confirmed. Fearing the partisan tensions, intensified media scrutiny, and distraction from other issues, administrations sought nominees who would achieve the consent of the Senate with minimal controversy. One result of the demands to find confirmable nominees is that presidents are increasingly unlikely to put forward unqualified individuals. Candidates with slim professional qualifications, like Nixon's Carswell would immediately pose confirmability problems and are thus more likely to not be nominated at all. Another consequence of such confirmability pressures, furthermore, is a tendency to find nominees to the Court who can be packaged and sanitized to prevent dispute and limit discussion.

The Reagan administration followed Bork's nomination with the naming of Douglas Ginsburg—a spectacular failure. Ginsburg was, arguably, more conservative than Bork, and special interest groups began scouring his record soon after he was named. They need not have bothered. Ginsburg's personal propensity for marijuana use as a Harvard law professor would be his undoing, as it became clear that his explanations for this illegal behavior were misleading.[3] Ultimately, the Reagan administration would find a successful nominee in California's Anthony Kennedy, a relatively unknown though certainly pleasant judge who testified effectively before the Senate and who sailed to easy confirmation.[4] But the damage, politically and historically, of two failed nominations to the Supreme Court was considerable. As such, when William Brennan resigned from the Court in 1990, the Bush administration faced intense pressure to find a confirmable nominee.

Stealth Nominees

One way to assure confirmability is to find a nominee for the Supreme
Court who is relatively unknown in the public eye, who has no real record
or "paper trail." A significant problem that the Reagan administration faced
with Robert Bork was the nominee's public record, amassed after years of
writing for law journals, giving speeches, crafting briefs, and writing opinions. The Bush administration was anxious to avoid a nominee who was
too conservative, who would provoke the ire of interest groups and Democratic senators, and who had too much of a record that would provide am-
munition for groups opposed to the administration. In David Souter, those
in the administration found their nominee.

An obscure, though well-respected, member of the New Hampshire
Supreme Court, David Souter came to the attention of the Bush administration through one of his patrons, New Hampshire senator Warren Rud-
man. Bush's chief of staff, John Sununu, was a former governor of New
Hampshire, giving Souter additional leverage in the administration's deliberations over Brennan's replacement. Moreover, as journalist David Savage
notes, "Souter had not written any articles or made speeches on controversial topics, and his New Hampshire court opinions dealt mostly with dry issues of state law."[5] In short, he was confirmable largely because he lacked
any record that might be attacked or dissected.

Souter's lack of a public record made his confirmation hearings an unfo-
cused rhetorical event characterized mostly by its collegiality. Henry Abraham notes that Souter's "views on specific issues, particularly abortion,
affirmative action, church-state relations, civil rights and liberties, generally, were plainly a cipher,"[6] and Judiciary Committee chair Joseph Biden
observed in his opening statement, "You come before us without an extensive record that details your views on important constitutional questions of
our time."[7]

Biden promised Souter a fair hearing, and it was defined largely by the
nominee's reluctance to commit to any specific position on controversial
constitutional cases. Thus, while Souter would not comment on *Roe v.
Wade*, he did surprise some by declaring his belief in a constitutional right
to privacy. An example of the caution that distinguished his testimony
emerges from a dialogue between Souter and Biden about the right to privacy, where the nominee concluded:

> My answer is that the most that I can legitimately say is that the spectrum of
> possible protection that would rank as an interest to be asserted under

liberty, but how that interest should be evaluated, and the weight that should be given to it in determining whether there is in any or all circumstances a sufficiently countervailing governmental interest is a question with respect, I cannot answer.[8]

This answer reveals just how delicate the hearings process of Supreme Court nominees had become since the Bork hearings three years earlier. No freewheeling academic discourses about rationales for constitutional rights, or the value and importance of neutral principles, or the historical significance of past Supreme Court decisions. Instead, care and caution typified the Souter hearings, and the result was a 13–1 positive referral of the nomination from the Judiciary Committee and a 90–9 vote for confirmation by the full Senate.

Calling Souter an "antiseptic nominee," *Newsweek* noted the feverish, but unsuccessful, attempts by special interest groups and others to discover the nominee's stand on important constitutional issues.[9] The same magazine observed, after the hearings, that Souter's responses worried conservatives and liberals alike. Conservatives, especially, fretted about Souter's praise of William Brennan and the nominee's unwillingness to sternly condemn "judicial activism."[10] Such is the danger of "stealth" nominees to the Supreme Court. Rather than the principled and serious debate about constitutional issues and jurisprudential theory that characterized the Bork hearings, the Souter process produced largely platitudes and equivocations designed to obscure instead of illuminate. In so doing, stealth nominations promise to rob the public of robust and productive debate about weighty constitutional questions.

Celebritized Nominees

On July 1, 1991, President George Bush proudly strode to the podium outside his palatial Kennebunkport home on the Maine coast and introduced his nominee to replace Thurgood Marshall as the 106th justice of the Supreme Court. The president hailed Federal Circuit Court Judge Clarence Thomas as the "best qualified" individual for Marshall's seat. The nomination of Clarence Thomas to the Supreme Court became, arguably, one of the most remarkable political events of the late twentieth century. What would have been a contentious but fairly typical Supreme Court nomination became a full-fledged media spectacle when an unknown law professor from Oklahoma, Anita Hill, came forward to accuse the nominee of sexual harassment. A clear indicator of the Thomas nomination's significance is the large number of treatments it has received in the popular and scholarly press. This single event has produced scores of articles,[11] books,[12] dissertations,[13] newspaper accounts, editorials, and television commentaries examining these events with a thoroughness that is virtually unmatched in Supreme Court confirmation history. Not even the Bork nomination occasioned this level of intense scrutiny.

The nomination of Clarence Thomas represented another strategy responsive to confirmability pressures—the marketing of nominees on the basis of their celebrity, their emotional, personal narrative. Simply put, Clarence Thomas was celebritized, and the rhetorical strategies of the Bush administration, supporters of the nomination, the nominee, and the news media prompted an affective and epideictic response to the nomination. The celebritization of Clarence Thomas sought to circumvent the deliberative nature of Supreme Court confirmations in the Senate and worked to divert attention away from the nominee's views of the law and society, away from his judicial character, and toward his compelling personal story.[14]

Unlike Souter, Thomas had both a political and a legal record, or paper trail, that would be fodder for Democrats in the Senate and interest groups seeking to derail the nomination. In response, the Bush administration's rhetorical strategy was to divert the focus away from Thomas's record and his fairly weak legal acumen and to "sell" the nominee on the basis of his personal story. A gradual process, the celebritization of Thomas began at Kennebunkport on July 1, 1991, when President Bush presented a listing of Thomas's accomplishments, and the nominee thanked those people in his life who made it possible for him to achieve and succeed.[15] Ultimately, as Jane Mayer and Jill Abramson recount, the "Pin Point Strategy" emerged at a White House meeting after the Fourth of July holiday weekend, when a Justice Department lobbyist named John Mackey urged the assembled officials "to bury ideology and sell biography" and to "tell the Pin Point story"[16]—to base the confirmation of Clarence Thomas on the emotive quality of his upbringing in the small Georgia town of Pin Point.

The administration's celebritizing rhetoric about Clarence Thomas emphasized the affective, the emotive, dimensions of the nominee's upbringing. As the story was told and retold over the duration of the confirmation process, it skillfully exploited deep-seated ideological and mythic themes embedded in American political culture, and its affective dimensions were routinely highlighted. Clarence Thomas was someone, the narrative maintained, who rose up from poverty and despair through hard work, a dedicated family, and a personal adherence to core values and principles. From this background, the story continued, Thomas overcame hardship and discrimination to achieve the highest pinnacles of power and influence. The conclusion of the story was obvious; because of his upbringing, because of his perseverance and triumph over adversity, and because he embodied everything good about America, this man deserved a seat on the U.S. Supreme Court.

The most powerful spokesperson for Thomas's cause, aside from the nominee himself, was President George Bush. Bush occasionally mentioned specific qualifications that Thomas possessed, but the primary focus of his rationalization for Thomas's elevation to the Supreme Court was the affective power of the Pin Point narrative.

Bush stressed the emotional power of Thomas's biography in a speech on July 8, a week after announcing the nomination:

> Our new nominee for the Supreme Court, Judge Clarence Thomas, offers what I think is a very stirring testament to what people can do when they refuse to take no for an answer; when through sheer determination they overcome obstacles that others have placed in their way. It was very emotional for me up there at our house in Maine when we announced his appointment because he outdistanced poverty and racism; because he possessed the greatest treasures of all, the love of family, the faith of teachers—remember what he said about teachers?—and then the belief in himself."[17]

Later, in an August 6 address, Bush commented on Thomas's "personal story," saying, "[W]hen you meet him you can't help but be impressed—in my case, deeply moved. It [his personal story] impresses everybody, everybody that's fair and openminded."[18] Just eleven days later, in a teleconference with the National Governors Association, Bush again underscored the emotional dimensions of Thomas's nomination: "I must say I got all choked up when I heard Clarence talk about his background. And he did it from the heart; there's no phoniness there."[19]

President Bush adeptly linked Clarence Thomas and his childhood narrative to enduring cultural, ideological values that marked the nominee as a representation of American ideals. As Bush told the National Association of Towns and Townships on September 6, "Clarence Thomas embodies the virtues America and all her towns and townships hold dear."[20] That same day, in an address to the nation about the Thomas nomination, Bush noted, "Most of you have heard his story, how Clarence Thomas was raised in Pin Point, Georgia, by stern and loving grandparents, educated in parochial schools, graduated from Holy Cross and the Yale Law School."

Though deprived of material wealth, the president remarked, Thomas was "blessed with the important treasures: a loving family, sturdy values, and a chance," and he "defined opportunity through education, dedication, and just plain hard work."[21] Bush reaffirmed the emotional power of Thomas's personal narrative when he told a fund-raising dinner in Philadelphia about his reaction to watching the opening statements at the confirmation hearings: "Parenthetically, I watched the opening presentation that he [Thomas] made to this committee, and I got kind of choked up listening, as I did at Kennebunkport when I nominated him."[22]

George Bush was correct when he said on September 6, "Most of you have heard his story." By the time the confirmation hearings commenced, the Clarence Thomas Pin Point story was a common staple of news media coverage of the nomination. In no small part because of the president's efforts, when he was sworn in at his confirmation hearings, Clarence Thomas was already an American political celebrity.

In her special report about the nomination, CBS News's Rita Braver described Thomas's personal story as "the stuff of American legends" complete with "a father who abandoned him, a mother who worked as a maid struggling just to feed her children, finally at age seven sent to live with the grandparents he credits with setting him on course."[23] ABC News also emphasized these themes in the July 1, 1991, edition of *Nightline*. In the introductory report by Forrest Sawyer, Senator Orrin Hatch is quoted as saying, "If anybody understands the needs and rights of minorities, if anybody has felt the sting of prejudice against him, if anybody has had to fight his or her way through society in almost every step that that person made, that has to be Clarence Thomas."[24]

CBS News again featured Thomas's Pin Point upbringing in its broadcast on July 2. Reporter Erin Hayes was dispatched to the small Georgia town, and from there she told viewers "Thomas' house is gone now. It was tiny with no plumbing. He lived there with his mother. His father left when he was two. Clarence Thomas's grandfather became his father figure and, his mother says, kept him from being embittered by the poverty and racism of the 1960s South." Hayes concluded her report with this observation: "[T]he confirmation hearings may be tough. But he [Thomas] grew up with tough times. Folks here are convinced he can handle them."[25] On CNN, Larry King began his broadcast concerning the Thomas nomination by retelling the Pin Point story and emphasizing the confirmation challenges that Thomas faced:

Clarence Thomas was born in rural Georgia with two strikes against him: He was black, desperately poor and, from an early age on, fatherless. Now, 43 years later and against seemingly impossible odds, he has become America's newest Supreme Court nominee. But as a black judge with a proven conservative record he has political enemies on the left and right side and his ascension to the lofty bench promises to be a battle.[26]

The news media became the Bush administration's accomplice in its Pin Point strategy. Virtually all the coverage of the nomination—especially that coverage immediately subsequent to its announcement—emphasized Thomas's compelling personal saga and the politics of the confirmation struggle. Some journalists noted the irony of Bush's selection of an African American conservative with such humble roots,[27] while other media sources employed the story to contextualize the growing debate within African American civil rights organizations about Thomas.[28] But however it was used, the Pin Point story, as persistently retold in news media accounts, came to define Clarence Thomas in the early days of his confirmation process.

The historical record and the committee testimony reflected that Clarence Thomas was an individual who claimed to have *never* discussed *Roe v. Wade*, who upheld the preeminent role of natural rights, who advocated judicial activism to overturn wrongly decided opinions, and who lent his name and reputation to supporters of the apartheid regime in South Africa.[29] Yet for the majority of Americans, because of the celebritizing power of the Pin Point strategy, Clarence Thomas was only a talented and hard-working man who had triumphed over adversity, overcome the shackles of segregation, and achieved the highest pinnacles of success in America. This was the Clarence Thomas as celebritized by the administration and offered to the Senate for confirmation to the Supreme Court, the Clarence Thomas portrayed and depicted in his own words in testimony to the Senate Judiciary Committee. This was the Clarence Thomas so frequently and compellingly displayed in the news media at every stage of his confirmation process. This was also the Clarence Thomas who would soon face charges from an unknown law professor in Oklahoma that attacked the very persona so carefully crafted over the span of ten weeks in 1991.

Anita Hill's charges were not caused by the Pin Point strategy and the celebritization of Clarence Thomas. They were, depending on the version one believes, either the result of the grossly inappropriate behavior of Clarence Thomas or invented in the mind of a vindictive and scornful woman seeking to inflict harm on an honorable man. But Hill's charges

and the ensuing hearings before the Judiciary Committee cannot be completely assessed without reference to the celebritization of Clarence
Thomas. Hill's charges and the responses made to those charges by Thomas
and his partisans were guided by the rhetorical parameters of the confirmation process as constructed by Thomas's celebritization.

Hill's incriminations offered a starkly opposing portrait of Clarence
Thomas to the one put forth in the Pin Point story. They presented a portrait of an individual who abused his power and was lascivious in his personal conduct. But just as they opposed the persona put forth in the Pin
Point story, they were also perfectly consistent with the trajectory of the
nomination. That is, Anita Hill's charges called forth a judgment of
Clarence Thomas based in an affective reaction to personal behavior and
circumstance. They capitalized on the tools of celebritization to construct
an alternative and dramatically converse image of Clarence Thomas. The
opponents of Thomas's nomination in the civil rights community used political speeches and legal texts to oppose the nomination—but such evidence was tame when placed next to the emotionally powerful and
resonant Pin Point narrative. Hill's accusations were different—they constructed a separate character of Clarence Thomas, a substitute vision of this
celebrity that worked in utter contrast to the hard-working, religious, inde-
fatigable Clarence Thomas of the Pin Point narrative. When Thomas was
confirmed on October 15, 1991, by the smallest approval margin in more
than one hundred years, the celebritization of Supreme Court nominees
received its ultimate validation, proving this to be an effective response to
the confirmability pressures that emerged from the Bork nomination.

Celebrity discourses are powerful in a political culture dominated by the
mass media, where emotion and hyperbole rule and where confirmability
pressures motivate their invocation. Realizing its power, the Clinton administration employed a similar strategy to achieve confirmation of its first
nominee to the Supreme Court—Ruth Bader Ginsburg. When he announced her nomination, President Clinton began the process of celebritizing his choice, noting that "many admirers of her work say that she is to
the women's movement what former Supreme Court Justice Thurgood
Marshall was to the movement for the rights of African-Americans." Later
at the announcement event, Ginsburg offered an emotional tribute to her
mother and the sacrifices her mother had made for her children. Her tribute elicited tears from an ever-emotional Bill Clinton and occasioned an
exchange between the president and ABC News's Brit Hume, who queried
Clinton about the selection process. Clinton replied, "How you could ask a

question like that after the statement she just made is beyond me."[30] Clinton's remarks signaled the coming celebritization of the nomination—a rhetorical trajectory that continued with Ginsburg's testimony before the Senate.

Ginsburg's nomination was received with near unanimous acclaim, and her testimony before the Senate Judiciary Committee, like David Souter's, was a relatively decorous event. Virtually all of the supportive statements favoring Ginsburg's elevation to the Supreme Court highlighted her triumphs over sex discrimination and her successes arguing such discrimination cases before the Supreme Court. Typical was Senator Dianne Feinstein's remarks, when she praised Ginsburg

> for the intellect and dedication to thrive in hostile academic environments, laying the groundwork for thousands of women, including your daughter and mine, who is today a lawyer, to follow; for the courage to persevere, with your husband's active participation, in pursuit of a life in the law, and perhaps most of all, for the fruits of that life as a litigator and a jurist.[31]

In her own testimony before the committee, the nominee repeatedly stressed her family, claiming that "neither of my parents had the means to attend college, but both taught me to love learning, to care about people, and to work hard for whatever I wanted or believe in. . . . What has become of me could happen only in America. Like so many others, I owe so much to the entry this Nation afforded to people yearning to breathe free."[32]

As with Clarence Thomas, the nominee's jurisprudential views were overwhelmed by her compelling personal narrative, and the news media actively disseminated that narrative to the larger community. Nina Totenburg, on National Public Radio, highlighted Ginsburg's opening statement and revealed, "Her message was one of womanhood, a message to her fellow women workers, fellow wives, mothers, and grandmothers. She introduced her family, proudly showed off a picture of her granddaughter, and mentioned a conversation she had had with her daughter on the telephone."[33] The *New York Times* began its coverage of the nomination by calling attention to the personal, emotional dimensions of the nominee's story: "If confirmed, Judge Ginsburg, whose first job out of Columbia University Law School was as a legal secretary, would be the second woman to serve on the High Court, joining Justice Sandra Day O'Connor. She would also be the first Jew to serve on the Court since Justice Abe Fortas resigned in 1969."[34] Interestingly, this coverage takes some time to get to a discussion of Ginsburg's legal philosophy; the dominant theme of the initial reporting was clearly on her remarkable personal narrative.

Clarence Thomas's nomination was complicated by the spectacular testimony of Anita Hill that altered the expected trajectory of this celebritized nomination. Ruth Bader Ginsburg's nomination was more typical. The emphasis on Ginsburg's personal narrative, her triumph over sexism and discrimination, and her elevation to near-heroic status as the female incarnation of Thurgood Marshall worked powerfully to secure her confirmation. This narrative blunted concerns by some pro-choice activists about her complaints concerning *Roe v. Wade*. It limited arguments against her judicial philosophy from conservatives and probing questions from the media. In short, the celebritizations of both Clarence Thomas and Ruth Bader Ginsburg were significant rhetorical moments in the confirmation of these individuals to the Supreme Court.

Celebritizing Supreme Court nominees, however, may have an unfortunate, and possibly unavoidable, "otherizing" tendency. The fact that the Bush administration used the Pin Point strategy to secure confirmation for Clarence Thomas but selected another approach in the case of David Souter is instructive. Indeed, even the most cursory review of Supreme Court confirmation debates reveals that elaborate renditions of personal narratives are rare. Except when such narratives are unusual, as in the case of football hero Byron White, the only tales of upbringing or extended discussions of personal background belong to those candidates for the Court who were nonwhite males or females. This "otherizing" capacity normalizes and naturalizes the presence of white males and marks nonwhite males and female candidates for the Court as unusual. So in 1981 Americans learned of the frontier upbringing of Sandra Day O'Connor, and ten years later they were treated to the humble and difficult origins of Clarence Thomas. In some cases, other life experiences are celebritized, as in the cases of Justices Marshall and Ginsburg.[35] In the case of all four individuals, some measure of their confirmability came from their celebrity, and not from their capabilities as jurists or legal thinkers. Moreover the childhood experiences and struggles of Justices Rehnquist, Kennedy, Scalia, Stevens, and Breyer would probably elude most observers, making their presence on the Court seem ordinary and typical and representing the disturbing capacity of the Supreme Court confirmation process to only celebritize "the other."[36]

Supreme Court confirmations may be more prone to celebritization than other processes of the U.S. government, such as the elections for the executive and legislative branches. Presidents may nominate individuals for the Court because of their celebrity, as when Bill Clinton eagerly sought to nominate Mario Cuomo for the Court.[37] Moreover, the Senate may confirm, or refuse to confirm, a nominee based solely on a constructed celebrity persona. For instance, the Senate confirmed Benjamin Cardozo ten seconds after his nomination was announced, while Louis Brandeis's nomination in 1916 elicited gasps of shock when announced on the floor of the Senate.[38] Though judges and legal scholars are not often well-known people, the compressed and fluid nature of the Supreme Court confirmation process invites the celebritization of nominees as a means of confirmation. As the Thomas and Ginsburg confirmations reveals, such a celebritizing tendency may be unfortunate and may undermine the very credibility of all branches of the U.S. government.

Safe Nominees

A final response to the intensified confirmability pressures facing presidents may be the selection of safe nominees—individuals who will be assured of confirmation because of their connections or past experiences. One way of assuring confirmation is to select a current or former member of the U.S. Senate. In such a case, as Laurence Tribe suggests, "the Senate's institutional prerogatives do not so vigorously counteract those of the President," and the Senate "confirms such nominations with almost no investigation and with amazing, rather than deliberate, speed."[39] Franklin Roosevelt's nomination of Hugo Black and Harry Truman's nominations of Harold Burton and Sherman Minton illustrate how expeditiously that body handles nominations from the Senate ranks. It is little wonder, then, that Orrin Hatch, Utah's senior senator, is repeatedly mentioned as a possible Republican nominee to the Supreme Court.

Another approach is to nominate an individual who is well known to senators and who has generated, for whatever reason, a wealth of goodwill in the Senate. This approach worked well for President Clinton when he named Judge Stephen Breyer to the Supreme Court in 1994 to replace Justice Harry Blackmun. Breyer had served, in various capacities, as a counsel with the Senate Judiciary Committee for several years in the 1970s and 1980s. He was well known and well liked by members of that committee from both parties. In his opening statement at Breyer's confirmation hearings, Judiciary Committee chair Joseph Biden described the nominee's background, noting, "As a professor of law at Harvard and, *to some of us here, more importantly*, as counsel to this committee, you are an established expert in regulation and its reform, in administrative law and processes, and in the intersection of science and law."[40] Republican Orrin Hatch similarly noted Breyer's connections to the Senate: "I first came to know and admire Judge Breyer when he worked for the Senate Judiciary Committee, first as a consultant, then as chief counsel. In his work, Judge Breyer was instrumental in bringing about airline deregulation."[41] The nominee himself also highlighted his relationship with the Senate, where, he said, he learned "a great deal about Congress, about government and about political life."[42] The result of this amity between the nominee and the committee was a highly civil, even bland, confirmation process, where questions of controversy and discord were minimal.

Calling Breyer "the safest choice," CNN's Al Hunt condemned Clinton for buckling to conservative pressures and not choosing Interior Secretary Bruce Babbitt. Hunt faulted Clinton, in other words, for succumbing to confirmability pressures that have become dominant in the Supreme Court confirmation process. The CNN coverage noted the wide support that the nomination elicited, from Strom Thurmond and Orrin Hatch to Edward Kennedy and Alan Dershowitz.[43] The *CBS Evening News* commented that the nominee was a consensus builder and that he was "[n]o stranger to Washington. . . . Breyer, in the '70s, served as an assistant Watergate special prosecutor and chief counsel to the Senate Judiciary Committee. His much-vaunted wit and political savvy are already the envy of some newcomers."[44] Perhaps no media source highlighted Breyer's connections with the Senate more than National Public Radio's Nina Totenburg: "The entire judiciary committee knows him; he was chief counsel for the committee. His political godfather is Edward Kennedy. Orrin Hatch helped get him on the court of appeals when Ronald Reagan had already been elected."[45]

Everyone saw Stephen Breyer for what he truly was—a highly qualified, thoroughly safe nominee assured of speedy confirmation to the Supreme Court. In that safety, President Clinton found confirmability and assured himself of little controversy in his staffing of the Supreme Court. Moreover, the process was so smooth that questions about Breyer's employment of an illegal alien—questions that derailed other non-judicial nominations earlier in the Clinton administration—were diminished, as were serious probes about judicial philosophy. Finding the confirmable nominee is the surest way to disarm opposition and truncate the important debate that often emerges from Supreme Court confirmations.

The Supreme Court Confirmation Process and U.S. Political Culture

"Advice and consent" is a relatively harmless phrase that, carefully expressed within Article II of the Constitution, possesses tremendous influence in U.S. political culture. These words and the power they confer have resulted in a remarkable history of controversy and debate—a history that has made the U.S. democratic experiment stronger.

As I have demonstrated in this analysis, the contemporary controversies over Supreme Court nominations, with all of their political wrangling and partisan polarizations, are rooted in the structural and rhetorical dynamics of the U.S. Constitution. Emerging as it did from the Articles of Confederation, the Constitution gave considerable attention to the character of people who would occupy the offices of the new federal government. In this way, the Constitution established a rhetorical framework for Supreme Court confirmations that I have labeled characterlogical.

An outgrowth of this constitutional characterology is the embodiment in particular nominees to the High Court of specific and powerful ideological commitments that demarcate the parameters of U.S. law. Such embodiment, I have suggested, is highly political and sometimes fragmenting, enacting ideological contests in the United States with considerable consequence for the constitutive formation of the community. This ideological embodiment defines, in part, the parameters of the polity itself, indicating what justifies collective belief and behavior, what motivates a sense of community. Another result of this characterological and embodying capacity of Supreme Court confirmations is that presidents face increasing confirmability pressures as they seek the best nominees for the Court. Moreover, it results in the personalization of this political process and invites, and has created in some high profile instances, a celebritization of Supreme Court nominees.

The power and importance of ideological embodiment in the Supreme Court confirmation process were dramatically displayed in the confirmations of the twentieth century. Supreme Court nominees from Brandeis to Bork embodied a range of ideological commitments that in many ways defined U.S. political and legal culture. Louis Brandeis represented an emerging commitment to social justice that had its roots in the progressivism characteristic of powerful economic, social, and political forces in the late nineteenth and early twentieth centuries. Sixteen years later, Herbert Hoover's nominations of Charles Evans Hughes and John J. Parker enacted

the debate over the limits of social justice, testing the boundaries of property rights and human rights. Parker's nomination, additionally, expressed
again in the legal conversation the important question of race and its role
in the U.S. commitment to human rights.

Race would again figure prominently in the contested nominations of
Thurgood Marshall, Clement Haynsworth, and G. Harrold Carswell. Indeed, these confirmation struggles articulated the persistent concern about
race and civil rights that was only briefly alluded to in the Parker debate.
Some forty years later, because of many social, political, and legal changes,
civil rights and race were the dominant issues confronting the United
States. These nominations beckoned a further reexamination of the nation's commitment to civil rights, from competing perspectives, inviting the
community to express and test the meanings of this important ideological
obligation.

All of these commitments, from social justice to property rights, from
human rights to civil rights, were in play in the political spectacle of the
Bork confirmation hearings. The Bork hearings were the culmination of
this process, with a richly detailed and highly relevant discussion of the
meaning of rights, the role of the Constitution, the power of judges, and
the meaning of judging for the United States. Regrettably, perhaps, much
of the discussion was lost in the political spectacle that the Bork hearings
became. Indeed, these hearings, while potentially a meaningful educational moment in the meaning of U.S. law, became instead a biting commentary on the limits of the confirmation process, testing the boundaries
of acceptability in confirmation politics.

Consistent with the hyperbole of the hearings themselves were the
overreactions of those who criticized the process and sought its reform.
Most of these proposals were historically myopic in their contention that
the process had suddenly, in the Bork hearings, become startlingly political.
Virtually every complete and thorough account of the history of both the
"advice and consent" provisions of the Constitution and the Supreme
Court nominations of the eighteenth and nineteenth centuries reveal a
highly political process.[46] At some point, curiously, a rhetoric took hold
that divorced law from politics and that articulated the mythology that judicial confirmations should be apolitical. Undoubtedly rooted in a commitment to legal formalism, this rhetoric was useful for presidents who
disliked the Senate's interference in the nomination process. It worked to
truncate arguments and questions about the judicial philosophy and

political viewpoints of nominees, and it upheld another mythology—the independent, apolitical judiciary.

This rhetoric of a depoliticized confirmation process must be resisted for a series of compelling reasons. First, politicized confirmations affirm our constitutional and historical heritage, carrying out the constitutional commandment of advice and consent and subjecting the appointment of Supreme Court justices to the checks and balances established by the Constitution. In addition, they enact the characterological meaning of the Constitution, reflecting the persistent concern for character and public virtue that the founders believed was critical for successful governance.

Second, the U.S. political culture is stronger for the politicized discussions occasioned by the various confirmation controversies of the twentieth century. Debates about the meanings of social justice, human rights, civil rights, and privacy rights are debates a free and democratic society should be having, and the advice and consent process provides a useful enactment for those debates. Rather than keep these discussions isolated in the courtrooms and judges' chambers, the confirmation process, for Supreme Court justices particularly, renews public attention to these important concerns. Moreover, the process of ideological embodiment articulated in those debates gives citizens a concrete, material manifestation of ideological meaning. Louis Brandeis represented social justice; Thurgood Marshall embodied civil rights—and the larger culture achieved a clearer, more specific understanding of what these commitments mean and how they function in collective life. In this way, confirmation debates are democraticizing as they materialize the remote, distant ideologies that are the basis of social knowledge and collective life in the U.S. polity.

Finally, depoliticized confirmations bankrupt an important democratic process, sanitizing its power to contribute meaningfully to national debate about vital ideological matters. In the wake of the Bork hearings, regrettably, the pressures for confirmability resulted in nominations that were either "stealth," celebritized, or safe. In each of these cases, the debate about the propriety and prudence of the nomination gave way and was subsumed by other, ancillary concerns. This tendency must be resisted. In the absence of rigorous scrutiny of political positions and judicial philosophy, the process becomes simply an assessment of qualifications and the vague quality of "judicial temperament." More politics, not less, makes the confirmation process of Supreme Court justices a meaningful enactment of the rhetorical, legal, and political culture in the United States. As Keith Whittington maintains, "The constitutional division of powers contributes to a

unique and unpredictable dynamic that can feed government action, encourage institutional development, and foster political and constitutional
deliberation."[47] Such enactments tell us much, in this ongoing democratic
experiment that we call the United States, about the mainstream of U.S.
law, the nature of rights and duties in the constitutional system, and the
power of legal ideologies in political life—indeed, a politicized Supreme
Court confirmation process communicates to the larger citizenry the true
American character of justice.

Epilogue

Of Baseball Analogies, Crying Spouses, and the Erosion of Advice and Consent

"He shall have Power . . . by and with the Advice and Consent of the Senate, [to] appoint Ambassadors, other public Ministers and Consuls, Judges of the supreme Court, and all other Officers of the United States." So says Article II of the U.S. Constitution as it delineates the powers of the president. Coordinating appointment powers in this manner, the framers of the Constitution invited, even commanded, that executive appointments be subject to the deliberative judgment of the Senate. When those appointments are for life, without likely removal from office, Senate deliberation is of even greater importance and, as Akhil Reed Amar remarks, for such posts, "more Senate scrutiny [is] appropriate."[1]

The framers of the Constitution appear to have recognized that in a constitutional democracy deliberation is a cornerstone of effective decision-making and political judgment. "Common deliberation," writes Ronald Beiner, "remedies (or at least mitigates) the imperfections of democracy."[2] Drawing on the ancient wisdom of Aristotle, Beiner notes that deliberative discourse concerns the future, proceeds in a prudent and wise manner, and is a mark of individuals seeking practical wisdom and true conviction. It is, in essence, the telos of rhetoric in a democratic society. In their coordination of appointment powers, in their construction of checks and balances, in the separation of powers, the Constitution's drafters and ratifiers instantiated and manifested this telos for the emerging American republic.

In *The Character of Justice*, I explore the manner in which the Constitution motivates and drives deliberative rhetorics about character in its construction of the appointments power of the presidency and the advice and consent function of the Senate. Examining various confirmation moments over the span of the twentieth century, I have endeavored to explain how such moments articulate and enact the ideological and political development of the law over several decades. As I hope is clear, each of these moments occasioned deliberation—from the "trial" of Louis Brandeis to the spectacle of Robert Bork, when presidents offered their nominees to the Senate, that deliberative body often took the time to debate the propriety of those nominations and what they could mean for the Supreme Court and the nation. In the end, I conclude that such deliberative moments are beneficial to the U.S. political culture and the community it constitutes, and that more politics, more deliberation, not less, is what is required for a healthy and productive advice and consent process.

The years since the Bork hearings have not been kind to the advice and consent process. Increased partisan polarization and an amplified sense of the judiciary's political and social importance have magnified the stakes of judicial nominations and created an environment in which presidential administrations avoid deliberation, to seek confirmation at any and all costs. During the Supreme Court nominations of Justices David Souter, Clarence Thomas, Ruth Bader Ginsburg, and Stephen Breyer, administrations have responded to increasing confirmability pressures in a variety of ways, from celebritization to stealth, all with the aim to limit the deliberative capacity of advice and consent and to ensure speedy confirmation. These strategies have, by and large, been successful.

It is, of course, important to remember that, despite contrary impressions in the media, most judicial appointments are confirmed with little or no controversy. This includes Supreme Court justices—every Supreme Court nominee since the rejection of Robert Bork has been confirmed by the Senate, except for those nominees withdrawn from consideration before a full Senate vote. The vast majority of lower court judges are also confirmed by the Senate. Put simply, administrations are increasingly skilled at finding, presenting, and securing the confirmations of their judicial nominees.

Sadly, the lesson that those administrations appear to have learned is that confirmability is likelier in the absence of meaningful deliberation. Nowhere is this lesson more clearly enacted than in the confirmation hearings of John Roberts and Samuel Alito.

Umpiring the Law

"Judges are like umpires," John Roberts remarked in his opening remarks to the Senate Judiciary Committee. "Umpires don't make the rules; they apply them," he continued, "The role of an umpire and a judge is critical. They make sure everybody plays by the rules. But it is a limited role. Nobody ever went to a ball game to see the umpire."[3] A clever analogy, Roberts's umpire comment functioned as an organizing principle for his hearings before the Committee, eliciting praise from his supporters and scrutiny from his opponents.[4] In the process, the analogy truncated the deliberative capacity of these hearings, diverting the discussion from weighty matters of law and political philosophy, toward the intricacies of calling balls and strikes on a baseball field.

As senators questioned Roberts, particularly about the character-based matter of judicial philosophy and temperament, the umpire analogy continually reappeared. As might be expected, Republican senators validated the analogy—Alabama's Senator Jeff Sessions, for instance, noted that "What we need is what you said—an umpire, fair and objective, that calls it like they see it, based on the discreet case that comes before the judge. And I think that's most important." Some Democrats, conversely, challenged the applicability of the analogy. Wisconsin's Herb Kohl, for example, pressed Roberts on the umpire analogy when he remarked "And ballplayers and basketball players understand that depending upon who the umpire is and who the referee is, the game can be called entirely differently. When we look at real legal cases, I wonder whether or not your analogy works." Delaware's Senator Joe Biden also questioned Roberts on the analogy, noting that "So, as much as I respect your metaphor, it's not very apt, because you get to determine the strike zone. What's unreasonable? Your strike zone on reasonable/unreasonable may be very different than another judge's view of what is reasonable or unreasonable search and seizure. And the same thing prevails for a lot of other parts of the Constitution. The one that we're all talking about—and everybody here, it wouldn't matter what we said, from left, right and center—is concerned about the liberty clause of the Fourteenth Amendment." Later in the hearings, Senator Kohl challenged the analogy again, forcing the nominee to admit that it breaks down when the Supreme Court is deciding not the merits of a case, but which cases to hear. Of course, what is significant here is that as senators debated the usefulness or accuracy of his umpire analogy, they were nonetheless committed to John Roberts's framework, his metaphorical boundary, in discussing the propriety of his nomination. Roberts thusly controlled the focus of his own hearings, constraining the limits of the possible deliberation about his fit as chief justice of the United States.

John Roberts was able, with an analogy, to frame his confirmation hearings in a benign and familiar manner that limited deliberation, and, despite their attempts to resist it, Democrats were generally unsuccessful at refuting its simplicity. If judges are umpires, the analogy holds, then they come to the "game" of the law as blank slates, as simply reactors to that which occurs before them. They use their familiarity with the rules of the game to make judgments about the actual particulars that they witness, without prior prejudice or bias. Advice and consent becomes not a deliberative interrogation about judicial philosophy, not an inquisition about constitutional jurisprudence, but simply an assessment of the potential umpire's knowledge of the rules and absence of bias. Moreover, the nominee is required, by virtue of upholding the analogy, to decline to answer questions that might reveal a bias or preexisting constitutional position. So, when asked about specific cases or issues that he might confront as the next chief justice of the United States, Roberts frequently invoked a precedent of previous nominees and declined to answer. When asked by Pennsylvania's Arlen Specter, for example, to reflect on the erosion of the *Roe v. Wade* precedent, the nominee replied "Well, again, I think I should stay away from discussions of particular issues that are likely to come before the court again. And in the area of abortion, there are cases on the courts docket, of course. It is an issue that does come before the court." The umpire/judge must not discuss specifics in advance of the actual case, Roberts's analogy suggested, lest he sacrifice his neutrality in the process. Roberts took full advantage of his analogy, and the rather shaky historical precedent from previous confirmations, to avoid answering many, many of the questions put to him by the Judiciary Committee.

John Roberts's umpire analogy served him well in the hearings. It also provided the news media with a convenient and uncomplicated theme with which to frame discussions concerning his suitability for the Supreme Court. National Public Radio found two judges who also worked as baseball umpires and interviewed them extensively regarding the analogy.[5] As it made the case for his confirmation, *USA Today* noted that "[Roberts] vowed to be an open-minded umpire. On the whole, he left the impression he'd be an establishment jurist and less of a firebrand than Scalia or Thomas."[6] Conversely, Jeff Jacoby, writing in the *Boston Globe*, fretted that Roberts was not answering questions that needed to be answered: "It is not enough for a nominee to say, as Roberts said last week, that precedents should not be lightly overturned, or that judges should be like umpires. Those are platitudes. But whether *Roe v. Wade* was rightly or wrongly decided and why whether racial preferences are consistent with the 14th Amendment's guarantee of equal protection . . . those are fair but pointed questions to which a Supreme Court nominee should be required to give nonevasive answers."[7] Citizens used the analogy, as well, to argue for and against the nomination. Eric Adams of Bow, New Hampshire, wrote to the *Boston Globe* to say that "an umpire controls the game and can decide its ultimate place in history . . . There is no doubt that Roberts will be confirmed, but will he be a good umpire?"[8] "We, the people, don't need an 'umpire' on the court," noted Marilyn Benioff in her letter to the *San Francisco Chronicle*, "We need an impartial justice who will serve all the people, not just those who have paid to sit in the stadium."[9] Carl Eifert, of Alexandria, Virginia, applauded Roberts's analogy, writing to the *Washington Post* that it "was a good illustration of his core belief about jurisprudence."[10] Even as they deliberated about the nomination, these citizens argued it on the basis of Roberts's own analogy, and thus ceded to him and the administration important deliberative ground. In short, the umpire analogy worked well to circumvent meaningful and inquisitive deliberation about John Roberts's constitutional positions, his views on important constitutional questions, and his understanding and opinions about important cases and issues that have been or will be put before the United States Supreme Court. Sadly, the outcome was a process of advice and consent that yielded little relevant information or argument.

Tears of Concern

To his credit, Samuel Alito was more willing than John Roberts to answer questions put to him during his confirmation hearings for the Supreme Court. This willingness, furthermore, may explain why Alito was confirmed by such a relatively small margin—he received only four votes from Democratic senators, and even lost the vote of one Republican. But at least he answered the questions, honoring the deliberative quality of the confirmation process.

Unfortunately, the larger, cultural discussion of his confirmation hearings was preoccupied not with the answers he provided to questions he was asked, or with his constitutional positions, but with an episode on the second day of his hearings. As South Carolina Senator Lindsey Graham asked the nominee if he was a "closeted bigot," Alito's wife, Martha-Ann, began to weep and was ultimately escorted from the hearing room to regain her composure. This single moment came to dominate the public discussion of the Alito nomination, from political rhetorics to talk radio to late night comedy. Again in the confirmation process, deliberation was lost and the hearings were hijacked by the personal and the mundane.

The line of questioning from Graham and other senators was focused on the nominee's membership in the Concerned Alumni of Princeton (CAP), a group at his alma mater that, among other views, believed in restricting the diversity of admissions to the university. When pressed by Illinois Senator Dick Durbin, Alito recalled that he joined the group to protest a decision to remove ROTC from the Princeton campus, and that "what bothered me about the Princeton administration over a period of time was the treatment of ROTC." He was subsequently challenged on his membership in CAP by several senators, forcing him to repudiate much that the group articulated as their beliefs. This line of questioning apparently affected the nominee's wife considerably. Her emotional reaction, in turn, affected the nature of deliberation about the nomination, shifting the focus away from Alito's membership in CAP and other aspects of his background to questions about the confirmation process and its "unfairness" to nominees. Later on the same day that Martha-Ann Alito[11] exited from the hearings, Texas Senator John Cornyn began his questioning by telling the nominee "how desperate your opponents are to defeat your nomination." Oklahoma's Tom Coburn told the nominee that his interrogators were engaged in guilt by association: "This idea of association with anything means you take it all, whether in fact that's the truth or not, and that's not good work on this committee and it's not truthful and it's not intellectually honest." And Utah's Senator Orrin Hatch concluded that the nominee has "been straightforward here, you've honestly answered the questions, you've answered more questions than almost any Supreme Court nominee in my 29 years in the Senate and I don't think you've been fairly treated."

While Republicans lamented the process and apologized to the nominee, Democrats were largely silenced, reluctant to trigger another emotional reaction. The concerns raised about the nominee's membership in CAP were largely dropped, and the hearings proceeded in a relatively uncontroversial manner toward the eventual confirmation of the nominee. And while important questions of privacy, constitutional law and judicial interpretation, presidential powers, and a range of other critical questions were discussed during the remainder of the hearings, larger public discussions about the nominee were largely focused on the breakdown of the nominee's spouse. Reporting that "Samuel Alito's wife fled weeping from her husband's high court confirmation," the *Daily News* concluded that any "headway the Democrats made was washed away with the tears of Alito's wife." The article quotes political analyst Larry Sábato who concluded "That is the very definition of how not to win over moderate votes . . . That's a disaster for the Democrats . . . It's over."[12] On ABC News, Claire Shipman praised the nominee for remaining "impassive," but noted that his spouse "reached her breaking point." Shipman compared Martha-Ann Alito's responses in the hearings to Pat Nixon's reactions during Watergate and Virginia Thomas's responses to attacks on her husband, though such comparisons may stretch credibility. Nixon was accused of subverting the Constitution, Thomas of severe acts of sexual harassment; all Alito stood accused of was joining an alumni group. But Shipman's account of the incident speaks to its emotional power and its ability to truncate deliberation—as she remarks in her report "It's never been easy to watch a spouse under political fire."[13]

Members of the public, moreover, were drawn to this episode in their commentary about the nomination, rather than to other more substantive questions. Reacting to a *Washington Post* Style section article about the crying instance, Richard Stukey of Germantown, Maryland, said he resented the implication that the weeping might have been planned: "What shocked me most about this statement is the suggestion that Martha-Ann Alito's feelings—stripped bare by a brutal confirmation process—were some sort of staged, manipulative device to help her husband." In the same letters column, Charles Springer of Toledo, Oregon, called the tears from Martha-Ann Alito "a genuine reaction from someone unfamiliar with the callous, crude, and roughshod communication that has become the 'standard American' image around the world."[14] An alternative view was expressed by Aaron Dellutri of Lake View, Illinois, in the *Chicago Sun-Times* when he labeled the crying an "emotional stunt" that "may have made a good image."[15] Of course, the most telling aspect of these letters is that the episode attracted as much attention as it did. The process is identified as brutal, callous, and crude. It is one that featured roughshod communication and, alternatively, emotional stunts. What Martha-Ann Alito's weeping accomplished, in short, was an end to deliberation about her husband's suitability for the Supreme Court. Instead, the discussion shifted to the nature of the process, the bullying of the Democrats, and the victimization of Samuel Alito.

The Future of Advice and Consent

What both the Roberts and Alito confirmations reveal is an erosion of the U.S. Senate's advice and consent power to presidential Supreme Court nominations. My indictment of these hearings is not a nostalgic call for a time that never was; the history of advice and consent is filled with fascinating episodes of meaningful and ideological relevant deliberation. My indictment of these hearings is also not a romantic call for serious, high-minded deliberation, though there are compelling instances of such deliberation in the memory of Supreme Court confirmations as well. Rather, my concerns about the Roberts and Alito hearings are meant to raise cautionary flags about the future of the Supreme Court confirmation process. The process must not be allowed to become simply a rhetorical exercise in display, where what matters is the cleverness of the nominee, his or her facility with meaningless analogies, or the spectacular, ancillary matters of family, emotion, and the alleged brutality of the process. It cannot become simply a résumé check, a time to make sure the nominee is talented and credentialed. And it cannot be hijacked by the politics of the moment, when majority status and the loss of minority voice and rights are more important than due consideration of a nominee.

Advice and consent, emergent as it is from the coordinated, joint power-sharing scheme of the U.S. Constitution, must instead reflect the legacy of the first president who saw a nominee for the Supreme Court rejected by the Senate. As I have already noted, George Washington was so concerned with the Senate's *deliberation* about executive nominees that he told senators that he would not appear to alter their discussion or inhibit its due consideration of nominees, because he did want to deter them from the "fullest and freest enquiry into the Character of the Person nominated."[16] With all of the politics, with all of the focus on character and reputation, with all of the concerns that so bother so many contemporary commentators, the deliberative advice and consent process envisioned by Washington may well prove to be the best way to assess and articulate the character of justice for the United States now and well into the future.

Notes

Chapter One. Character and the Constitution: Politics in the Supreme Court Confirmation Process

1. *Bush v. Gore*, 531 U.S. 98 (2000). See also Theodore O. Prosise and Craig R. Smith, "The Supreme Court's Ruling in *Bush v. Gore*: A Rhetoric of Inconsistency," *Rhetoric and Public Affairs* 4 (2001): 605–32.

2. See Glenda Conway, "Inevitable Reconstructions: Voice and Ideology in Two Landmark U.S. Supreme Court Opinions," *Rhetoric and Public Affairs* 6 (2003): 487–507; Carrie Crenshaw, "The 'Protection' of 'Woman': A History of Legal Attitudes toward Women's Workplace Freedom," *Quarterly Journal of Speech* 81 (1995): 63–82; Carrie Crenshaw, "The Normality of Man and Female Otherness: (Re)Producing Patriarchal Lines of Argument in the Law and the News," *Argumentation and Advocacy* 32 (1996): 170–85; Todd F. McDorman, "Challenging Constitutional Authority: African American Responses to *Scott v. Sanford*," *Quarterly Journal of Speech* 83 (1997): 192–210; Todd F. McDorman, "Uniting Legal Doctrine and Discourse to Rethink Women's Workplace Rights," *Women's Studies in Communication* 21 (1998): 27–55; and Roger Stahl, "Carving Up Free Exercise: Dissociation and 'Religion' in Supreme Court Jurisprudence," *Rhetoric and Public Affairs* 5 (2002): 439–58.

3. The change in the publicity surrounding the nomination of individuals to the Supreme Court is discussed fully in John Anthony Maltese, *The Selling of Supreme Court Nominees* (Baltimore: Johns Hopkins University Press, 1995); Richard Davis, "Supreme Court Nominations and the News Media," *Albany Law Review* 57 (1994): 1061–79; and Richard Davis and Vincent James Strickler, "The Invisible Dance: The Supreme Court and the Press," *Perspectives on Political Science* 29 (2000): 85–92.

4. The most comprehensive history of Supreme Court nominations is offered in Henry J. Abraham, *Justices, Presidents, and Senators: A History of the U.S. Supreme Court Appointments from Washington to Clinton*, new and rev. ed. (Lanham, Md.: Rowman and Littlefield, 1999). Other historical surveys include Jonathan L. Entin, "Judicial Selection and

Political Culture," *Capital University Law Review* 30 (2002): 523–57; John P. Frank, "The Appointment of Supreme Court Justices: Prestige, Principles and Politics," *Wisconsin Law Review* 1941 (1941): 172–210, 343–79, 461–512; Paul A. Freund, "Appointment of Justices: Some Historical Perspectives," *Harvard Law Review* 101 (1988): 1146–63; Maltese, *Selling of Supreme Court Nominees;* Paul Simon, *Advice and Consent: Clarence Thomas, Robert Bork and the Intriguing History of the Supreme Court's Nomination Battles* (Washington, D.C.: National Press Books, 1992); and Laurence H. Tribe, *God Save This Honorable Court: How the Choice of Supreme Court Justices Shapes Our History* (New York: Random House, 1985).

5. The history of presidential appointments to the Supreme Court is replete with instances of rejection on the basis of the unpleasant and personal. See Simon, *Advice and Consent,* 163–68; Henry J. Abraham, *Justices and Presidents: A Political History of Appointments to the Supreme Court,* 3rd ed. (New York: Oxford University Press, 1992); Maeva Marcus and James R. Perry, eds., *The Documentary History of the Supreme Court of the United States, 1789–1800* (New York: Columbia University Press, 1985), 1:94–100 (hereafter cited as *DHSC*); and Tribe, *God Save This Honorable Court,* 79–80. The early history of such nominations is a story of political intrigue and personal vilification resulting in the rejection or withdrawal of eleven nominees by the turn of the twentieth century. By contrast, the Senate has only rejected outright four nominees to the Supreme Court in the twentieth century (John J. Parker, Clement F. Haynsworth Jr., G. Harrold Carswell, and Robert Bork). See Tribe, *God Save This Honorable Court,* 142–47. This last figure does not count the nominations that were declined or postponed or those where no action was taken by the Senate.

6. Stephen L. Carter, *The Confirmation Mess: Cleaning up the Federal Appointments Process* (New York: Basic Books, 1994), 6. Carter's book elicited considerable commentary in the legal/academic community. See Michael J. Gerhardt, "The Confirmation Mystery," *Georgetown Law Journal* 83 (1994): 395–431; Elena Kagan, "Confirmation Messes, Old and New," *University of Chicago Law Review* 62 (1995): 919–42; Michael Stokes Paulsen, "Straightening Out *The Confirmation Mess,*" *Yale Law Journal* 105 (1995): 549–79; and Gary J. Simson, "Mired in the Confirmation Mess," *University of Pennsylvania Law Review* 143 (1995): 1035–63. Carter is not alone in his critical scrutiny of the appointments process. See Robert H. Bork, *The Tempting of America: The Political Seduction of the Law* (New York: Free Press, 1990); "Essays on

the Supreme Court Appointment Process," *Harvard Law Review* 101 (1988): 1146–229; Frank Guliuzza III, Daniel J. Reagan, and David M. Barrett, "Character, Competency, and Constitutionalism: Did the Bork Nomination Represent a Fundamental Shift in Confirmation Criteria?" *Marquette Law Review* 75 (1992): 409–37; Simon, *Advice and Consent*; David A. Strauss and Cass R. Sunstein, "The Senate, the Constitution, and the Confirmation Process," *Yale Law Journal* 101 (1992): 1491–524; "Symposium, Confirmation Controversy: The Selection of a Supreme Court Justice," *Northwestern University Law Review* 84 (1990): 832–1046; and "Symposium Issue: The Selection of Judges in the United States," *Kentucky Law Journal* 77 (1988–89): 481–644.

7. Mark Silverstein, *Judicious Choices: The New Politics of Supreme Court Confirmations* (New York: W. W. Norton, 1994), 6. Silverstein is a bit hasty in his criticism of President Clinton's nomination of Ruth Bader Ginsburg to the Supreme Court. He argues that she was not "a public figure of great stature, well known to the citizenry and likely to alter dramatically the evolution of American constitutional law." By these criteria many, if not most, of the greatest jurists to serve on the Supreme Court would never have been appointed. See Mark Silverstein and William Haltom, "You Can't Always Get What You Want: Reflections on the Ginsburg and Breyer Nominations," *Journal of Law and Politics* 12 (1996): 459–79. See also G. Calvin Mackenzie, ed., *Innocent Until Nominated: The Breakdown of the Presidential Appointments Process* (Washington, D.C.: Brookings Institution Press, 2001). An alternative view that directly challenges Silverstein's reading of contemporary confirmation politics is found in Jeffrey K. Tulis, "Constitutional Abdication: The Senate, the President, and Appointments to the Supreme Court," *Case Western Reserve Law Review* 47 (1997): 1331–57.

8. See Brannon P. Denning, "The Judicial Appointments Process: The 'Blue Slip': Enforcing Norms of the Judicial Confirmation Process," *William and Mary Bill of Rights Journal* 10 (2001): 75–101; Emery G. Lee III, "The Federalist in an Age of Faction: Rethinking Federalist No. 76 on the Senate's Role in the Judicial Confirmations Process," *Ohio Northern Law Review* 30 (2004): 235–66; and Gerald Walpin, "Take Obstructionism Out of the Judicial Nominations Confirmation Process," *Texas Review of Law and Politics* 8 (2003): 89–112.

9. Joshua Meyrowitz offers a complete discussion of the impact of television and other electronic media on the political environment and those who occupy that public space. See Joshua Meyrowitz, *No Sense*

of Place: The Impact of Electronic Media on Social Behavior (New York: Oxford University Press, 1985). See also Roderick P. Hart, *Seducing America: How Television Charms the Modern Voter* (New York: Oxford University Press, 1994); and Timothy Luke, *Screens of Power: Ideology, Domination, and Resistance in Informational Society* (Urbana: University of Illinois Press, 1989). For a specific discussion of the news media coverage of Supreme Court nominations, see Michael Comiskey, "Not Guilty: The News Media in the Supreme Court Confirmation Process," *Journal of Law and Politics* 15 (1999): 1–36; and Davis, "Supreme Court Nominations."

10. See Carter, *Confirmation Mess*, 16–20; and Silverstein, *Judicious Choices*, 146–53.

11. See Twentieth Century Fund, *Judicial Roulette: Report of the Twentieth Century Fund Task Force on Judicial Selection* (New York: Priority, 1988), 3–12.

12. See Charles L. Black Jr., "A Note on Senatorial Consideration of Supreme Court Nominees," *Yale Law Journal* 79 (1970): 657–64; Michael John Burton, "Propriety in Confirmation Questioning: The Appearance of Supreme Court Nominees Before the Senate Judiciary Committee" (Ph.D. diss., University at Albany, State University of New York, 1995); Kenneth C. Cole, "Judicial Affairs The Rôle of the Senate in the Confirmation of Judicial Nominations," *American Political Science Review* 28 (1934): 875–94; Michael Comiskey, "Can the Senate Examine the Constitutional Philosophies of Supreme Court Nominees?" *PS: Political Science and Politics* 26 (1993): 495–500; James E. Gauch, "The Intended Role of the Senate in Supreme Court Appointments," *University of Chicago Law Review* 56 (1989): 337–65; Ruth Bader Ginsburg, "Confirming Supreme Court Justices: Thoughts on the Second Opinion Rendered by the Senate," *University of Illinois Law Review* 1988 (1988): 101–17; Joel B. Grossman and Stephen L. Wasby, "The Senate and Supreme Court Nominations: Some Reflections," *Duke Law Journal* 1972 (1972): 557–91; Matthew D. Marcotte, "Advice and Consent: A Historical Argument for Substantive Senatorial Involvement in Judicial Nominations," *NYU Journal of Legislation and Public Policy* 5 (2001/2002): 519–62; Adam Mitzner, "The Evolving Role of the Senate in Judicial Nominations," *Journal of Law and Politics* 5 (1989): 387–428; William G. Ross, "The Functions, Roles, and Duties of the Senate in the Supreme Court Appointment Process," *William and Mary Law Review* 28 (1987): 633–82; and Scott R. Ryther,

"Advice and Consent: The Senate's Political Role in the Supreme Court Appointment Process," *Utah Law Review* 1988 (1988): 411–33.

13. The various proposed reforms include shortening the process, resurrecting the Senate's role in advising on nominations as well as offering consent, removing the Senate from the process, closing hearings, and involving the House of Representatives. See Mary Katherine Boyte, "The Supreme Court Confirmation Process in Crisis: Is the System Defective, or Merely the Participants?" *Whittier Law Review* 14 (1993): 542–46; Joseph Faria and David Markey, "Supreme Court Appointments After the Thomas Nomination: Reforming the Confirmation Process," *St. John's Journal of Legal Commentary* 7 (1991): 407–16; John M. Lawlor, "Court Packing Revisited: A Proposal for Rationalizing the Timing of Appointments to the Supreme Court," *University of Pennsylvania Law Review* 134 (1986): 967–1000; Maltese, *Selling of Supreme Court Nominees;* Richard D. Manoloff, "The Advice and Consent of Congress: Toward a Supreme Court Appointment Process for Our Time," *Ohio State Law Journal* 54 (1993): 1104–7; Terri Jennings Peretti, "Restoring the Balance of Power: The Struggle for Control of the Supreme Court," *Hastings Constitutional Law Quarterly* 20 (1992): 69–103; William G. Ross, "The Supreme Court Appointment Process: A Search for a Synthesis," *Albany Law Review* 57 (1994): 993–1042; Simon, *Advice and Consent,* 303–19; Strauss and Sunstein, "Senate," 1517–20; and Twentieth Century Fund, *Judicial Roulette.* During the 2000 presidential campaign, George W. Bush proposed that the Senate pass judgment on presidential judicial nominations within sixty days of the naming of the nominee. See George W. Bush, "A New Approach," June 8, 2000, http://www.georgewbush.com/speeches/newapproach.asp (June 15, 2000).

14. See Charles M. Cameron, Albert D. Cover, and Jeffrey A. Segal, "Senate Voting on Supreme Court Nominees: A Neoinstitutional Model," *American Political Science Review* 84 (1990): 525–34; John D. Felice and Herbert F. Weisberg, "The Changing Importance of Ideology, Party, and Region in Confirmation of Supreme Court Nominees, 1953–1988," *Kentucky Law Journal* 77 (1988–89): 509–30; Katherine M. Gannon, "The Template-Driven Construal Model: An Application to Decision Making of the Senate Judiciary Committee in Supreme Court Justice Nomination Hearings" (Ph.D. diss., Ohio State University, 1995); Frank Guliuzza III, Daniel J. Reagan, and David M. Barrett, "The Senate Judiciary Committee and Supreme Court Nominees: Measuring the Dynamics of Confirmation Criteria," *Journal of*

Politics 56 (1994): 773–87; Thomas R. Marshall, *Public Opinion and the Supreme Court* (Boston: Unwin Hyman, 1989), 104–30; Jan Palmer, "Senate Confirmation of Appointments to the U.S. Supreme Court," *Review of Social Economy* 41 (1983): 152–62; Ronald Hale Romine, "The 'Politics' of Supreme Court Nominations from Theodore Roosevelt to Ronald Reagan: The Construction of a 'Politicization Index'" (Ph.D. diss., University of South Carolina, 1984); P. S. Ruckman Jr., "The Supreme Court, Critical Nominations, and the Senate Confirmation Process," *Journal of Politics* 55 (1993): 793–805; Jeffrey A. Segal, "Senate Confirmation of Supreme Court Justices: Partisan and Institutional Politics," *Journal of Politics* 49 (1987): 998–1015; Jeffrey A. Segal and Albert D. Cover, "Ideological Values and the Votes of U.S. Supreme Court Justices," *American Political Science Review* 83 (1989): 559–65; Donald R. Songer, "The Relevance of Policy Values for the Confirmation of Supreme Court Nominees," *Law and Society* 13 (1979): 927–48; and Stuart E. Teger, "Presidential Strategy for the Appointment of Supreme Court Justices" (Ph.D. diss., University of Rochester, 1976).

15. This dimension of legal practice and jurisprudence is the source of recent scholarship that attempts to reconceptualize the nature of how the law is seen and understood. Some critics liken the law to literature and other nonlegal practices, noting its rhetorical dimensions, particularly in the law's use of narrative. See Peter Brooks and Paul Gewirtz, eds., *Law's Stories: Narrative and Rhetoric in the Law* (New Haven, Conn.: Yale University Press, 1996); Robert Ferguson "The Judicial Opinion as Literary Genre," *Yale Journal of Law and the Humanities* 2 (1990): 201–19; Jody Freeman, "Constitutive Rhetoric: Law as a Literary Activity," *Harvard Women's Law Journal* 14 (1991): 305–25; Fredric G. Gale, *Political Literacy: Rhetoric, Ideology, and the Possibility of Justice* (Albany: State University of New York Press, 1994); Anselm Haverkamp, "Rhetoric, Law, and the Poetics of Memory," *Cardozo Law Review* 13 (1992): 1639–53; L. H. LaRue, *Constitutional Law as Fiction: Narrative in the Rhetoric of Authority* (University Park: Pennsylvania State University Press, 1995); Sanford Levinson and Steven Mailloux, eds., *Interpreting Law and Literature* (Evanston, Ill.: Northwestern University Press, 1988); William Lewis, "Law's Tragedy," *Rhetoric Society Quarterly* 21 (1991): 11–21; William Lewis, "Of Innocence, Exclusion, and the Burning of Flags: The Romantic Realism of the Law," *Southern Communication Journal* 60 (1994): 4–21; Daniela K. Pacher, "Aesthetics and Ideology: The Motives behind 'Law and Literature,'" *Columbia-*

VLA Journal of Law and the Arts 14 (1990): 587–614; Austin Sarat and Thomas R. Kearns, eds., *The Rhetoric of Law* (Ann Arbor: University of Michigan Press, 1994); Robert Weisberg, "The Law-Literature Enterprise," *Yale Journal of Law and the Humanities* 1 (1988): 1–67; and James Boyd White, *Justice as Translation* (Chicago: University of Chicago Press, 1990). More specifically, critical and rhetorical interpretations of the relationship between rhetoric and law are found in Julia M. Allen, "'That Accursed Aesopian Language': Prosecutorial Framing of Linguistic Evidence in *U.S. v. Foster*, 1949," *Rhetoric and Public Affairs* 4 (2001): 109–34; Peter Goodrich, *Legal Discourse: Studies in Linguistics, Rhetoric and Legal Analysis* (New York: St. Martin's Press, 1987); Marouf Hasian Jr., "Critical Legal Rhetorics: The Theory and Practice of Law in a Postmodern World," *Southern Communication Journal* 60 (1994): 44–56; Marouf Hasian Jr., *Legal Memories and Amnesias in America's Rhetorical Culture* (Boulder, Colo.: Westview, 2000); Marouf Hasian Jr., Celeste Michelle Condit, and John Louis Lucaites, "The Rhetorical Boundaries of 'the Law': A Consideration of the Rhetorical Culture of Legal Practice and the Case of the 'Separate but Equal' Doctrine," *Quarterly Journal of Speech* 82 (1996): 323–42; Marouf Hasian Jr., and Earl Croasmun, "Rhetoric's Revenge: The Prospect of a Critical Legal Rhetoric," *Philosophy and Rhetoric* 29 (1996): 384–99; Geoffrey Klinger, "Law as Communicative *Praxis:* Toward a Rhetorical Jurisprudence," *Argumentation and Advocacy* 30 (1994): 236–47; John Louis Lucaites, "Between Rhetoric and 'the Law': Power, Legitimacy, and Social Change," *Quarterly Journal of Speech* 76 (1990): 435–49; and Joseph Pilotta et al., "The Contemporary Rhetoric of the Social Theories of Law," *Central States Speech Journal* 34 (1983): 211–20. Useful surveys of the evolving relationship between rhetoric and law are Victoria Kahn, "Rhetoric and the Law," *Diacritics* 19 (1989): 21–34; Dennis R. Klinck, *The Word of the Law* (Ottawa, Canada: Carleton University Press, 1992); Martha Minow, "Law Turning Outward," *Telos* 73 (1987): 79–100; "Symposium: Rhetoric and Skepticism," *Iowa Law Review* 74 (1989): 755–836; and Brook Thomas, "Reflections on the Law and Literature Revival," *Critical Inquiry* 17 (1991): 510–39.

16. Michael J. Hyde and Craig R. Smith, "Hermeneutics and Rhetoric: A Seen but Unobserved Relationship," *Quarterly Journal of Speech* 65 (1979): 348.

17. Gerald B. Wetlaufer, "Rhetoric and Its Denial in Legal Discourse," *Virginia Law Review* 76 (1990): 1548. The specific philosophical and

hermeneutic bases for the interaction between the law and language/rhetoric are discussed fully in Brian Bix, *Law, Language, and Legal Determinacy* (Oxford: Clarendon Press, 1993); and Patrick Nerhot, ed., *Law, Interpretation, and Reality: Essays in Epistemology, Hermeneutics and Jurisprudence* (Dordrecht, The Netherlands: Kluwer Academic Publishers, 1990).

18. James Boyd White, *Heracles' Bow: Essays on the Rhetoric and Poetics of the Law* (Madison: University of Wisconsin Press, 1985), 35. A useful commentary on White's work is offered by Joseph W. Dellapenna and Kathleen Farrell, "Law and the Language of Community: On the Contributions of James Boyd White," *Rhetoric Society Quarterly* 21 (1991): 38–58. See also Samuel J. M. Donnelly, *The Language and Uses of Rights: A Biopsy of American Jurisprudence in the Twentieth Century* (Lanham, Md.: University Press of America, 1994).

19. Lucaites, "Between Rhetoric and 'the Law,'" 445.

20. To focus on ideological commitments as a unit of analysis is not to ignore the other dimensions of public debate and rhetoric. Indeed, analysis of such commitments is incomplete without attention to their relationship to myths, narratives, metaphors, and so forth. See Marouf Hasian Jr., *The Rhetoric of Eugenics in Anglo-American Thought* (Athens: University of Georgia Press, 1996), 8. See also Michael J. Gerhardt, "The Rhetoric of Judicial Critique: From Judicial Restraint to the Virtual Bill of Rights," *William and Mary Bill of Rights Journal* 10 (2002): 585–645.

21. See Joseph R. Biden Jr., "The Constitution, the Senate, and the Court," *Wake Forest Law Review* 24 (1989): 951–58; Bork, *Tempting of America*; Robert A. Friedlander, "Judicial Selection and the Constitution: What Did the Framers Originally Intend?" *Saint Louis University Public Law Review* 8 (1989): 1–11; Michael J. Gerhardt, *The Federal Appointments Process: A Constitutional and Historical Analysis* (Durham, N.C.: Duke University Press, 2000); Orrin G. Hatch, "More Marbury Myths," *Cincinnati Law Review* 57 (1989): 891–901; Nathaniel R. Jones, "Whither Goest Judicial Nominations, *Brown* or *Plessy?*— Advice and Consent Revisited," *SMU Law Review* 46 (1992): 735–49; Joseph S. Larisa Jr., "Popular Mythology: The Framers' Intent, the Constitution, and Ideological Review of Supreme Court Nominees," *Boston College Law Review* 30 (1989): 969–86; Charles H. Percy, "Advice and Consent: A Reevaluation," *Southern Illinois University Law Journal* 1978 (1978): 31–43; Tribe, *God Save This Honorable Court*; Norman Vieira and Leonard E. Gross, "The Appointments Clause: Judge

Bork and the Role of Ideology in Judicial Confirmations," *Journal of Legal History* 11 (1990): 311–52; and Christopher Wolfe, "The Senate's Power to Give 'Advice and Consent' in Judicial Appointments," *Marquette Law Review* 82 (1999): 355–79.

22. The futility of trying to ascertain the framers' original intent is clearly revealed in Paul Brest, "The Misconceived Quest for the Original Understanding," *Boston University Law Review* 60 (1980): 204–38.

23. James Jasinski maintains that the "liberty" central to the origins of the Constitution is "feminized" and that it compelled the selection of individuals who "displayed the most virtue" for public office as a means of enacting public virtue. See James Jasinski, "The Feminization of Liberty, Domesticated Virtue, and the Reconstitution of Power and Authority in Early American Political Discourse," *Quarterly Journal of Speech* 79 (1993): 146–64.

24. Kenneth Burke, *A Grammar of Motives* (Berkeley and Los Angeles: University of California Press, 1969), 377. See also Kenneth Burke, *The Philosophy of Literary Form: Studies in Symbolic Action* (Berkeley and Los Angeles: University of California Press, 1973), 109–11. For commentaries on Burke's view of the dialectics of constitutions, see Stephen Bygrave, *Kenneth Burke: Rhetoric and Ideology* (London: Routledge, 1993), 89–94; Henry L. Ewbank, "The Constitution: Burkeian, Brandeisian, and Borkian Perspectives," *Southern Communication Journal* 61 (1996): 220–32; Robert L. Heath, *Realism and Relativism: A Perspective on Kenneth Burke* (Macon, Ga.: Mercer University Press, 1986); and Thomas Meisenhelder, "Law as Symbolic Action: Kenneth Burke's Sociology of Law," *Symbolic Interaction* 4 (1981): 43–57. A similar view of the substantiality of the U.S. Constitution is offered in Levinson and Mailloux's argument that constitutional requirements and prohibitions are not only legal facts but are "normative principle[s] with moral weight" because the Constitution functions as a "repository of wisdom." See Levinson and Mailloux, *Interpreting Law and Literature*, 3; and Sheldon S. Wolin, *The Presence of the Past: Essays on the State and the Constitution* (Baltimore: Johns Hopkins University Press, 1989), 9.

25. Burke, *Grammar of Motives*, 389.

26. Burke, *Grammar of Motives*, 363.

27. Walter Fisher, *Human Communication as Narration: Toward a Philosophy of Reason, Value, and Action* (Columbia: University of South Carolina Press, 1987), 47. Bruce Gronbeck suggests that the term "characterological" as an adjective for argument or rhetoric comes from Forbes Hill's analysis of Nixon's Vietnamization speech. Gronbeck applies the term to the

arguments advanced in political campaign films. See Bruce E. Gron-beck, "Characterological Argument in Bush's and Clinton's Convention Films," in *Argument and the Postmodern Challenge: Proceedings of the Eighth SCA/AFA Conference on Argumentation*, ed. Raymie E. McKerrow, 397 (Annandale, Va.: Speech Communication Association, 1993); and Forbes Hill, "Conventional Wisdom—Traditional Form—The Presi-dent's Message of November 3, 1969," *Quarterly Journal of Speech* 58 (1972): 373–86.

28. Forrest McDonald, *Novus Ordo Seclorum: The Intellectual Origins of the Constitution* (Lawrence: University Press of Kansas, 1985), 193.

29. Paul K. Longmore, *The Invention of George Washington* (Charlottesville: University Press of Virginia, 1999), 2.

30. John Adams, *Discourses on Davila: A Series of Papers on Political History* (1790; reprint, New York: DaCapo Press, 1973), 25–26.

31. Isocrates, "Antidosis," in *Speeches and Letters*, ed. George Norlin, 15.278, http://www.perseus.tufts.edu/ (June 14, 2000).

32. Aristotle, *The "Art" of Rhetoric*, 1.2.1356a3–7. For an extended discus-sion of Aristotle on character, see Thomas B. Farrell, *Norms of Rhetori-cal Culture* (New Haven, Conn.: Yale University Press, 1993); and Eugene Garver, *Aristotle's Rhetoric: An Art of Character* (Chicago: Uni-versity of Chicago Press, 1994).

33. [Cicero], *Ad C. Herennium*, 4.49.62–51.65. For more contemporary ex-aminations of ethos, see James S. Baumlin and Tita French Baumlin, eds., *Ethos: New Essays in Rhetorical and Critical Theory* (Dallas: Southern Methodist University Press, 1994). See also Cal M. Logue and Eugene F. Miller, "Rhetorical Status: A Study of Its Origins, Functions, and Consequences," *Quarterly Journal of Speech* 81 (1995): 20–47.

34. Philip Bobbitt, *Constitutional Fate: Theory of the Constitution* (New York: Oxford University Press, 1982), 94.

35. Jerry Frug, "Argument as Character," *Stanford Law Review* 40 (1988): 875. A critique of Frug's position is offered by Brian Leiter, "Intellec-tual Voyeurism in Legal Scholarship," *Yale Journal of Law and the Hu-manities* 4 (1992): 79–104.

36. Alasdair MacIntyre, *After Virtue: A Study in Moral Theory* (Notre Dame, Ind.: University of Notre Dame Press, 1981), 27.

37. Celeste Michelle Condit, "Democracy and Civil Rights: The Universal-izing Influence of Public Argumentation," *Communication Monographs* 54 (1987): 4.

38. Robert Hariman, *Political Style: The Artistry of Power* (Chicago: Univer-sity of Chicago Press, 1995), 3, 4.

39. Hariman, *Political Style*, 4.

40. Hariman, *Political Style*, 114–15.

41. A frequently cited source for this interpretation of the Articles of Confederation is Merrill Jensen, *The Articles of Confederation* (Madison: University of Wisconsin Press, 1940).

42. Robert W. Hoffert, *A Politics of Tensions: The Articles of Confederation and American Political Ideas* (Niwot: University Press of Colorado, 1992), xiii.

43. Eric M. Freedman, "Why Constitutional Lawyers and Historians Should Take a Fresh Look at the Emergence of the Constitution from the Confederation Period: The Case of the Drafting of the Articles of Confederation," *Tennessee Law Review* 60 (1993): 784. See also Arthur R. Landever, "Those Indispensable Articles of Confederation—Stage in Constitutionalism, Passage for the Framers, and Clue to the Nature of the Constitution," *Arizona Law Review* 31 (1989): 79–125; and Donald S. Lutz, "The Articles of Confederation as the Background to the Federal Republic," *Publius* 20 (1990): 55–70.

44. Wolin, *Presence of the Past*, 3.

45. The *Articles of Confederation*, Art. V, cl. 2, provides: "No state shall be represented in Congress by less than two, nor by more than seven members; and no person shall be capable of being a delegate for more than three years in any term of six years; nor shall any person, being a delegate, be capable of holding any office under the United States, for which he, or another for his benefit receives any salary, fees or emolument of any kind."

46. The *Articles of Confederation*, Art. IX, cl. 5, requires: "The United States in Congress assembled shall have authority to appoint a committee, to sit in the recess of Congress, to be denominated 'A Committee of the States,' and to consist of one delegate from each state; and to appoint such other committees and civil officers as may be necessary for managing the general affairs of the United States under their direction—to appoint one of their number to preside, provided that no person be allowed to serve in the office of president more than one year in any term of three years."

47. John Leubsdorf, "Deconstructing the Constitution," *Stanford Law Review* 40 (1987): 193–94.

48. *U.S. Constitution*, Preamble.

49. *U.S. Constitution*, Art. I, sec. 5, cl. 2.

50. *U.S. Constitution*, Art. II, sec. 1, cl. 9.

51. *U.S. Constitution*, Art. II, sec. 2, cl. 2.

52. *U.S. Constitution*, Art. III, sec. 1, cl. 1.

53. See Richard A. Posner, *An Affair of State: The Investigation, Impeachment, and Trial of President Clinton* (Cambridge, Mass.: Harvard University Press, 1999), 97–98.

54. Albert Furtwangler, *The Authority of Publius: A Reading of the Federalist Papers* (Ithaca, N.Y.: Cornell University Press, 1984), 18.

55. George Carey, *The Federalist: Design for a Constitutional Republic* (Urbana: University of Illinois Press, 1989), xi. See also David F. Epstein, *The Political Theory of the Federalist* (Chicago: University of Chicago Press, 1984); Robert Ferguson, "Ideology and the Framing of the Constitution," *Early American Literature* 22 (1987): 157–65; Furtwangler, *Authority of Publius*; and Edward Millican, *One United People: The Federalist Papers and the National Idea* (Lexington: University Press of Kentucky, 1990).

56. James Madison, Alexander Hamilton, and John Jay, *The Federalist Papers*, ed. Isaac Kramnick (Middlesex, England: Penguin Books, 1987), 87–322.

57. Madison, Hamilton, and Jay, *Federalist Papers*, 323–24.

58. Madison, Hamilton, and Jay, *Federalist Papers*, 366.

59. Madison, Hamilton, and Jay, *Federalist Papers*, 394–5.

60. Madison, Hamilton, and Jay, *Federalist Papers*, 428.

61. Madison, Hamilton, and Jay, *Federalist Papers*, 437–8.

62. Sanford Levinson, "'The Constitution' in American Civil Religion," in *The Supreme Court Review 1979*, ed. Philip B. Kurland and Gerhard Casper, 123–51 (Chicago: University of Chicago Press, 1979).

63. Kathleen Hall Jamieson, *Packaging the Presidency: A History and Criticism of Presidential Campaign Advertising*, 3rd ed. (New York: Oxford University Press, 1996).

64. See Abraham, *Justices and Presidents*; Albert P. Melone, "The Senate's Confirmation Role in Supreme Court Nominations and the Politics of Ideology versus Impartiality," *Judicature* 75, no. 2 (1991): 68–79; Simon, *Advice and Consent*; and Tribe, *God Save This Honorable Court*.

65. John B. Thompson, *Ideology and Modern Culture* (Stanford, Calif.: Stanford University Press, 1990), 292.

66. Michael Calvin McGee, "The 'Ideograph': A Link Between Rhetoric and Ideology," *Quarterly Journal of Speech* 66 (1980): 1–16. The study of ideographs is different from standard explanations of the history of ideas or conceptual history. For such explanations, see Terence Ball, James Farr, and Russell L. Hanson, *Political Innovation and Conceptual Change* (Cambridge: Cambridge University Press, 1989). Ideographic

analysis is useful for its blending of materialist and symbolic views of language and its concern with social consequence and lived experience. See Hasian, *Rhetoric of Eugenics*; and Shawn J. Parry-Giles, "The Rhetorical Tension Between 'Propaganda' and 'Democracy': Blending Competing Conceptions of Ideology and Theory," *Communication Studies* 44 (1993): 127–28.

67. Hasian, *Rhetoric of Eugenics*, 9.

68. For more on the rhetorical construction of community, see Maurice Charland, "Constitutive Rhetoric: The Case of the *Peuple Québécois*," *Quarterly Journal of Speech* 73 (1987): 133–50; Michael Calvin McGee, "In Search of 'The People': A Rhetorical Alternative," *Quarterly Journal of Speech* 61 (1975): 235–49; and Edmund S. Morgan, *Inventing the People: The Rise of Popular Sovereignty in England and America* (New York: W. W. Norton, 1988).

69. Abraham, *Justices and Presidents*, 206.

70. For instance, Douglas Ginsburg, who was by some estimates a very conservative extremist appointed as revenge for the Senate's rejection of Robert Bork, saw his nomination withdrawn by President Ronald Reagan because of disclosures of significant marijuana usage as a student and law professor. See Abraham, *Justices and Presidents*, 359.

71. "South Carolina State-Gazette, July 17, 1795, Charleston, South Carolina," *DHSC*, 765–67.

72. "Edmund Randolph to George Washington, July 29, 1795, Philadelphia, Pennsylvania," *DHSC*, 773.

73. "William Bradford Jr., to Alexander Hamilton, August 4, 1795, Philadelphia, Pennsylvania," *DHSC*, 775.

74. "George Washington to Edward Carrington, December 23, 1795, Philadelphia, Pennsylvania," *DHSC*, 817. In early January, Washington would write to Henry Lee about his concern that the bench be filled by the time they were scheduled by law to reconvene. See "George Washington to Henry Lee, January 11, 1796, Philadelphia, Pennsylvania," *DHSC*, 829.

75. George Washington, "Conference with a Committee of the United States Senate," August 8, 1789, in *The Papers of George Washington: Presidential Series*, Vol. 3, edited by W. W. Abbot (Charlottesville: University Press of Virginia, 1987), 401.

76. "John Adams to Abigail Adams, December 17, 1795, Philadelphia, Pennsylvania," *DHSC*, 813.

77. "Thomas Jefferson to William B. Giles, December 31, 1795, Monticello, Albemarle County, Virginia," *DHSC*, 821.

78. Abraham, *Justices, Presidents, and Senators*, 66.

79. James Madison, "To the Senate of the United States, July 6, 1813," in *A Compilation of the Messages and Papers of the Presidents, 1789–1897*, 10 vols., ed. James D. Richardson (Washington, D.C.: Government Printing Office, 1897), 1:531.

80. Andrew Jackson, "To the Senate of the United States, February 10, 1835," in Richardson, *Compilation of the Messages and Papers of the Presidents*, 3:133. For more on Jackson's struggles over advice and consent, see Joseph P. Harris, *The Advice and Consent of the Senate: A Study of the Confirmation of Appointments by the United States Senate* (Berkeley: University of California Press, 1953), chapter 4.

81. Andrew Jackson, "To the Senate, March 11, 1834," in Richardson, *Compilation of the Messages and Papers of the Presidents*, 3:42.

82. Tyler's opposition to Jackson's spoils system is discussed in Dan Monroe, *The Republican Vision of John Tyler* (College Station: Texas A&M University Press, 2003), 150–53.

83. John Tyler, "Special Session Message, June 1, 1841," in Richardson, *Compilation of the Messages and Papers of the Presidents,* 4:50.

84. Tyler, "Special Session Message," 50.

85. Harris, *Advice and Consent of the Senate*, 66. See also William F. Swindler, "John Tyler's Nominations: 'Robin Hood,' Congress, and the Court," *Yearbook of the Supreme Court Historical Society* (1977): 39–43.

86. John Tyler, "To the House of Representatives of the United States, March 23, 1842," in Richardson, *Compilation of the Messages and Papers of the Presidents*, 4:106.

87. Robert J. Morgan, *A Whig Embattled: The Presidency under John Tyler* (Lincoln: University of Nebraska Press, 1954), 87. See also Oscar Doane Lambert, *Presidential Politics in the United States, 1841–1844* (Durham, N.C.: Duke University Press, 1936); and Monroe, *Republican Vision of John Tyler*.

88. For a discussion of Tyler's attempt to fill Baldwin's seat, see Henry A. Wise, *Seven Decades of Union* (Philadelphia: J. B. Lippincott, 1881).

89. Abraham, *Justices, Presidents, and Senators*, 80–81. For a discussion of the role of geography in Supreme Court appointments, see William J. Daniels, "The Geographic Factor in Appointments to the United States Supreme Court: 1789–1976," *Western Political Quarterly* 31 (1978): 226–37.

90. James K. Polk, *The Diary of a President, 1845–1849*, ed. Allan Nevins (London: Longmans, Green, 1929), 37.

91. Polk, *Diary*, 39.
92. Polk, *Diary*, 45.
93. Abraham, *Justices, Presidents, and Senators*, 85–86. There is no mention of the appointment or the Senate's rejection in the authorized biography of Black. See Mary Black Clayton, *Reminiscences of Jeremiah Sullivan Black* (St. Louis: Christian Publishing, 1887). Buchanan commented on the president's power of appointments in a response to the Senate dated January 15, 1861, which had requested information concerning a temporary appointment. Buchanan upheld the president's autonomy: "I take it for granted that the Senate did not mean to call for the reasons upon which I acted in performing an Executive duty nor to demand an account of the motives which governed me in an act which the law and the Constitution left to my own discretion." See James Buchanan, "To the Senate of the United States, January 15, 1861," in Richardson, *Compilation of the Messages and Papers of the Presidents*, 5:661.
94. See *The Papers of Ulysses S. Grant*, ed. John Y. Simon (Carbondale: Southern Illinois University Press, 1995), 20:54–57, 92, 405. Importantly, Hoar was Grant's attorney general and had generated considerable hostility in the Senate. Upon his rejection, Senator Cameron was reported to have said, "What could you expect for a man who had snubbed seventy senators?" See Moorfield Storey and Edward W. Emerson, *Ebenezer Rockwood Hoar: A Memoir* (Boston: Houghton Mifflin, 1911), 197.
95. "George Williams to USG," in Simon, *Papers of Ulysses S. Grant*, 24:287.
96. Richard E. Welch Jr., *The Presidencies of Grover Cleveland* (Lawrence: University Press of Kansas, 1988), 207.
97. Allan Nevins, ed., *Letters of Grover Cleveland, 1850–1908* (Boston: Houghton Mifflin, 1933), 332.
98. 410 U.S. 113 (1973).
99. For more on the power of "celebrity," see P. David Marshall, *Celebrity and Power: Fame in Contemporary Culture* (Minneapolis: University of Minnesota Press, 1997).

Chapter Two. For the Soul of the Supreme Court: The 1916 Nomination of Louis D. Brandeis

1. Alpheus Thomas Mason, *Brandeis: A Free Man's Life* (New York: Viking Press, 1946), 466. The surprise occasioned by the Brandeis appointment was reported in the *Washington Star* when it noted that "the appointment of Louis D. Brandeis came to the Senate as an

absolute surprise." See "Louis D. Brandeis Named for Place on Supreme Bench," *Washington Star*, January 28, 1916.

2. Daniel T. Rodgers, "In Search of Progressivism," *Reviews in American History* 10 (1982): 123.

3. David L. Waterhouse, *The Progressive Movement of 1924 and the Development of Interest Group Liberalism* (New York: Garland, 1991), 68.

4. Barry D. Karl, *The Uneasy State* (Chicago: University of Chicago Press, 1983), 20.

5. Karl, *Uneasy State*, 60. Brandeis's progressive views of the law and social justice are put forth in an oft-reprinted speech to the Chicago Bar Association, January 3, 1916. See Louis D. Brandeis, "The Living Law," *Illinois Law Review* 10 (1916): 461–71.

6. Brandeis's progressivism is discussed fully in the following: Richard P. Adelstein, "'Islands of Conscious Power': Louis D. Brandeis and the Modern Corporation," *Business History Review* 63 (1989): 614–56; Stephen W. Baskerville, *Of Laws and Limitations: An Intellectual Portrait of Louis Dembitz Brandeis* (Rutherford, N.J.: Fairleigh Dickinson University Press, 1994); David W. Levy, "Brandeis and the Progressive Movement," in *Brandeis and America*, ed. Nelson L. Dawson, 99–117 (Lexington: University Press of Kentucky, 1989); and Philippa Strum, "Louis Brandeis: Lawyer and Judge," *Journal of Supreme Court History* 1993 (1993): 29–40. Opposing views of Brandeis's brand of progressivism also exist. One such perspective holds that Brandeis actually went beyond progressivism by rejecting governmental regulation of business in favor of individual liberty. See Philippa Strum, *Brandeis: Beyond Progressivism* (Lawrence: University Press of Kansas, 1993). A Brandeis critic holds that the future Supreme Court justice lacked conceptual intelligence and advocated economic regulations based on a set of faulty economic assumptions. See Thomas K. McCraw, *Prophets of Regulation: Charles Francis Adams, Louis D. Brandeis, James M. Landis, Alfred E. Kahn* (Cambridge, Mass.: Belknap Press, 1984).

7. Thomas K. McCraw, "Louis D. Brandeis Reappraised," *American Scholar* 54 (1985): 527. In retrospect, Brandeis's progressivism may have been a bit more limited or constrained than his historical legend/legacy would suggest. The creation and manifestation of the Brandeis legacy and legend are discussed in G. Edward White, "The Canonization of Holmes and Brandeis: Epistemology and Judicial Reputations," *New York University Law Review* 70 (1995): 576–621. The extent to which Brandeis rhetorically contributed to this legacy is the subject of Walter Ulrich, "The Creation of a Legacy: Brandeis's

Concurring Opinion in *Whitney v. California*," *Southern Speech Communication Journal* 50 (1985): 143–55.

One historical revisionist maintains that Brandeis's view of antitrust policy, for example, privileged a belief in competition and an antigiantism that mitigated against activist trust-busting. See Philip Cullis, "The Limits of Progressivism: Louis Brandeis, Democracy and the Corporation," *Journal of American Studies* 30 (1996): 381–404. Clyde Spillenger argues that Brandeis was not the "people's lawyer" but was rather an "elusive advocate" who saw his role in lawyering as more judicial than advocative. See Clyde Spillenger, "Elusive Advocate: Reconsidering Brandeis as People's Lawyer," *Yale Law Journal* 105 (1996): 1445–535. Even Brandeis's famous brief in *Muller v. Oregon* (208 U.S. 412 [1908]), long a testament to legal realism, is reasonably faulted for establishing a legal framework of "protectionism" and inferiority for women. See Crenshaw, "'Protection' of 'Woman,'" 63–83. Indeed, Brandeis was arguably more of a legal pragmatist than a legal progressive or reformer, though such distinctions might be a bit too facile for a complete understanding of the Brandeisian legacy. For a forceful assertion of Brandeis's pragmatic tendencies, see Daniel A. Farber, "Reinventing Brandeis: Legal Pragmatism for the Twenty-First Century," *University of Illinois Law Review* 1995 (1995): 163–90. This view is also noted, though not explicitly, in Ewbank, "Constitution," 220–32.

8. See, for example, "A 'People's Lawyer' for the Supreme Court," *Literary Digest*, February 12, 1916, 362–64.

9. "Press Comment on Appointment of Brandeis to Supreme Court Shows Wide Diversity of Views," *Washington Post*, January 29, 1916.

10. Louis J. Jacoves, "Brandeis and Briand," *New York Times*, February 5, 1916.

11. "Big Fight Brews against Brandeis," *Washington Star*, January 29, 1916.

12. See McCraw, "Louis D. Brandeis Reappraised," 531. Along this same vein, Christopher Bracey argues the Brandeis's nomination to the Court was stalled because "Brandeis was sympathetic to blacks." Bracey is virtually alone in this judgment. See Christopher A. Bracey, "Louis Brandeis and the Race Question," *Alabama Law Review* 52 (2001): 878.

13. The impact of progressivism on the Supreme Court, as well as the impact of the Supreme Court on progressive reform, is decidedly ambiguous. On one level, the Supreme Court remained remarkably

insulated against the sweeping changes in intellectual and political thought wrought by progressivism. As Alexander Bickel and Benno Schmidt observe, by 1916 "nothing of the ferment, nothing of the new intellectual currents in economics, philosophy, and law, nothing even of the new methods of inquiry had reached the Court." They also note that state courts were far more likely to overrule progressive legislation than were the federal courts. See Alexander M. Bickel and Benno C. Schmidt Jr., *The Judiciary and Responsible Government, 1910–21*, vol. 9 of *History of the Supreme Court of the United States* (New York: Macmillan, 1984), 201, 367.

At the same time, the Supreme Court generally upheld federal and state reform legislation as constitutional, despite perceptions to the contrary. During the period from 1887 to 1911, according to a contemporaneous account by Charles Warren, the Court heard 560 cases concerning what he calls "social justice" legislation, and such legislation was only deemed unconstitutional in three cases. See Charles Warren, "The Progressiveness of the United States Supreme Court," *Columbia Law Review* 13 (1913): 294–95. Warren's account is supported by Ernest Sutherland Bates, *The Story of the Supreme Court* (Indianapolis, Ind.: Bobbs-Merrill, 1936). Some of the most profound cases from this period include *Second Employers' Liability Cases* (223 U.S. 1 [1912]), which upheld legislation that forced compensation for victims of industrial accidents; *United States v. Chandler-Dunbar Co.* (229 U.S. 53 [1913]), which upheld the Tennessee Valley Authority; and *Hipolite Egg Co. v. United States* (220 U.S. 45 [1911]), which declared the Pure Food and Drug Act of 1906 constitutional. These and other cases are discussed fully in Bickel and Schmidt, *Judiciary and Responsible Government*. The case that probably cemented perceptions of the Court as reactionary in this period was the 1905 *Lochner* decision (198 U.S. 45). This decision rejected maximum working hours legislation for New York bakers. The case, according to Gerald Gunther, "symbolizes the rise of substantive due process as a protection of economic and property rights." See Gerald Gunther, *Constitutional Law*, 11th ed. (Mineola, N.Y.: Foundation Press, 1985), 441. See also Eileen A. Scallen, William Wiethoff, Warren Sandmann, and James Arnt Aune, "Rhetorical Criticism of Legal Texts: Four Rhetoricians on *Lochner v. New York*," *Hastings Constitutional Law Quarterly* 23 (1996): 621–70.

14. See Melvin I. Urofsky, "The 'Outrageous' Brandeis Nomination," in *Supreme Court Historical Society Yearbook 1979*, ed. William F. Swindler, 8–19 (Washington, D.C.: Supreme Court Historical Society, 1980).

15. Melvin I. Urofsky, *Louis D. Brandeis and the Progressive Tradition* (Boston: Little, Brown, 1981), 104. Wilson biographer Arthur S. Link also reflects on the significance of the nomination when he concludes that it "was an open defiance of and a personal affront to the masters of capital as well as to conservative Republicans like [William Howard] Taft." See Arthur S. Link, *Woodrow Wilson and the Progressive Era, 1910-1917* (New York: Harper and Brothers, 1954), 225; Ray Stannard Baker, *Woodrow Wilson: Life and Letters, Facing War 1915–1917*, vol. 6 (Garden City, N.Y.: Doubleday, 1937); and John Morton Blum, *The Progressive Presidents* (New York: W. W. Norton, 1980). A contrasting view is offered by Jonathan Entin, who reads the historical record of the Brandeis nomination as largely concerned with "symbolic questions of ethics and character because explicit consideration of ideology was regarded as inappropriate." See Entin, "Judicial Selection and Political Culture," 541.

16. Senate Committee on the Judiciary, *Nomination of Louis D. Brandeis: Report*, 64th Cong., 1st sess., June 1, 1916, Ex. Rept. No. 2, pt. 1, 234 (hereafter cited as *Brandeis Report*).

17. Warren, "Progressiveness of the United States Supreme Court," 294–95.

18. The best historical account of the Brandeis confirmation debates foregrounds the forensic nature of the proceedings. See A. L. Todd, *Justice on Trial: The Case of Louis D. Brandeis* (Chicago: University of Chicago Press, 1964).

19. Josephus Daniels, *The Wilson Era: Years of Peace, 1910–1917* (1944; reprint, Westport, Conn.: Greenwood Press, 1974), 543.

20. Philippa Strum, "Louis D. Brandeis, the New Freedom and the State," *Mid-America* 69 (1987): 107. See also Baker, *Woodrow Wilson*.

21. Urofsky, *Louis D. Brandeis*, 105.

22. The rejections of Hornblower and Peckham are fully discussed in Carl A. Pierce, "A Vacancy on the Supreme Court: The Politics of Judicial Appointment 1893–94," *Tennessee Law Review* 39 (1972): 555–612.

23. A full treatment of the Matthews confirmation struggle is offered by Maltese, *Selling of Supreme Court Nominees*, 37–44. The discussion of this confirmation in the Brandeis hearings is found in *Brandeis Report*, 245–47.

24. The Senators were William Edwin Chilton (D-WV), Duncan Fletcher (D-FL), Thomas J. Walsh (D-MT), Clarence Clark (R-WY), and Albert Baird Cummins (R-IA). Clark was replaced by John D. Works (R-CA)

in the midst of the proceedings. For background on these individuals, see Todd, *Justice on Trial*, 96–97, 114.

25. Todd, *Justice on Trial*, 112–14.
26. Brandeis's involvement is evident from his published letters. See Melvin I. Urofsky and David W. Levy, eds., *Letters of Louis D. Brandeis* (Albany: State University of New York Press, 1975), 4:86–198.
27. *Brandeis Report*, 298–99.
28. John P. Frank, "The Legal Ethics of Louis D. Brandeis," *Stanford Law Review* 17 (1965): 683–709. Frank's essay is an extremely succinct and clear distillation of the case presented in opposition to the Brandeis appointment. His breakdown of the charges is the structure I am employing in this discussion.

    The five charges that Frank dismisses as trivial involve: (1) the advance rate case, in which Brandeis represented the "public interest" and opposed increasing railroad freight rates; (2) the Illinois Central matter, where Brandeis was charged with representing a client "in whose activities he did not personally believe"; (3) the Boston and Maine merger, where Brandeis opposed a railroad merger as hostile to the public interest; (4) the liquor hearings, in which Brandeis represented the liquor industry in hearings before the Massachusetts legislature; and (5) the Liggett Drug matter, in which Brandeis represented the drug industry in antitrust actions.

    The remaining seven charges are more complicated. The first of these charges was that Brandeis tried to destroy the New York and New England Railroad Company via a series of lawsuits that sought to give control of the railroad to his clients. This charge was put forth primarily by two individuals: Clarence W. Barron, the publisher of the *Wall Street Journal*, the *Boston News Bureau*, and the *Philadelphia News Bureau*, and Moorfield Storey, a Boston attorney and former president of the American Bar Association. Barron had written a scathing editorial in the *Boston News Bureau* that called the Brandeis nomination an "unfit appointment," and he appeared at the hearings to substantiate his charges. Their testimony and Barron's anti-Brandeis editorial are found in Senate Committee on the Judiciary, *Hearings Before the Subcommittee of the Committee on the Judiciary United States Senate, on the Nomination of Louis D. Brandeis to Be an Associate Justice of the Supreme Court of the United States*, 2 vols., 64th Cong., 1st sess., 1916, 116–34 (hereafter cited as *Brandeis Hearings I* and *Brandeis Hearings II*).

The second significant charge made against Brandeis was that he simultaneously represented the Equitable Life Assurance Society and the Equitable Policyholders' Protective Committee. While representing the Equitable Company, Brandeis also provided free counsel to a group of policyholders and, in that capacity, actively criticized the management and practices of the company.

The third charge against Brandeis concerned his failure to disclose his employment by *Collier's* magazine in his appearance before Congress in 1910 on behalf of Louis Glavis, an Interior Department official during the Taft administration in a dispute about the conservation of Alaskan resources. An excellent summary of this incident is found in Todd, *Justice on Trial*, 75–77. For a discussion of Taft's reaction and the impact of the Ballinger controversy on his antipathy toward Brandeis, see Henry F. Pringle, *The Life and Times of William Howard Taft* (New York: Farrar and Rinehart, 1939), 2:952. Taft's dislike of Brandeis was undoubtedly affected by his view of progressivism, which he feared would lead to "a modification of then controlling case law, [which was] the substance of the judicial product." See Peter G. Fish, "William Howard Taft and Charles Evans Hughes: Conservative Politicians as Chief Judicial Reformers," in *Supreme Court Review 1975*, ed. Philip B. Kurland, 126–27 (Chicago: University of Chicago Press, 1976).

The fourth charge was especially complicated and concerned Brandeis's simultaneous representation of two parties who had competing interests in a case concerning the S. D. Warren Company, a paper manufacturer.

The fifth charge asserted that "Mr. Brandeis was guilty of unprofessional conduct in accepting employment as counsel for P. Lennox & Co., or James Lennox, and then acting against them." See *Brandeis Report*, 192.

The sixth and seventh charges concern the United Shoe Machinery case.

29. Frank notes that the United Shoe Machinery case was of considerable importance, especially to the minority members of the subcommittee. See Frank, "Legal Ethics," 703.

30. *Brandeis Hearings I*, 160.

31. *Brandeis Hearings I*, 160.

32. *Brandeis Hearings I*, 160–67. Winslow introduced into the record several pages of transcripts. See *Brandeis Hearings I*, 1023–54.

33. *Brandeis Report*, 314.

34. *Brandeis Report*, 335.
35. *Brandeis Report*, 371.
36. *Brandeis Hearings I*, 702–6, 713–47.
37. *Brandeis Hearings I*, 742.
38. *Brandeis Report*, 182–83.
39. *Brandeis Report*, 190.
40. "The Brandeis Hearings," *Nation*, March 9, 1916, 272–73. The *Literary Digest* also presented considerable coverage of the charges in this case and the condemnation of Brandeis in several newspapers as a result. See "Mr. Brandeis 'On Trial,'" *Literary Digest*, April 1, 1916, 888.
41. William Hard, "Brandeis," *Outlook*, May 31, 1916, 274–75.
42. "Brandeis and the Shoe Machinery Company," *New Republic*, March 4, 1916, 119.
43. "Mr. Brandeis 'On Trial,'" 889.
44. "Brandeis and the Shoe Machinery Company," 119.
45. *Brandeis Hearings I*, 611.
46. *Brandeis Hearings I*, 750
47. *Brandeis Hearings I*, 622–23.
48. *Brandeis Report*, 305. One of the minority members of the committee was William Borah, a noted progressive from Idaho. His biographer reports that the senator later came to regret his opposition to Brandeis. See Claudius O. Johnson, *Borah of Idaho* (New York: Longmans, Green, 1936), 157.
49. "'Up from Aristocracy'—The Career of the Bohemian Jew Named for a Seat in the Supreme Court," *Current Opinion*, March 1916, 166.
50. "Mr. Brandeis 'On Trial,'" 888.
51. "Brandeis Hearings," 272. The *Literary Digest* also printed the attacks on Brandeis's reputation from Boston lawyers Moorfield Storey and Sherman Whipple. See "Mr. Brandeis 'On Trial,'" 888.
52. "Mr. Brandeis for the Supreme Court," *New York Times*, January 29, 1916.
53. "Mr. Brandeis," *New York Times*, January 31, 1916.
54. Grossman and Wasby, "Senate and Supreme Court Nominations," 572.
55. Max Lerner, "The Social Thought of Mr. Justice Brandeis," in *Mr. Justice Brandeis*, ed. Felix Frankfurter, 22 (1932; reprint, New York: Da Capo Press, 1972).
56. *Brandeis Hearings I*, 620.
57. *Brandeis Hearings I*, 620.
58. Todd, *Justice on Trial*, 146.

59. *Brandeis Report*, 251.

60. *Brandeis Report*, 241–42. Brandeis biographer Alfred Lief refers to Eliot as the "first citizen of the land, next to the President." See Alfred Lief, *Brandeis: The Personal History of an American Ideal* (New York: Stackpole Sons, 1936), 392.

61. The *New Republic*'s promotion of the nominee was largely the efforts of Walter Lippmann and Felix Frankfurter. See Richard Rovere, "Walter Lippmann," *American Scholar* 44 (1975): 589.

62. "Editorial," *New Republic*, March 11, 1916, 139.

63. "The Case against Brandeis," *New Republic*, March 25, 1916, 203–4.

64. "The Brandeis Heresy Trial," *Independent*, May 22, 1916, 266 (emphasis added).

65. Alexander Sidney Lanier, "Objections to Mr. Brandeis," *New York Times*, February 1, 1916.

66. "'People's Lawyer,'" 362–64.

67. "Brandeis," *New Republic*, February 5, 1916, 6. Baker asserts that the author of this editorial was Felix Frankfurter. See Leonard Baker, *Brandeis and Frankfurter: A Dual Biography* (New York: Harper and Row, 1984), 103.

68. "Is This a Good Appointment?" *Outlook*, February 9, 1916, 296.

69. Hamilton Holt, "Just the Man for Judge," *Independent*, February 7, 1916, 185.

70. "Brandeis or—? Portrait of Mr. Brandeis Altered to Bring Out the Resemblance to Abraham Lincoln," *Independent*, May 29, 1916, 323. Oddly, the *Nation's* "Tattler" also noted the resemblance, though it argued that "Lincoln was most noted for his leadership of men, Brandeis for his advocacy of causes and his energy as a propagandist." See "Notes from the Capital," *Nation*, February 10, 1916, 159.

71. Jacoves, "Brandeis and Briand."

72. *Brandeis Report*, 211.

73. *Brandeis Report*, 234.

74. *Brandeis Report*, 234. Walsh's biographer credits the senator's statements with securing Brandeis's confirmation, though such a judgment seems a bit overstated. See Josephine O'Keane, *Thomas J. Walsh, a Senator from Montana* (Francestown, N.H.: Marshall Jones, 1955), 60. Walsh apparently was quite proud of his role in the vindication of Brandeis. See Miles William Dunnington, *Senator Thomas J. Walsh and the Vindication of Louis D. Brandeis* (Chicago: University of Chicago, 1943), 1.

75. Until 1916, only one other Jew was even considered for appointment to the Supreme Court. In 1852, President Millard Fillmore offered an appointment to Judah P. Benjamin, who declined the nomination in favor of his position as a U.S. senator from Louisiana. See Abraham, *Justice and Presidents*, 112; and Thomas Karfunkel and Thomas W. Ryley, *The Jewish Seat: Anti-Semitism and the Appointment of Jews to the Supreme Court* (Hicksville, N.Y.: Exposition Press, 1978). For a full discussion of the religious, racial, and gendered nature of Supreme Court appointments, see Barbara A. Perry, *A "Representative" Supreme Court? The Impact of Race, Religion, and Gender on Appointments* (New York: Greenwood, 1991).

76. *Brandeis Hearings I*, 754.

77. Todd, *Justice on Trial*, 152.

78. Baker, *Brandeis and Frankfurter*, 99. See also Urofsky and Levy, *Letters of Louis D. Brandeis*, 43 n. 2. One commentator concludes that Jewish support was instrumental in the confirmation struggle, arguing that Brandeis only worked for Zionist causes to advance his political career. See Yonathan Shapiro, "American Jews in Politics: The Case of Louis D. Brandeis," *American Jewish Historical Quarterly* 15 (1965): 199–211. A story from the time period has Samuel Untermyer speaking passionately in favor of Brandeis's nomination to President Wilson and the impact of the nomination for Jews in the United States. The president, according to the report, was moved to tears by Untermyer's testimony. See Arthur Pound and Samuel Taylor Moore, eds., *They Told Barron: Conversations and Revelations of an American Pepys in Wall Street* (New York: Harper and Brothers, 1930), 234–35.

79. Baker, *Brandeis and Frankfurter*, 102.

80. "'People's Lawyer,'" 363.

81. "Brandeis as a Jew," *Literary Digest*, February 26, 1916, 520.

82. "Is This a Good Appointment?" 295.

83. "'Up from Aristocracy'—The Career of the Bohemian Jew Named for a Seat in the Supreme Court," *Current Opinion*, March 1916, 166.

84. Richard D. Friedman, "Tribal Myths: Ideology and the Confirmation of Supreme Court Nominations," *Yale Law Journal* 95 (1986): 1310.

85. Ronald D. Rotunda, "Innovations Disguised as Traditions: A Historical Review of the Supreme Court Nominations Process," *University of Illinois Law Review* 1995 (1995): 127. See also Freund, "Appointment of Justices," 1151; and Melvin I. Urofsky, *A Mind of One Piece: Brandeis and American Reform* (New York: Charles Scribner's Sons, 1971), 119. Brandeis is reputed to have believed that the opposition to his

elevation to the Court was primarily due to his radicalism and the fact that he was Jewish. See Mason, *Brandeis*, 491.

86. Link, *Papers of Woodrow Wilson*, 611.

87. See Lief, *Brandeis*, 391; Dewey W. Grantham Jr., *Hoke Smith and the Politics of the New South* (Baton Rouge: Louisiana State University Press, 1958), 298. Richard Rovere offers a slightly different interpretation of the confirmation. He credits the unflagging work of Walter Lippmann and Felix Frankfurter, who "in letters, articles, and conversations . . . worked tirelessly for Brandeis." Rovere labels the confirmation "Lippmann's greatest triumph." See Rovere, "Walter Lippmann," 589.

88. See Todd, *Justice on Trial*, 232–34. Southern support for the nomination was tenuous at best, and great effort was expended to assure party loyalty in the vote for confirmation by the Judiciary Committee. Only Florida senator Duncan Fletcher, a member of the subcommittee investigating the nomination, was unreservedly for Brandeis among southern senators. See Wayne Flynt, *Duncan Upshaw Fletcher: Dixie's Reluctant Progressive* (Tallahassee: Florida State University Press, 1971), 73.

89. *Congressional Record*, 64th Cong., 1st sess., 1916, 53, pt. 9: 9032. As was the custom at the time, debate concerning the nomination was held in executive session and thus was not recorded in the *Congressional Record*. In late April 1916, there was a discussion on the Senate floor regarding the conduct of the hearings and their openness and decorum. See *Congressional Record*, 64th Cong., 1st sess., 1916, 53, pt. 7: 6970–73. President Wilson's letter was entered into the *Record* on May 9, 1916. See *Congressional Record*, 64th Cong., 1st sess., 1916, 53, pt. 8: 7627–8.

90. Friedman, "Tribal Myths," 1310.

91. See Abraham, *Justices and Presidents*; Simon, *Advice and Consent*; Mark Silverstein, *Judicious Choices: The New Politics of Supreme Court Confirmations* (New York: W. W. Norton, 1994); and Tribe, *God Save This Honorable Court*.

92. See, for example, the remarks of Kentucky senator Marlow Cook in *Congressional Record*, 91st Cong., 1st sess., 1969, 115, pt. 25: 34269. President Nixon made similar comparisons. See "Remarks at an Informal Meeting with Members of the White House Press Corps on Judge Haynsworth's Nomination to the Supreme Court. October 20, 1969," *Public Papers of the Presidents of the United States: Richard Nixon, 1969*

(Washington, D.C.: Government Printing Office, 1971), 819; and chapter 5.

93. "Mr. Brandeis for the Supreme Court."

94. Bickel and Schmidt, *Judiciary and Responsible Government*, 367.

Chapter Three.
From Property Rights to Human Rights:
The Hughes and Parker Nominations of 1930

1. For an account of the Cardozo nomination, see Andrew L. Kaufman, *Cardozo* (Cambridge, Mass.: Harvard University Press, 1998). See also Silverstein, *Judicious Choices*.

2. John Anthony Maltese argues that organized interests began to influence Supreme Court nominations as early as 1881, with President Garfield's nomination of Stanley Matthews. Maltese may be right, but such interests lay dormant for fifty years until they organized again to oppose Parker. Even during the highly contentious Brandeis nomination, organized interest groups per se were largely quiet in their reaction to Wilson's nominee. The Matthews nomination thus was more an aberration than the beginnings of a shift in the process. Following 1930, organized interest groups regularly and significantly weighed in on Supreme Court nominations. See Maltese, *Selling of Supreme Court Nominees*. See also Lauren Cohen Bell, *Warring Factions: Interest Groups, Money, and the New Politics of Senate Confirmation* (Columbus: Ohio State University Press, 2002).

3. See Warren, "Progressiveness of the United States Supreme Court," 294–313

4. Tribe, *God Save This Honorable Court*, 11. For a revisionist account of laissez-faire constitutionalism that pays particular attention to its ideological roots in nineteenth-century America, see Michael Les Benedict, "Laissez-Faire and Liberty: A Re-Evaluation of the Meaning and Origins of Laissez-Faire Constitutionalism," *Law and History Review* 3 (1985): 293–331.

5. William E. Leuchtenburg, *The Perils of Prosperity, 1914–1932* (Chicago: University of Chicago Press, 1958), 99.

6. 236 U.S. 1 (1915).

7. The Court relied on its 1908 ruling in *Adair v. United States* (208 U.S. 161 [1908]) in deciding *Coppage*. As will be clear, the yellow-dog contract issue was of considerable importance in the confirmation debates for both Hughes and Parker.

8. 208 U.S. 412 (1908).

9. 243 U.S. 426 (1917).

10. *Adkins v. Children's Hospital,* 261 U.S. 525 (1923).

11. 247 U.S. 251 (1918).

12. 259 U.S. 20 (1922).

13. 244 U.S. 590 (1917).

14. 278 U.S. 105 (1928).

15. 278 U.S. 235 (1929).

16. Alpheus Thomas Mason, *The Supreme Court from Taft to Warren* (Baton Rouge: Louisiana State University Press, 1958), 40–41.

17. Bates, *Story of the Supreme Court,* 263.

18. The Butler nomination is the subject of David J. Danelski, *A Supreme Court Justice Is Appointed* (New York: Random House, 1964).

19. A complete account of the 1925 Stone nomination is found in Alpheus Thomas Mason, *Harlan Fiske Stone: Pillar of the Law* (New York: Viking Press, 1956), 181–200.

20. A very complete biography of Charles Evans Hughes is Merlo J. Pusey, *Charles Evans Hughes,* 2 vols. (New York: Columbia University Press, 1963). A clear and specific discussion of the Hughes nomination is found in Hugh David Jones, "The Confirmation of Charles Evans Hughes as Chief Justice of the Supreme Court of the United States" (A.M. thesis, Duke University, 1962).

21. Pusey, *Charles Evans Hughes,* 651.

22. David J. Danelski and Joseph S. Tulchin, eds., *The Autobiographical Notes of Charles Evans Hughes* (Cambridge, Mass.: Harvard University Press, 1973), 291.

23. Such is the judgment of Pusey, *Charles Evans Hughes,* 659.

24. Richard L. Neuberger and Stephen B. Kahn, *Integrity: The Life of George W. Norris* (New York: Vanguard Press, 1937), 343.

25. *Congressional Record,* 71st Cong., 2d sess., 1930, 72, pt. 3: 3372.

26. *Congressional Record,* 71st Cong., 2d sess., 1930, 72, pt. 3: 3373.

27. *Congressional Record,* 71st Cong., 2d sess., 1930, 72, pt. 4: 3450.

28. *Congressional Record,* 71st Cong., 2d sess., 1930, 72, pt. 4: 3499 (emphasis added).

29. G. Gould Lincoln, "Dill Continues Attack in Senate on Supreme Court," *Washington Star,* February 14, 1930.

30. *Congressional Record,* 71st Cong., 2d sess., 1930, 72, pt. 4: 3514.

31. *Congressional Record,* 71st Cong., 2d sess., 1930, 72, pt. 4: 3519.

32. "The New Chief Justice," *Nation,* February 19, 1930, 208.

33. William C. Murphy Jr., "Is Mr. Hughes a Federalist?" *Commonweal*, March 5, 1930, 499.

34. "Fashions from London," *New York Times*, February 16, 1930.

35. "Conscientious Performance," *New York Times*, April 30, 1930.

36. Caleb S. Miller, "What Hughes Did for American Policy-Holders," *Washington Star*, March 5, 1930.

37. *Congressional Record*, 71st Cong., 2d sess., 1930, 72, pt. 4: 3452.

38. *Congressional Record*, 71st Cong., 2d sess., 1930, 72, pt. 4: 3452.

39. *Congressional Record*, 71st Cong., 2d sess., 1930, 72, pt. 4: 3503.

40. *Congressional Record*, 71st Cong., 2d sess., 1930, 72, pt. 4: 3512.

41. *Congressional Record*, 71st Cong., 2d sess., 1930, 72, pt. 4: 3514.

42. Silas Hardy Strawn, "Chief Justice Hughes," *Washington Star*, February 23, 1930.

43. *Congressional Record*, 71st Cong., 2d sess., 1930, 72, pt. 4: 3591.

44. Such is the judgment of Zechariah Chafee, who maintained that the acts of Hughes's public life "were not those of a reactionary." See Zechariah Chafee Jr., *Free Speech in the United States* (Cambridge, Mass.: Harvard University Press, 1946), 361. Hughes suggests that several senators expressed their regret for opposing his nomination. See Danelski and Tulchin, *Autobiographical Notes of Charles Evans Hughes*, 297.

45. Francis Wilson O'Brien, "Bicentennial Reflections on Herbert Hoover and the Supreme Court," *Iowa Law Review* 61 (1975): 402.

46. Donald J. Lisio, *Hoover, Blacks, and Lily-Whites: A Study of Southern Strategies* (Chapel Hill: University of North Carolina Press, 1985), 208. Hoover presents a different view of the Parker nomination in his memoirs, where he asserts that the nomination was made solely on the basis of qualification. See Herbert C. Hoover, *The Memoirs of Herbert Hoover: The Cabinet and the Presidency, 1920–1933* (New York: Macmillan, 1952).

47. Richard L. Watson Jr., "The Defeat of Judge Parker: A Study in Pressure Groups and Politics," *Mississippi Valley Historical Review* 50 (1963): 231. See also Grossman and Wasby, "Senate and Supreme Court Nominations," 557–91.

48. Watson, "Defeat of Judge Parker," 213.

49. See "AF of L Opposes Parker on Supreme Bench," *New York Times*, March 26, 1930.

50. 18 F.2d 839 (4th Circ. 1927).

51. 245 U.S. 229 (1917).

52. *Red Jacket*, 849.

53. Peter G. Fish, "Torchbearer for Pre–New Deal Southern Economic Development: Judge John J. Parker of the U.S. Court of Appeals for the Fourth Circuit," in *An Uncertain Tradition: Constitutionalism and the History of the South*, ed. Kermit L. Hall and James W. Ely Jr., 274 (Athens: University of Georgia Press, 1989). See also Peter G. Fish, "*Red Jacket* Revisited: The Case That Unraveled John J. Parker's Supreme Court Appointment," *Law and History Review* 5 (1987): 51–104.

54. The president of the AFL, William Green, dispatched a letter to President Hoover advising him of labor's objections and noting that Parker's decision in *Red Jacket* clearly indicated his support of yellow-dog contracts, not just his adherence to precedent. See letter from William Green to Herbert Hoover, Presidential Papers—Subject File, Box 192, Herbert Hoover Presidential Library, West Branch, Iowa.

55. Senate Subcommittee of the Committee on the Judiciary, *Confirmation of Hon. John J. Parker to Be an Associate Justice of the Supreme Court of the United States*, 71st Cong., 2d sess., April 5, 1930, 24, (hereafter cited as *Parker Hearings*).

56. *Parker Hearings*, 27–28.

57. *Parker Hearings*, 25, 55, 56.

58. *Congressional Record*, 71st Cong., 2d sess., 1930, 72, pt. 7: 7301.

59. *Congressional Record*, 71st Cong., 2d sess., 1930, 72, pt. 8: 7977.

60. *Congressional Record*, 71st Cong., 2d sess., 1930, 72, pt. 8: 8183.

61. *Congressional Record*, 71st Cong., 2d sess., 1930, 72, pt. 8: 8486 (emphasis added).

62. *Congressional Record*, 71st Cong., 2d sess., 1930, 72, pt. 7: 7809.

63. "Judge Parker and the Injunction," *New Republic*, April 16, 1930, 230.

64. "The Protest against Judge Parker," *Nation*, April 23, 1930, 477; "In Appointing Judge John J. Parker," *Nation*, April 2, 1930, 381.

65. "Parker Rejected," *Outlook and Independent*, May 21, 1930, 94.

66. "Parker Only and 'Incident,'" *New York Times*, May 8, 1930.

67. "Labor and Judge Parker," *New York Times*, April 30, 1930.

68. Herbert W. Gediman, "Judge Parker's Record Is Warmly Defended," *Washington Star*, April 16, 1930.

69. "Politics and the Supreme Court," *New York Times*, April 24, 1930.

70. *Parker Hearings*, 28.

71. Kenneth W. Goings, *"The NAACP Comes of Age": The Defeat of Judge John J. Parker* (Bloomington: Indiana University Press, 1990), 90. See also Darlene Clark Hine, "The NAACP and the Supreme Court: Walter F. White and the Defeat of Judge John J. Parker," *Negro History Bulletin* 40 (1977): 753–57.

72. See Maltese, *Selling of Supreme Court Nominees.*

73. 163 U.S. 537 (1896). See also Hasian, Condit, and Lucaites, " Rhetorical Boundaries," 323–43.

74. Celeste Michelle Condit and John Louis Lucaites, *Crafting Equality: America's Anglo-African Word* (Chicago: University of Chicago Press, 1993), 162.

75. Condit and Lucaites, *Crafting Equality*, 177.

76. Sheldon Avery, *Up from Washington: William Pickens and the Negro Struggle for Equality, 1900–1954* (Newark: University of Delaware Press, 1989). See also Lisio, *Hoover, Blacks, and Lily-Whites.*

77. "Sanford's Successor," *Outlook and Independent*, April 2, 1930, 532.

78. See Lisio, *Hoover, Blacks, and Lily-Whites.*

79. This campaign is discussed fully in Raymond. L. Zangrando, *The NAACP Crusade against Lynching, 1909–1950* (Philadelphia: Temple University Press, 1980).

80. See Avery, *Up from Washington.*

81. The quotation is found in "Sharp Protests Hit Parker as Justice," *New York Times*, March 30, 1930.

82. See Lisio, *Hoover, Blacks, and Lily-Whites.*

83. "NAACP Prepares for Senate Hearing on Parker Confirmation," 1930, box C-397, Records of the National Association for the Advancement of Colored People, Manuscript Division, Library of Congress, Washington, D.C. (hereafter cited as NAACP Records).

84. "Judge Parker Not the Right Man," 1930, box C-397, NAACP Records.

85. See "Country Stirred by Fight on Judge Parker Confirmation," 1930, box C-397, NAACP Records; and "Senator Wheeler Tells Negroes He Will Vote Against Parker," 1930, box C-397, NAACP Records.

86. Walter White, *A Man Called White: The Autobiography of Walter White* (New York: Viking, 1948), 106. Roy Wilkins recounts the hostility that White faced in Roy Wilkins, *Standing Fast: The Autobiography of Roy Wilkins* (New York: Viking, 1982), 91–93.

87. *Parker Hearings*, 75.

88. *Congressional Record*, 71st Cong., 2d sess., 1930, 72, pt. 7: 7794.

89. *Congressional Record*, 71st Cong., 2d sess., 1930, 72, pt. 7: 7810.

90. *Congressional Record*, 71st Cong., 2d sess., 1930, 72, pt. 8: 8435–37.

91. White, *Man Called White*, 107.

92. "Judicial Independence," *New York Times*, April 24, 1930.

93. "Judge Parker and the Negro," *New York Times*, April 30, 1930.

94. "North Carolinian Not Wanted on Supreme Bench," *Afro-American*, April 5, 1930, 1.

95. "For—Dr. Shepard's Letter Endorsing J. J. Parker of North Carolina for the U.S. Supreme Court," *Afro-American*, April 12, 1930, 6.

96. "Against," *Afro-American*, April 12, 1930, 6.

97. "Protests Pour In against Anti-Negro Judge," *Afro-American*, April 19, 1930, 1.

98. "Press on Parker," *Afro-American*, April 26, 1930, 1.

99. "The Parker Case," *Afro-American*, April 26, 1930, 6.

100. The White House was silent in response to the nomination. See "Hoover Silent on Rejection," *New York Times*, May 9, 1930. A draft of a statement is found in the files at the Hoover Presidential Library. Marked "Final Draft," the statement claims that "propaganda among certain groups to advance the causes to which they are devoted has, by appeal to senatorial constituents for pressure, carried the question of selection of a Justice into the field of political issues rather than personal and professional fitness." Despite the rejection of Parker, the statement concludes, "I [Hoover] shall not depart from the course of seeking for men not only fitted by ability and experience but of independent and courageous character as well." See "Final Draft, May 8, 1930," Presidential Papers—Subject File, Box 193, Herbert Hoover Presidential Library.

101. Martin L. Fausold, *The Presidency of Herbert C. Hoover* (Lawrence: University Press of Kansas, 1985), 91.

102. Calvin R. Massey, "Getting There: A Brief History of the Politics of Supreme Court Appointments," *Hastings Constitutional Law Quarterly* 19 (1991): 6. Henry Abraham is similarly charitable in the assessment of Parker's record. See Abraham, *Justices and Presidents*. Similar assessments of Parker were offered upon his death in 1958. One eulogist went so far as to assert that only Learned Hand was more qualified to sit on the Supreme Court than Parker. See Harold Medina, "John Johnston Parker 1885–1958," *North Carolina Law Review* 38 (1960): 299–306; and Morris Soper, Fred B. Helms, and Orie L. Phillips, "A Tribute to Judge John J. Parker—'The Gladsome Light of Jurisprudence,'" *North Carolina Law Review* 37 (1958): 1–16. Peter G. Fish, Parker's main academic champion, concludes that the judge was a spirited advocate of a "New South" constitutional jurisprudence who was not appreciated by his critics. See Fish, "Torchbearer for Pre–New Deal Southern Economic Development"; and Peter G. Fish, "The Hushed Case against a Supreme Court Appointment: Judge Parker's

'New South' Constitutional Jurisprudence, 1925–1933," *Duke Law Magazine* 9 (1990): 12–21. An extremely careful and moderate analysis of Parker's voting and decisions vis-à-vis the Supreme Court is offered by William C. Burris, "John J. Parker and Supreme Court Policy: A Case Study in Judicial Control" (Ph.D. diss., University of North Carolina, 1964). See also William C. Burris, *Duty and the Law: Judge John J. Parker and the Constitution* (Bessemer, Ala.: Colonial Press, 1987).

103. Goings, *"NAACP Comes of Age,"* 81.

104. Goings, *"NAACP Comes of Age,"* 89.

105. 347 U.S. 483 (1954).

106. Donald E. Lively, "The Supreme Court Appointment Process: In Search of Constitutional Roles and Responsibilities," *Southern California Law Review* 59 (1986): 571.

107. See Barbara J. Ross, *J. E. Spingarn and the Rise of the NAACP, 1911–1939* (New York: Atheneum, 1972), 165. In the midst of the Parker confirmation debate, J. Edgar Hoover of the Federal Bureau of Investigation (FBI) sent to the White House a file of information marked "Personal and Confidential" concerning Spingarn. See letter from J. Edgar Hoover to Walter Newton, April 25, 1930, Presidential Papers—Subject File, Box 192, Herbert C. Hoover Presidential Library. Kenneth O'Reilly reads this letter and its accompanying documents as evidence of a "troubling precedent" by the Hoover White House in their use of the FBI against the NAACP. See Kenneth O'Reilly, *Nixon's Piano: Presidents and Racial Politics from Washington to Clinton* (New York: Free Press, 1995), 105–6.

108. W. E. B. DuBois, "The Negro and Social Reconstruction," in *Against Racism: Unpublished Essays, Papers, Addresses, 1897–1961,* ed. Herbert Aptheker, 111 (Amherst: University of Massachusetts Press, 1985). See also George F. Garcia, "Black Disaffection from the Republican Party during the Presidency of Herbert Hoover, 1928–1932," *Annals of Iowa* 45 (1981): 462–77.

Chapter Four. The Character of Civil Rights: The Thurgood Marshall Nomination

1. Lyndon B. Johnson, "Remarks to the Press Announcing the Nomination of Thurgood Marshall as Associate Justice of the Supreme Court," *Public Papers of the Presidents of the United States: Lyndon B. Johnson, 1967* (Washington, D.C.: Government Printing Office, 1968),

611. The last sentence was undoubtedly referring to the fact that President Kennedy's nomination of Marshall to the Second Circuit Court of Appeals in New York in 1961 was stalled in the Senate for almost a year by opposing southern senators, notably Strom Thurmond of South Carolina. See Richard L. Revesz, "Thurgood Marshall's Struggle," *New York University Law Review* 68 (1993): 237–64; and Carl T. Rowan, *Dream Makers, Dream Breakers: The World of Justice Thurgood Marshall* (Boston: Little, Brown, 1993), 279. These remarks appear to be the thoughts and feelings of LBJ and not the product of a speechwriter or aide. The substance of the speech is found in handwritten notes prepared by LBJ prior to the introduction of Marshall. See Notes, "June 1967 (3 of 3)," Handwriting File, Box 23, Lyndon B. Johnson Library, Austin, Texas.

2. Transcript, Thurgood Marshall Oral History, Interview I, 7/10/69, by T. H. Baker, Internet Copy, 10–11, Lyndon B. Johnson Library. Different accounts of this story are also found. A review of those accounts is available in Howard Ball, *A Defiant Life: Thurgood Marshall and the Persistence of Racism in America* (New York: Crown, 1998), 192–99. Ball points out the irony that the only two justices of the High Court to come from Maryland were Marshall and Roger Taney, the author of the notorious 1857 decision *Scott v. Sandford* 19 How. (60 U.S.) 393 (1857).

3. See Perry, *"Representative" Supreme Court?* 100. Roy Wilkins suggests that Johnson's motives were based more in Marshall's judicial qualifications than in his ethnic origins. Wilkins quotes LBJ telling Clarence Mitchell: "You know, I wanted a Justice on the Supreme Court who knew the law and was respected for his knowledge of the law, but also had never lost touch with ordinary people. That was the reason I appointed Justice Marshall." See Wilkins, *Standing Fast*, 299.

4. Michael D. Davis and Hunter R. Clark, *Thurgood Marshall: Warrior at the Bar, Rebel on the Bench* (New York: Carol, 1992), 267.

5. William O. Douglas, *The Court Years, 1939–1975: The Autobiography of William O. Douglas* (New York: Random House, 1980), 251.

6. Roscoe Drummond, "The Race Revolution . . . Marshall—A Symbol of Change," *Washington Post*, June 17, 1967.

7. For more on the Black nomination, see Martín Carcasson and James Arnt Aune, "Klansman on the Court: Justice Hugo Black's 1937 Radio Address to the Nation," *Quarterly Journal of Speech* 89 (2003): 154–70; Gerald T. Dunne, *Hugo Black and the Judicial Revolution* (New York: Simon and Schuster, 1977); William E. Leuchtenburg, "A

Klansman Joins the Court: The Appointment of Hugo L. Black," *University of Chicago Law Review* 41 (1973): 1–31; William E. Leuchtenburg, *The Supreme Court Reborn: The Constitutional Revolution in the Age of Roosevelt* (New York: Oxford University Press, 1995); and Roger K. Newman, *Hugo Black: A Biography* (New York: Pantheon Books, 1994), 233–63.

8. Frankfurter's "communism" was said to come from his ties to the American Civil Liberties Union. In responding to the charges before the Senate Judiciary Committee, Frankfurter became only the second nominee to testify before the committee. See Liva Baker, *Felix Frankfurter* (New York: Coward-McCann, 1969); Max Freedman, comp. and ann., *Roosevelt and Frankfurter: Their Correspondence, 1928–1945* (Boston: Little, Brown, 1967), 481–86; and Senate Subcommittee of the Committee on the Judiciary, *Nomination of Felix Frankfurter*, 76th Cong., 1st sess., January 11 and 12, 1939.

9. Brennan faced fairly hostile questioning from Senator Joseph McCarthy at his 1957 confirmation hearings. See Hunter R. Clark, *Justice Brennan: The Great Conciliator* (New York: Birch Lane Press, 1995), 104–12; and Senate Committee on the Judiciary, *Nomination of William Joseph Brennan, Jr.*, 85th Cong., 1st sess., February 26 and 27, 1957.

10. See Senate Subcommittee of the Committee on the Judiciary, *Executive Session on the Nomination of Earl Warren of California to Be Chief Justice of the United States*, February 20, 1954, Library of Congress. For a specific examination of the Warren appointment, see Ed Cray, *Chief Justice: A Biography of Earl Warren* (New York: Simon and Schuster, 1997), 247–55; John P. Frank and Julie Katz, "The Appointment of Earl Warren as Chief Justice of the United States," *Arizona State Law Journal* 23 (1991): 725–32; and Earl Warren, *The Memoirs of Earl Warren* (Garden City, N.Y.: Doubleday, 1977), 274. On Eisenhower's appointments in general, see Michael A. Kahn, "Shattering the Myth about President Eisenhower's Supreme Court Appointments," *Presidential Studies Quarterly* 22 (1992): 47–56.

11. Taylor Branch, *Parting the Waters: America in the King Years, 1954–63* (New York: Simon and Schuster, 1988), 113.

12. Most notable, of course, are the 1964 Civil Rights Act and the Supreme Court cases of *Brown v. Board of Education (Brown II)* (349 U.S. 294 [1955]) and *Baker v. Carr* (369 U.S. 186 [1962]).

13. Condit and Lucaites, *Crafting Equality*, 188.

14. See, e.g., Richard Kluger, *Simple Justice* (New York: Knopf, 1975); and Mark V. Tushnet, *The NAACP's Legal Strategy against Segregated Education, 1925–1950* (Chapel Hill: University of North Carolina Press, 1987).

15. See, e.g., J. Harvie Wilkinson III, *From Brown to Bakke: The Supreme Court and School Integration, 1954–1978* (New York: Oxford University Press, 1979); Bob Smith, *They Closed Their Schools* (Chapel Hill: University of North Carolina Press, 1965); and Raymond Wolters, *The Burden of Brown: Thirty Years of School Desegregation* (Knoxville: University of Tennessee Press, 1984).

16. Wilkinson, *From Brown to Bakke*, 4.

17. For a useful collection of Marshall's pre-1954 writings, as well as his commentary about being labeled a Communist, see Mark V. Tushnet, ed., *Thurgood Marshall: His Speeches, Writings, Arguments, Opinions, and Reminiscences* (Chicago: Lawrence Hill Books, 2001).

18. Juan Williams, *Thurgood Marshall: American Revolutionary* (New York: Times Books, 1998), 239.

19. Williams, *Thurgood Marshall*, 240.

20. Todd Gitlin, *The Sixties: Years of Hope, Days of Rage* (New York: Bantam, 1987), 242.

21. David Zarefsky, *President Johnson's War on Poverty: Rhetoric and History* (University: University of Alabama Press, 1986), 160–61. A similar assessment is offered in Davis and Clark, *Thurgood Marshall*, 267.

22. A comprehensive account of the chronology of the nomination and confirmation of Thurgood Marshall is offered in Linda S. Greene, "The Confirmation of Thurgood Marshall to the Supreme Court," *Harvard Blackletter Journal* 6 (Spring 1989): 27–50. See also Neil D. McFeeley, *Appointment of Judges: The Johnson Presidency* (Austin: University of Texas Press, 1987), 110–13.

23. Carter, *Confirmation Mess*, 3.

24. This tension is discussed, albeit in different terms, in Condit and Lucaites, *Crafting Equality*.

25. *Congressional Record*, 90th Cong., 1st sess., 1967, 113, pt. 12: 15726.

26. *Congressional Record*, 90th Cong., 1st sess., 1967, 113, pt. 12: 16631.

27. *Congressional Record*, 90th Cong., 1st sess., 1967, 113, pt. 13: 17506.

28. *Congressional Record*, 90th Cong., 1st sess., 1967, 113, pt. 18: 23870.

29. *Congressional Record*, 90th Cong., 1st sess., 1967, 113, pt. 18: 24640.

30. *Congressional Record*, 90th Cong., 1st sess., 1967, 113, pt. 18: 24647.

31. *Congressional Record*, 90th Cong., 1st sess., 1967, 113, pt. 12: 15843.

32. *Congressional Record*, 90th Cong., 1st sess., 1967, 113, pt. 13: 17506.

33. *Congressional Record*, 90th Cong., 1st sess., 1967, 113, pt. 18: 23870.

34. Senate Committee on the Judiciary, *Nomination of Thurgood Marshall*, 90th Cong., 1st sess., July 1967, 15 (hereafter cited as *Marshall Hearings*). See also Senate Committee on the Judiciary, *Nomination of Thurgood Marshall: Report together with Minority Views*, 90th Cong., 1st sess., August 1967, 2.

35. Such was the judgment of *Business Week* magazine and the *National Review*. See "High Court Hints a Softer Tone," *Business Week*, June 17, 1967, 40; and James J. Kilpatrick, "Term's End," *National Review*, July 25, 1967, 789. In its cautionary editorial, the *Wall Street Journal* assumed Marshall's confirmation. See "Mr. Justice Marshall," *Wall Street Journal*, June 14, 1967. Citing likely opposition by southern senators, Roy Reed's coverage in the *New York Times* quoted Republican minority leader Everett Dirksen's prediction that confirmation would occur "without undue difficulty or delay." See Roy Reed, "Marshall Named for High Court, Its First Negro," *New York Times*, June 14, 1967. Kennedy and Johnson aide Louis Martin maintains that LBJ secured Dirksen's support prior to announcing the appointment publicly. See Transcript, Louis Martin Oral History Interview, 5/14/69, by David G. McComb, tape 1, 30, Lyndon B. Johnson Library.

36. *Congressional Record*, 90th Cong., 1st sess., 1967, 113, pt. 12: 15967.

37. *Congressional Record*, 90th Cong., 1st sess., 1967, 113, pt. 12: 15967–68.

38. Aside from the District of Columbia Republican Committee, which drafted a statement in support of Marshall's nomination, the Liberty Lobby is the only organization featured in the Judiciary Committee hearings. This, of course, changes in future nominations, where various interest groups become important players in the assessment and definition of nominees and their fitness for the Supreme Court. For a study of the impact of interest groups on nomination voting patterns in the Senate, see Gregory A. Caldeira and John R. Wright, "Lobbying for Justice: Organized Interests, Supreme Court Nominations, and the United States Senate," *American Journal of Political Science* 42 (1998): 499–523. See also Bell, *Warring Factions*.

39. *Marshall Hearings*, 183.

40. See *Marshall Hearings*, 164.

41. *Congressional Record*, 90th Cong., 1st sess., 1967, 113, pt. 18: 24649.

42. *Congressional Record*, 90th Cong., 1st sess., 1967, 113, pt. 18: 24638.

43. Alexander M. Bickel, *The Least Dangerous Branch: The Supreme Court at the Bar of Politics* (Indianapolis, Ind.: Bobbs-Merrill, 1962), 59.

Compare John Hart Ely, *Democracy and Distrust: A Theory of Judicial Review* (Cambridge, Mass.: Harvard University Press, 1980).

44. *Marshall Hearings*, 4 (emphasis added).

45. *Marshall Hearings*, 53.

46. *Congressional Record*, 90th Cong., 1st sess., 1967, 113, pt. 18: 24589. In his autobiography, Ervin would note that Marshall, on the Court, "manifested his devotion to civil liberties as well as civil rights." See Sam J. Ervin Jr., *Preserving the Constitution: The Autobiography of Senator Sam J. Ervin, Jr.* (Charlottesville, Va.: Michie, 1984), 91.

47. *Congressional Record*, 90th Cong., 1st sess., 1967, 113, pt. 18: 24635.

48. *Congressional Record*, 90th Cong., 1st sess., 1967, 113, pt. 18: 24640.

49. Greene, "Confirmation of Thurgood Marshall," 27.

50. L. Marvin Overby, Beth M. Henschen, Julie Strauss, and Michael H. Walsh, "African-American Constituents and Supreme Court Nominees: An Examination of the Senate Confirmation of Thurgood Marshall," *Political Research Quarterly* 47 (1994): 849.

51. Louis M. Kohlmeier Jr., *"God Save This Honorable Court!"* (New York: Charles Scribner's Sons, 1972), 70.

52. Michael J. Klarman, *From Jim Crow to Civil Rights: The Supreme Court and the Struggle for Racial Equality* (New York: Oxford University Press, 2004), 190.

53. Mary L. Dudziak, *Cold War Civil Rights: Race and the Image of American Democracy* (Princeton, N.J.: Princeton University Press, 2000), 125.

54. Williams, *Thurgood Marshall*, 332.

55. *Marshall Hearings*, 183.

56. See Transcript, Everett Dirksen Oral History Interview, 3/21/69, by Joe B. Frantz, tape 1, 15, Lyndon B. Johnson Library.

57. 342 F.2d 255 (2nd Circ.), 1965. Marshall's citation of Aptheker occurs on page 279 of the opinion as support for the following statement: "First, peaceful protest, speech and petition, is a form of self-help not unknown during the era of reconstruction when section 1443 (2) was forged."

58. *Marshall Hearings*, 176.

59. *Congressional Record*, 90th Cong., 1st sess., 1967, 113, pt. 18: 24642.

60. *Congressional Record*, 90th Cong., 1st sess., 1967, 113, pt. 18: 24656.

61. *Congressional Record*, 90th Cong., 1st sess., 1967, 113, pt. 18: 24657.

62. Carter, *Confirmation Mess*, 4.

63. Michael Calvin McGee, "Text, Context, and the Fragmentation of Contemporary Culture," *Western Journal of Speech Communication* 54 (1990): 285.

64. See Davis and Clark, *Thurgood Marshall*, 276; and Transcript, Thurgood Marshall Oral History Interview, 7/10/69, by T. H. Baker, tape 1, 15–16, Lyndon B. Johnson Library. Despite the significance of this appointment, Johnson barely mentions it in his memoirs, though he devotes four pages defending his nomination of Abe Fortas as chief justice in 1968. See Lyndon Baines Johnson, *The Vantage Point: Perspectives on the Presidency, 1963–1969* (New York: Holt, Rinehart and Winston, 1971), 179, 543–47.
65. McGee, "Text, Context," 288.
66. "Pres. Johnson Picks Thurgood Marshall," *Afro-American*, June 24, 1967, 2.
67. "Right Thing, Right Time, Right Place, Right Man," *Afro-American*, June 24, 1967, 5.
68. "What *Afro* Readers Say—Only a Beginning," *Afro-American*, July 1, 1967, 4.
69. Joseph Kraft, "Insight and Outlook . . . Hung Court," *Washington Post*, June 15, 1967.
70. Willliam S. White, "Marshall to the Court . . . Can Moderation Survive?" *Washington Post*, June 19, 1967.
71. "Letters to the Editor: Thurgood Marshall," *Washington Star*, June 24, 1967.

Chapter Five. Nixon's Southern Strategy and the Supreme Court: The Haynsworth and Carswell Nominations

1. Theodore H. White, *The Making of the President, 1968* (New York: Atheneum, 1969), 34.
2. As Joan Hoff suggests, "Before Nixon became president, the Supreme Court had initiated at least five major domestic policies, independent of Congress or the executive branch, in the areas of school desegregation, reapportionment, privacy rights, criminal justice reform, and obscenity law." See Joan Hoff, *Nixon Reconsidered* (New York: Basic Books, 1994), 44. For additional commentary on the impact of the Warren Court, see Archibald Cox, *The Warren Court: Constitutional Decision as an Instrument of Reform* (Cambridge, Mass.: Harvard University Press, 1968); Philip B. Kurland, *Politics, the Constitution, and the Warren Court* (Chicago: University of Chicago Press, 1970); and Alpheus Thomas Mason, *The Supreme Court from Taft to Burger*, 3rd ed. (Baton Rouge: Louisiana State University Press, 1979).

3. 370 U.S. 421 (1962).

4. 374 U.S. 203 (1963).

5. 384 U.S. 436 (1966).

6. 372 U.S. 335 (1963).

7. 367 U.S. 643 (1961).

8. 369 U.S. 186 (1962).

9. 377 U.S. 533 (1964).

10. 383 U.S. 301 (1966).

11. Cray, *Chief Justice*, 494–515; see also G. Edward White, *Earl Warren: A Public Life* (New York: Oxford University Press, 1982), 307. Warren would later deny that Nixon's impending election had anything to do with his resignation.

12. A complete account of the Fortas incident is Bruce Allen Murphy, *Fortas: The Rise and Ruin of a Supreme Court Justice* (New York: William Morrow, 1988). Johnson would claim in his memoirs that "Fortas was too progressive for the Republicans and Southern conservatives in the Senate, all of whom were horrified at the thought of a continuation of the philosophy of the Warren court." See Johnson, *Vantage Point*, 546. Many of the charges against Justice Fortas and the defense of his nomination are found in Senate Committee on the Judiciary, *Nominations of Abe Fortas and Homer Thornberry*, 90th Cong., 2nd sess., July 11–23, 1968; and in Senate Committee on the Judiciary, *Nomination of Abe Fortas: Report Together with Individual Views*, 90th Cong., 2nd sess., September 20, 1968.

13. See Senate Committee on the Judiciary, *Nomination of Warren E. Burger*, 91st Cong., 1st sess., June 3, 1969. An account of the Supreme Court's operations and decision-making under Chief Justice Burger is found in Bob Woodward and Scott Armstrong, *The Brethren* (New York: Simon and Schuster, 1979). Nixon soon discovered he "made a tremendous mistake with Burger," who "was more concerned with being on the winning side of a decision than with voting his conscience." See John Robert Greene, *The Limits of Power: The Nixon and Ford Administrations* (Bloomington: Indiana University Press, 1992), 41.

14. See Greene, *Limits of Power*, 36–37.

15. Richard Nixon, *RN: The Memoirs of Richard Nixon* (New York: Warner Books, 1978), 1:517. See also Stephen E. Ambrose, *Nixon: Volume 2, The Triumph of a Politician, 1962–1972* (New York: Simon and Schuster, 1989).

16. Richard M. Nixon, "Acceptance Speech: Candidate for President," *Vital Speeches of the Day* 34 (September 1, 1968): 674–77.

17. This refrain becomes a rather persistent theme in Republican politics for the next thirty years. As a candidate, and later as president, even President George W. Bush pledges to appoint "strict constructionists" to the Court, often using the exact same language as Nixon, Reagan, and Bush, the father, before him.

18. Harry S. Dent, *The Prodigal South Returns to Power* (New York: John Wiley and Sons, 1978), 207.

19. Rowland Evans Jr. and Robert D. Novak, *Nixon in the White House: The Frustration of Power* (New York: Random House, 1971), 160.

20. Quoted in Dan T. Carter, *George Wallace, Richard Nixon, and the Transformation of American Politics* (Waco, Tex.: Markham Press Fund, 1992), 21. See also O'Reilly, *Nixon's Piano*.

    Nixon's southern strategy was of such importance to him and his campaign that he convened a meeting of southern Republicans in May 1968. Present at the meeting, held in Atlanta, were Senators Strom Thurmond of South Carolina and John Tower of Texas, among others. Nixon expressed his concern for the increased pace of desegregation efforts by the federal government as well as his feeling that liberal judges had taken over the judiciary. He pledged that he would regularly consult with southern GOP leaders and that he would seek to appoint "strict constructionists" to the federal bench. As Theodore White concludes in his account of this meeting, when it was over, Nixon's "nomination was secure." See White, *Making of the President*, 138. See also Nadine Cohodas, *Strom Thurmond and the Politics of Southern Change* (New York: Simon and Schuster, 1993); and Bruce H. Kalk, "Wormley's Hotel Revisited: Richard Nixon's Southern Strategy and the End of the Second Reconstruction," *North Carolina Historical Review* 71 (1994): 85–105. The apparent connection between Nixon and southern Republicans would fuel speculation that the Haynsworth appointment was the result of a deal struck at this and other meetings. See John P. Frank, *Clement Haynsworth, the Senate, and the Supreme Court* (Charlottesville: University Press of Virginia, 1991), 66.

21. See Senate Committee on the Judiciary, *Nomination of Warren E. Burger*, 91st Cong., 1st sess., June 3, 1969.

22. Keith E. Whittington, "Taking What They Give Us: Explaining the Court's Federalism Offensive," *Duke Law Journal* 51 (2001): 505.

23. Richard G. Kleindienst, *Justice: The Memoirs of Attorney General Richard Kleindienst* (Ottawa, Ill.: Jameson Books, 1985), 116.

24. See most notably Joel B. Grossman and Stephen L. Wasby, "Haynsworth and Parker: History Does Live Again," *South Carolina Law Review* 23 (1971): 345–59; and Stephen L. Wasby and Joel B. Grossman, "Judge Clement F. Haynsworth, Jr.: New Perspective on His Nomination to the Supreme Court," *Duke Law Journal* 1990 (1990): 74–80. Judge Haynsworth even noted the comparison in his letter to President Nixon following his rejection. Haynsworth wrote that "I am beginning to think that the travail of the last few months and the action of the Senate, instead of impairing my usefulness on the Court of Appeals may have conditioned me for even better service. Judge Parker made it that way and I believe I can do it, too." See "Letter to Richard Nixon, November 25, 1969," Haynsworth, Clement: White House Special Files, Staff Member and Office Files: President's Personal File, Box 9, Richard M. Nixon Materials Project, National Archives, College Park, Md.

25. Evans and Novak, *Nixon in the White House*, 161.

26. 308 F.2d 920 (4th Cir. 1962).

27. 322 F.2d 332 (4th Cir. 1963).

28. "His Kind of Man," *Afro-American*, August 23, 1969, 4.

29. Roy Wilkins, "Judge Haynsworth's Deeds," *Afro-American*, September 6, 1969, 4.

30. "Anti-Haynsworth Drive: How Strong?" *U.S. News and World Report*, September 15, 1969, 18.

31. Ambrose, *Nixon*, 296.

32. Senate Committee on the Judiciary, *Clement F. Haynsworth, Jr.*, 91st Cong., 1st sess., September 16–19, 23–26, 1969, 35 (hereafter cited as *Haynsworth Hearings*).

33. *Haynsworth Hearings*, 44.

34. *Haynsworth Hearings*, 75.

35. For instance, in an exchange between the nominee and Senator Charles Mathias, Haynsworth was given the opportunity to showcase his pro–civil rights opinions. See *Haynsworth Hearings*, 307–8.

36. *Haynsworth Hearings*, 141.

37. *Haynsworth Hearings*, 211–18.

38. Senate Committee on the Judiciary, *Nomination of Clement F. Haynsworth, Jr.: Report together with Individual Views*, 91st Cong., 1st sess., November 12, 1969, Ex. Rept. No. 91–12, 17 (hereafter cited as *Haynsworth Report*).

39. *Haynsworth Report*, 21.

40. *Haynsworth Report*, 22.

41. *Congressional Record*, 91st Cong., 1st sess., 1969, 115, pt. 25: 34057.

42. *Congressional Record*, 91st Cong., 1st sess., 1969, 115, pt. 25: 34433.

43. *Congressional Record*, 91st Cong., 1st sess., 1969, 115, pt. 25: 34453–34457.

44. *Haynsworth Hearings*, 314.

45. *Haynsworth Hearings*, 355. Union leaders were quick to take up the civil rights charge with the Haynsworth nomination. Just thirty-nine years earlier, in the Parker nomination, organized labor worked hard to distance itself from the concerns of African Americans. See chapter 3.

46. *Haynsworth Hearings*, 394. The testimony highlights several cases in which Haynsworth either opposed integration efforts or opted for an incremental approach to desegregation. The most notorious of these cases was *Griffin v. Board of Supervisors of Prince Edward County*, which involved the famous school closings in Prince Edward County, Virginia. In his majority opinion for the Fourth Circuit Court of Appeals, Haynsworth reversed a decree ordering the opening of the schools, arguing that such a decree must wait until the Virginia state courts ruled on the validity of the legislation. The Supreme Court reversed Haynsworth and unanimously held that the tactic of closing the schools to avoid integration was unconstitutional. See *Griffin v. County Board of Prince Edward County* (377 U.S. 218 [1964]).

47. *Haynsworth Hearings*, 423–24.

48. *Haynsworth Hearings*, 429, 436.

49. *Haynsworth Hearings*, 451.

50. *Haynsworth Hearings*, 464. This testimony was supported by others, including a Richmond attorney who testified that the nominee tried to stall desegregation (525) and the chair of the Committee for a Fair, Honest, and Impartial Judiciary, who argued that the nomination was simply an attempt to secure southern support for Republicans in the 1970 and 1972 elections (544).

51. *Haynsworth Hearings*, 555. It is noteworthy that the minority members of the Judiciary Committee in their reports on the nomination did not mention his civil rights record, preferring instead to focus on the ethical issues surrounding the nominee. Only one senator, Philip Hart of Michigan, even mentioned civil rights in the report, noting that "in the very recent past the nominee was writing and joining in decisions which would have further delayed reforms recognized as within reach of the law by some of his colleagues on his own court." See *Haynsworth Report*, 48.

52. *Congressional Record*, 91st Cong., 1st sess., 1969, 115, pt. 25: 34275.

53. *Congressional Record*, 91st Cong., 1st sess., 1969, 115, pt. 26: 35130.

54. "Paying Political Debts," *New York Times*, August 26, 1969.

55. "Haynsworth's Qualities," *New York Times*, August 31, 1969.

56. "Rejecting Haynsworth," *New York Times*, September 10, 1969.

57. "A Nomination Rejected: Why, How and by Whom," *U.S. News and World Report*, December 1, 1969, 32.

58. David Lawrence, "The Haynsworth Tragedy," *U.S. News and World Report*, December 1, 1969, 88.

59. "Another Gray Man?" *Newsweek*, July 28, 1969, 39.

60. "In Fortas's Seat—Or Shoes?" *Newsweek*, October 20, 1969, 35.

61. "Haynsworth," *Nation*, September 1, 1969, 162.

62. "The 'Sharpie' Judge," *Commonweal*, October 3, 1969, 4.

63. The tendency of the news media to highlight difference is also a characteristic of the Brandeis nomination in 1916, when news outlets consistently and repeatedly emphasized the nominee's religion as a marker of his difference. See chapter 2.

64. "Haynsworth at Home," *Time*, October 24, 1969, 25.

65. "Judge Clement Haynsworth," *Time*, August 29, 1969, 12.

66. "Symbolic Logic," *Newsweek*, September 1, 1969, 20.

67. "The Haynsworth Taint," *New Republic*, October 25, 1969, 12. The impression that the nomination was a "deal" between the White House and southern senators persisted despite efforts to prevent such an impression. One such strategy called for Thurmond to publicly support another judge for the nomination. See Cohodas, *Strom Thurmond*, 407; and Dent, *Prodigal South*, 208.

68. "In Fortas's Seat—or Shoes?" 35.

69. "A Southern Justice," *Time*, August 29, 1969, 12.

70. "The Judge Comes to Judgment," *Newsweek*, November 24, 1969, 36.

71. "The Haynsworth Record," *Time*, October 17, 1969, 54.

72. See James F. Simon, *In His Own Image: The Supreme Court in Richard Nixon's America* (New York: David McKay, 1973), 97–115.

73. Senator Hugh Scott, the Republican leader, was asked about this new standard on CBS's *Face the Nation*. Scott replied that presidents generally have a right to appoint and have their nominees confirmed, unless there is the appearance of significant impropriety. See CBS News, *Face the Nation, 1969* (New York: Holt Information Systems, 1972), 268.

74. The nominee's stock and real estate portfolio were printed in the *Congressional Record*, 91st Cong., 1st sess., 1969, 115, pt. 25: 34064–77.

75. 325 F.2d 682 (4th Circ. 1963).

76. See *The Haynsworth Nomination: An Analysis by the AFL-CIO* (Washington, D.C.: AFL-CIO, 1970).

77. *Congressional Record*, 91st Cong., 1st sess., 1969, 115, pt. 25: 33415.

78. *Haynsworth Hearings*, 38. These analogies are, of course, rather silly ones given that it is unlikely a judge would financially profit from a telephone case because of the telephone's presence in the home. If the judge, though, owned stock in the telephone company, profit might result from favorable rulings on the company's behalf.

79. *Haynsworth Hearings*, 111, 115. Frank would later elaborate his testimony in a volume devoted to the Haynsworth nomination. See Frank, *Clement Haynsworth*.

80. *Haynsworth Hearings*, 65.

81. *Haynsworth Hearings*, 66.

82. *Haynsworth Hearings*, 92.

83. *Haynsworth Hearings*, 94.

84. *Congressional Record*, 91st Cong., 1st sess., 1969, 115, pt. 25: 34288.

85. *Congressional Record*, 91st Cong., 1st sess., 1969, 115, pt. 25: 34062–63.

86. 392 F.2d 348 (4th Circ. 1968).

87. This account of the case comes from Judge Haynsworth's testimony before the Judiciary Committee and from Senator Bayh's statement on the Senate floor regarding the case. See *Haynsworth Hearings*, 270–72; and *Congressional Record*, 91st Cong., 1st sess., 1969, 115, pt. 25: 34060.

88. *Haynsworth Hearings*, 272.

89. *Congressional Record*, 91st Cong., 1st sess., 1969, 115, pt. 25: 34378.

90. *Congressional Record*, 91st Cong., 1st sess., 1969, 115, pt. 25: 34059.

91. *Haynsworth Report*, 53.

92. *Congressional Record*, 91st Cong., 1st sess., 1969, 115, pt. 25: 34426.

93. *Congressional Record*, 91st Cong., 1st sess., 1969, 115, pt. 25: 33829.

94. *Congressional Record*, 91st Cong., 1st sess., 1969, 115, pt. 25: 34269.

95. *Congressional Record*, 91st Cong., 1st sess., 1969, 115, pt. 25: 34385.

96. "A Question of Ethics," *Time*, September 26, 1969, 21.

97. "The Haynsworth Hassle," *Time*, October 10, 1969, 16.

98. "Haynsworth Under Fire," *Newsweek*, October 6, 1969, 76.

99. "'The Nomination Is Rejected,'" *Newsweek*, December 1, 1969, 21.

100. "Haynsworth Nomination," *New Republic*, October 4, 1969, 8.

101. Alexander M. Bickel, "Does It Stand Up?" *New Republic*, November 1, 1969, 14.

102. Patrick Owens, "A Jury of His Club Mates," *Nation*, November 3, 1969, 462.

103. "Remarks at an Informal Meeting with Members of the White House Press Corps on Judge Haynsworth's Nomination to the Supreme Court. October 20, 1969," *Public Papers of the Presidents of the United States: Richard Nixon, 1969*, 815.

104. "Remarks at an Informal Meeting," 818, 819.

105. *Congressional Record*, 91st Cong., 1st sess., 1969, 115, pt. 26: 35395.

106. *Congressional Record*, 91st Cong., 1st sess., 1969, 115, pt. 26: 35398.

107. Grossman and Wasby, "Senate and Supreme Court Nominations," 580.

108. "Statement Following the Senate Vote on the Nomination of Judge Clement F. Haynsworth, Jr., as Associate Justice of the Supreme Court. November 21, 1969," *Public Papers of the Presidents of the United States: Richard Nixon, 1969*, 957.

109. Evans and Novak, *Nixon in the White House*, 163. See also Dent, *Prodigal South*, 210–12. Dent also records how popular the Haynsworth nomination was in the South and how the rejection of the judge, and Nixon's outrage, was particularly effective in that region of the country. Dent's view of the political benefits of Nixon's defense of Haynsworth are also noted in Michael A. Genovese, *The Nixon Presidency: Power and Politics in Turbulent Times* (New York: Greenwood Press, 1990) 43.

110. See Hoff, *Nixon Reconsidered*, 46.

111. Dean J. Kotlowski, "Trial by Error: Nixon, the Senate, and the Haynsworth Nomination," *Presidential Studies Quarterly* 26 (1996): 72. This view was reflected in the comments by Democratic senator Russell Long on *Face the Nation* when he faulted President Nixon for failing to lobby personally on behalf of Haynsworth's nomination. See CBS News, *Face the Nation, 1969* (New York: Holt Information Systems, 1972), 298.

112. See Joseph Calluori, "The Supreme Court Under Siege: The Battle over Nixon's Nominees," in *Richard M. Nixon: Politician, President, Administrator*, ed. Leon Friedman and William F. Levantrosser, 369 (New York: Greenwood Press, 1991); and H. R. Haldeman, *The Haldeman Diaries: Inside the Nixon White House* (New York: G. P. Putnam's Sons, 1994), 93.

113. Edward N. Beiser, "The Haynsworth Affair Reconsidered: The Significance of Conflicting Perceptions of the Judicial Role," *Vanderbilt Law Review* 23 (1970): 263–91.

114. William Safire, *Before the Fall: An Inside View of the Pre-Watergate White House* (New York: Ballantine Books, 1977), 342.

115. Richard E. Vatz and Theodore Otto Windt Jr., "The Defeats of Judges Haynsworth and Carswell: Rejection of Supreme Court Nominees," *Quarterly Journal of Speech* 60 (1974): 488.

116. Safire, *Before the Fall*, 342.

117. Ambrose, *Nixon*, 330.

118. Grossman and Wasby, "Senate and Supreme Court Nominations," 579.

119. Quoted in Richard Harris, *Decision* (New York: E. P. Dutton, 1971), 15–16. Civil rights activist Joseph Rauh called these comments "the worst statement ever made by a candidate for the U.S. Supreme Court . . . in this century." See Senate Committee on the Judiciary, *George Harrold Carswell*, 91st Cong., 2nd sess., January 27–29 and February 2–3, 1970, 278 (hereafter cited as *Carswell Hearings*).

120. *Carswell Hearings*, 4.

121. *Carswell Hearings*, 10.

122. *Carswell Hearings*, 23 (emphasis added).

123. *Carswell Hearings*, 25.

124. *Carswell Hearings*, 69.

125. *Carswell Hearings*, 81.

126. *Carswell Hearings*, 91.

127. The novelty of sex discrimination as a grounds for opposing a Supreme Court nominee was evident in *Newsweek*'s report that these "militant women" diverted attention from the real charges against Carswell concerning his racist past. See "The Carswells of Tallahassee," *Newsweek*, February 9, 1970, 23.

128. *Carswell Hearings*, 114.

129. *Carswell Hearings*, 213.

130. *Carswell Hearings*, 227.

131. Fred P. Graham, "Carswell's Credo Is Restraint," *New York Times*, January 21, 1970.

132. Bruce H. Kalk, "The Carswell Affair: The Politics of a Supreme Court Nomination in the Nixon Administration," *American Journal of Legal History* 42 (1998): 274.

133. 306 F.2d 862 (5th Circ., 1962).

134. 333 F.2d 630 (5th Circ., 1964).

135. 9 R.R.L.R. 1206 (1964).

136. "Carswell's Deed," *Newsweek*, February 23, 1970, 24.

137. "Haynsworth to Carswell," *New Republic*, January 31, 1970, 8.

138. "No to Carswell," *New Republic*, February 28, 1970, 8.

139. "Here Comes the Judge," *Newsweek*, February 2, 1970, 19.

140. "Once More, with Feeling," *Time*, February 2, 1970, 9.

141. "The Seventh Crisis of Richard Nixon," *Time*, April 20, 1970, 13.

142. "Pity the South," *Nation*, March 30, 1970, 355. Florida senator Edward J. Gurney also commented that Carswell was facing additional scrutiny because he was from the South. Gurney maintained on *Face the Nation* that those who asserted an antisouthern bias in this case had a "valid point." See CBS News, *Face the Nation, 1970*, 105.

143. "Carswell Opposed," *New York Times*, January 29, 1970.

144. "Carswell Opposed," *New York Times*, February 17, 1970.

145. "Sop to Southerners?" *New York Times*, March 1, 1970.

146. Senate Committee on the Judiciary, *Nomination of George Harrold Carswell: Report together with Individual Views*, 91st Cong., 2nd sess., February 27, 1970, Ex. Rept. No. 91–14, 3 (hereafter cited as *Carswell Report*).

147. *Carswell Report*, 7–8.

148. *Carswell Report*, 13.

149. *Carswell Report*, 33.

150. *Carswell Report*, 36.

151. *Congressional Record*, 91st Cong., 2nd sess., 1970, 116, pt. 6: 7497.

152. *Congressional Record*, 91st Cong., 2nd sess., 1970, 116, pt. 6: 7661.

153. *Congressional Record*, 91st Cong., 2nd sess., 1970, 116, pt. 6: 7853.

154. *Congressional Record*, 91st Cong., 2nd sess., 1970, 116, pt. 6: 8064.

155. As John Ehrlichman records in his memoirs, "Nixon knew instinctively that he should keep some distance between the Carswell debacle and the White House, but he couldn't let the fight alone." See John Ehrlichman, *Witness to Power: The Nixon Years* (New York: Pocket Books, 1982), 106.

156. "Exchange of Letters with Senator William B. Saxbe on the Nomination of Judge G. Harrold Carswell to the Supreme Court. April 1, 1970," *Public Papers of the Presidents of the United States: Richard Nixon, 1970* (Washington, D.C.: Government Printing Office, 1971), 332. This exchange of letters prompted responses from senators upset with President Nixon's characterization of his prerogative on Supreme Court nominations. See, for example, *Congressional Record*, 91st Cong., 2nd sess., 1970, 116, pt. 8: 10158–92.

157. Greene, *Limits of Power*, 40.

158. "The Carswell File," *Newsweek*, March 16, 1970, 29.

159. "Counting Out Carswell," *Newsweek*, April 6, 1970, 26.

160. "Haynsworth to Carswell," 7.

161. "The Carswell Nomination—New Direction for High Court," *U.S. News and World Report*, February 2, 1970, 19.

162. "Judge Carswell's Mediocrity," *National Review*, April 21, 1970, 429.

163. *Carswell Hearings*, 114.

164. *Carswell Hearings*, 136.

165. *Carswell Hearings*, 242.

166. *Carswell Report*, 15.

167. *Carswell Hearings*, 63.

168. *Carswell Report*, 3.

169. *Congressional Record*, 91st Cong., 2nd sess., 1970, 116, pt. 8: 10188–89.

170. Vatz and Windt, "Defeats of Judges Haynsworth and Carswell," 484. John Dean, President Nixon's legal counsel, suggests also that Carswell was a "known homosexual" and that this may have contributed to his defeat. This aspect of Carswell's background came to light when he was arrested for propositioning a vice squad officer in the men's bathroom at a Tallahassee shopping mall. See John W. Dean, *The Rehnquist Choice: The Untold Story of the Nixon Appointment that Redefined the Supreme Court* (New York: Free Press, 2001), 18–23. In a memo to Bryce Harlow, presidential aide Charles Colson concluded that the White House mishandled liberal and moderate Republican senators, specifically Maryland's Charles Mathias. Colson argued that "I do not believe that we will ever win this group over by being vindictive or by retaliating." See "Memorandum for Bryce Harlow," Carswell [1 of 3]: White House Special Files, Staff Member and Office Files: Charles W. Colson, Box 44, Richard M. Nixon Materials Project, National Archives.

171. See e.g., Hoff, *Nixon Reconsidered*, 46; and Kotlowski, "Trial by Error," 72.

172. See Madeline Morris, "The Grammar of Advice and Consent: Senate Confirmation of Supreme Court Nominees," *Drake Law Review* 38 (1988–89): 871.

173. See Kohlmeier, *"God Save This Honorable Court!"*, 168–69. Nixon would also appoint, of course, William Rehnquist to the Supreme Court. For a fascinating "insider" account of the decision-making involved in the Rehnquist selection, see Dean, *Rehnquist Choice*.

Chapter Six. "Bork's America": Supreme Court Confirmations as Political Spectacle

1. Bork, *Tempting of America*. Bork has supporters. Henry Abraham's account of the Bork confirmation is laced with adjectives and invective

against Bork's rejection. See Abraham, *Justices, Presidents, and Senators,* 291–330. In her analysis of the role of special interests in Senate confirmations, Lauren Cohen Bell acknowledges that the role of interest groups "has long been blamed for the defeat of Robert Bork." See Bell, *Warring Factions,* 9.

2. Michael Schaller, *Reckoning with Reagan: America and Its President in the 1980s* (New York: Oxford University Press, 1992), 79.

3. "Constitutional Rules by 'Gut' Feelings," *Washington Post,* October 20, 1980.

4. "Reagan, Carter and the Future U.S. Supreme Court," *New York Times,* October 16, 1980. De Gregory's faith in advice and consent was also expressed by Dean Alfange, who wrote to the *Times* that "so long as Presidential appointees must pass the test of Senate scrutiny, there is virtually no chance that an ideologically oriented Court committed to a single purpose can be imposed upon the nation." "Presidents and 'Their' Supreme Courts," *New York Times,* October 21, 1980.

5. Reagan Bush Committee, "Ronald Reagan Will Take Partisan Politics Out of Judicial Selection," *New York Times,* October 28, 1980.

6. Americans Concerned for the Judiciary, "Reagan and the Courts: The Class of '81?" *New York Times,* November 2, 1980.

7. For a compelling discussion of the abortion controversy and its enunciation in public discourse, see Céleste Michelle Condit, *Decoding Abortion Rhetoric: Communicating Social Change* (Urbana: University of Illinois Press, 1990). See also Mari Boor Tonn, "Donning Sackcloth and Ashes: *Webster vs. Reproductive Health Services* and Moral Agony in Abortion Rights Rhetoric," *Communication Quarterly* 44 (1996): 265–79.

8. 438 U. S. 265 (1978).

9. See Tinsley Yarbrough, "Reagan and the Courts," in *The Reagan Presidency: An Incomplete Revolution?* ed. Dilys M. Hill, Raymond A. Moore, and Phil Williams, 68 (New York: St. Martin's Press, 1990). Yarbrough also notes, in his more complete treatment of the Rehnquist Court, that Reagan was more successful than Nixon in his campaign for "the hearts of a more amorphous, yet larger, constituency incensed at Supreme Court rulings expanding the rights of suspects and defendants in criminal cases." See Tinsley E. Yarbrough, *The Rehnquist Court and the Constitution* (New York: Oxford University Press, 2000), ix. Additional discussions of the attacks on the Supreme Court by conservatives are found in William C. Berman, *America's Right Turn: From Nixon to Clinton,* 2nd ed. (Baltimore: Johns Hopkins University Press, 1998).

John Judis and Ruy Teixeira also note the power of Reagan's message with Protestant evangelicals as he forged a new Republican majority. See John B. Judis and Ruy Teixeira, *The Emerging Democratic Majority* (New York: Scribner, 2002).

10. See Elder Witt, *A Different Justice: Reagan and the Supreme Court* (Washington, D.C.: Congressional Quarterly, 1986).

11. Yarbrough, "Reagan and the Courts," 85.

12. See Bernard Schwartz, *The New Right and the Constitution: Turning Back the Legal Clock* (Boston: Northeastern University Press, 1990). For a discussion of the debates that emerged between New Right legal advocate and Reagan confidante, attorney general, and counselor Edwin Meese and Justice William Brennan, see Marouf Hasian Jr., "The Public Addresses of Meese and Brennan: Voices in the American Legal Wilderness," *Communication Studies* 44 (1993): 299–319. Morton Horwitz notes the almost religious power of "originalism" in American jurisprudence. See Morton J. Horwitz, "The Bork Nomination and American Constitutional History," *Syracuse Law Review* 39 (1988): 1033.

13. Senate Committee on the Judiciary, *Nomination of Justice William Hubbs Rehnquist*, 99th Cong., 2nd sess., July 29–31, August 1, 1986; Senate Committee on the Judiciary, *Nomination of Judge Antonin Scalia*, 99th Cong., 2nd sess., August 5–6, 1986. For a discussion of Rehnquist's initial selection by Richard Nixon, see Dean, *Rehnquist Choice*.

14. Senate Committee on the Judiciary, *Nomination of Sandra Day O'Connor*, 97th Cong., 1st sess., September 9–11, 1981. See also Grover Rees III, "Questions for Supreme Court Nominees at Confirmation Hearings: Excluding the Constitution," *Georgia Law Review* 17 (1983): 913–67.

15. Richard L. Pacelle Jr., *The Transformation of the Supreme Court's Agenda* (Boulder, Colo.: Westview, 1991), 206.

16. For a discussion of Robert Bork's view of constitutional interpretation and its failure to recognize the linguistic dimensions of judicial analysis, see Ewbank, "Constitution," 220–32.

17. See Robert Bork, "Neutral Principles and Some First Amendment Problems," *Indiana Law Journal* 47 (1971): 1–19. Most notably, Bork discussed the problems of judicial review by neutral principles in the cases of desegregation, privacy, and First Amendment law, concluding that all of these legal domains involved some degree of nonneutral, value-laden decision-making.

18. Ethan Bronner, *Battle for Justice: How the Bork Nomination Shook America* (New York: W. W. Norton, 1989), 27.

19. *Public Papers of the Presidents of the United States: Ronald Reagan, 1987*, Book 1 (Washington, D.C.: Government Printing Office, 1989), 736.

20. A fascinating discussion of the press's gingerly treatment of the Reagan administration is found in Mark Hertsgaard, *On Bended Knee: The Press and the Reagan Presidency* (New York: Farrar, Strauss, Giroux, 1988).

21. See Bork, *Tempting of America*; Bronner, *Battle for Justice*; Mark Gitenstein, *Matters of Principle: An Insider's Account of America's Rejection of Robert Bork's Nomination to the Supreme Court* (New York: Simon and Schuster, 1992); Michael Pertschuk and Wendy Schaetzel, *The People Rising: The Campaign against the Bork Nomination* (New York: Thunder's Mouth Press, 1989); Simon, *Advice and Consent*; and Norman Vieira and Leonard Gross, *Supreme Court Appointments: Judge Bork and the Politicization of Senate Confirmations* (Carbondale: Southern Illinois University Press, 1998).

22. Horwitz likens the Bork hearings to the Lincoln-Douglas and Webster-Hayne debates of the nineteenth century. They were, Horwitz says, "an extraordinary event in American constitutional history." See Horwitz, "Bork Nomination," 1029.

23. The role of spectacle in political culture is discussed in Luke, *Screens of Power*; Murray Edelman, *Constructing the Political Spectacle* (Chicago: University of Chicago Press, 1988); Virginia Sapiro and Joe Soss, "Spectacular Politics, Dramatic Interpretations: Multiple Meanings in the Thomas/Hill Hearings," *Political Communication* 16 (1999): 285–314; and Sanford F. Schram, "The Post-Modern Presidency and the Grammar of Electronic Electioneering," *Critical Studies in Mass Communication* 8 (1991): 210–16.

24. Guy Debord, *The Society of the Spectacle*, trans. Donald Nicholson-Smith (New York: Zone Books, 1995), 12, 19. For the role of spectacle in political scandal, see John B. Thompson, *Political Scandal: Power and Visibility in the Media Age* (Cambridge: Polity, 2000).

25. See Edelman, *Constructing the Political Spectacle*, chapters 3 and 4.

26. Edelman, *Constructing the Political Spectacle*, 66.

27. Pertschuk and Schaetzel, *People Rising*, 15.

28. Bronner writes of one episode in the confirmation hearings where Vermont senator Patrick Leahy questioned Bork about a sudden spike in his consulting work in the early 1980s, only to realize that this increase in income was necessary to pay for Claire Bork's medical bills.

Leahy retreated from this line of questioning, but the impact on the hearings and their tone was palpable. See Bronner, *Battle for Justice*, 262–63.

29. Kennedy's ability to set the tone for the entire confirmation process was noted by Bork. See Bork, *Tempting of America*, 268. Pertschuk and Schaetzel also describe the parameters of the anti-Bork message and how the themes of the anti-Bork efforts emerged. See Pertschuk and Schaetzel, *People Rising*, 117–45.

30. *Congressional Record*, 100th Cong., 1st sess., 1987, 133, pt. 14: 18519.

31. Barry Brummett, *Contemporary Apocalyptic Rhetoric* (New York: Praeger, 1991), 9–10.

32. J. Michael Hogan, *The Nuclear Freeze Campaign: Rhetoric and Foreign Policy in the Telepolitical Age* (East Lansing: Michigan State University Press, 1994), 40. See also Stephen D. O'Leary, *Arguing the Apocalypse: A Theory of Millennial Rhetoric* (New York: Oxford University Press, 1994).

33. Hogan, *Nuclear Freeze Campaign*, 39–40. The power of religiously rooted rhetorics to restore feelings and assurances of order and stability is discussed in Kenneth Burke, *The Rhetoric of Religion: Studies in Logology* (Berkeley and Los Angeles: University of California Press, 1970).

34. Bronner, *Battle for Justice*, 99.

35. Pertschuk and Schaetzel provide a complete list of groups opposing the Bork nomination. See Pertschuk and Schaetzel, *People Rising*, 303–5.

36. Vieira and Gross, *Supreme Court Appointments*, 28.

37. American Civil Liberties Union, *Report on the Civil Rights Record of Judge Robert H. Bork* (New York: American Civil Liberties Union, 1987), 1–2.

38. Ellen J. Vargyas, Suzanne E. Meeker, Marcia D. Greenberger, and Nancy Duff Campbell, *Setting the Record Straight: Judge Bork and the Future of Women's Rights* (N.p.: National Women's Law Center, 1987), 39.

39. People for the American Way, *Robert Bork: The Wrong Man, the Wrong Place, the Wrong Time: Editorial Memorandum* (Washington, D.C.: People for the American Way, 1987), 1–2.

40. *Judge Bork's Views Regarding Supreme Court Constitutional Precedents: A Report of the NAACP Legal Defense and Educational Fund, Inc. and People for the American Way Action Fund* (N.p.: 1987), 3.

41. See Edelman, *Constructing the Political Spectacle*.

42. *ABC World News Tonight*, July 1, 1987.

43. "Bork Appointment to Supreme Court," ABC News, *Nightline*, July 1, 1987.

44. Ted Gest, "Reagan's Choice to Shape the Supreme Court," *U.S. News and World Report*, July 13, 1987, 28.

45. Aric Press and Ann McDaniel, "Trying to Leave a Conservative Legacy," *Newsweek*, July 13, 1987, 22.

46. See "How to Judge Judge Bork," *New York Times*, July 7, 1987; and "The Bork Nomination," *Washington Post*, July 2, 1987. Gitenstein offers an interesting discussion of the initial strategy by Democrats in response to the Bork nomination and the role of the news media, and specifically newspaper editorials, in this process. See Gitenstein, *Matters of Principle*, 55–67.

47. Bork, *Tempting of America*, 268.

48. *ABC World News Tonight*, July 1, 1987.

49. For more detailed discussions of the tensions between the White House and the Justice Department, see Bronner, *Battle for Justice*; and Gitenstein, *Matters of Principle*.

50. Lloyd Cutler, "Saving Bork from Both Friends and Enemies," *New York Times*, July 16, 1987, 27.

51. See "The White House Report: Information on Judge Bork's Qualifications, Judicial Record and Related Subjects," reprinted in *Cardozo Law Review* 9 (1987): 187–217.

52. U.S. Department of Justice, *A Response to the Critics of Judge Robert H. Bork* (Washington, D.C.: U.S. Department of Justice, Office of Public Affairs, 1987).

53. Both Bork and Bronner spend considerable time discussing how the physical layout of the hearing room was planned to avoid the problems faced by Congress during the Iran-contra hearings, where Oliver North appeared beneath the members of the committee and was often photographed from below. See Bork, *Tempting of America*, 295–96; Bronner, *Battle for Justice*, 209–12.

54. Senate Committee on the Judiciary, *Nomination of Robert H. Bork to Be Associate Justice of the Supreme Court of the United States*, pt. 1, 100th Cong., 1st sess., September 15–19, 21–23, 25, 28–30, 1987, 12 (hereafter cited as *Bork Hearings*).

55. *Bork Hearings*, 17.

56. *Bork Hearings*, 33–34.

57. *Bork Hearings*, 44.

58. *Bork Hearings*, 67.

59. At the very outset of the hearings, one of the moderate Democrats on the committee, Arizona's Dennis DeConcini, asked former president Gerald Ford, who offered his supporting statement for Bork's nomination, if he had ever read any of Bork's writings or opinions. Ford was not anticipating questions and was forced to concede he had not read many of the nominee's writings. In asking his question, DeConcini had violated the ceremonial propriety of the occasion and revealed that the moderates were concerned about Bork's record. See *Bork Hearings*, 11; and Bronner, *Battle for Justice*, 215–17.

60. *Bork Hearings*, 75.

61. *Bork Hearings*, 79.

62. *Bork Hearings*, 104–5.

63. 381 U.S. 479 (1965). In this case, Justice Douglas articulated a right of privacy that formed the basis for later decisions, including but not limited to *Roe v. Wade*.

64. *Bork Hearings*, 116.

65. *Bork Hearings*, 148.

66. *Bork Hearings*, 186.

67. "The Bork Hearings, Day One," *Washington Post*, September 16, 1987.

68. R. W. Apple Jr., "The Bork Hearings: Trying to Sway the Doubters," *New York Times*, September 16, 1987.

69. Peter Osterlund, "Bork Explains His Judicial Philosophy," *Christian Science Monitor*, September 16, 1987.

70. 347 U.S. 497 (1954).

71. *Bork Hearings*, 287.

72. *Bork Hearings*, 288.

73. These changes in outlook prompted Vermont senator Patrick Leahy to accuse Bork of a "confirmation conversion." The most dramatic of his changes was his acceptance of the *Brandenburg v. Ohio* (395 U.S. 444 [1969]) criteria of imminent lawless action in First Amendment jurisprudence, a position he had opposed as recently as 1984. See *Bork Hearings*, 274.

74. *Bork Hearings*, 470. This case, *Oil, Chemical, and Atomic Workers v. American Cyanamid* (239 U.S. App. D.C. 222 [1984]), involved a policy by American Cyanamid called the "fetus protection policy" where women who worked with lead were told either to be sterilized or to lose their positions with the company. Bork's comments were refuted by a telegram from one of the women involved in the case. She expressed indignation at Bork's statement, saying, "I cannot believe that Judge Bork thinks we were glad to have the choice of getting

sterilized or getting fired. . . . This was the most awful thing that happened to me." Senator Metzenbaum entered this statement vocally into the record immediately before Senator Robert Byrd's (then majority leader of the Senate) questioning of Bork. The woman who wrote the telegram was from West Virginia, Byrd's home state. See *Bork Hearings*, 678.

75. Stuart Taylor Jr., "In Un-Socratic Exchanges, Bork Delineates Several Selves," *New York Times*, September 20, 1987.

76. David Broder, "Bork: Of Principles and Pain," *Washington Post*, September 20, 1987.

77. Aric Press, "The Grilling of Judge Bork," *Newsweek*, September 28, 1987, 27.

78. Gloria Borger, "The Stakes Are Extraordinarily High in the Battle over Bork; For All the Marbles," *U.S. News and World Report*, September 21, 1987, 20.

79. These witnesses articulated many of the same themes discussed previously, the same themes that dominated the questioning of Bork by the senators. Bork's opponents characterized him as a dangerous extremist who could possibly undue the legal progress beginning with the Warren Court and who would overrule existing precedent. His advocates emphasized his extraordinary qualifications and his place within the mainstream of U.S. law. The hearings also featured pages of submissions, including cases, news media articles, memoranda, and petitions.

80. *ABC World News Tonight*, October 6, 1987.

81. "Recommended Telephone Calls for the President," September 30, 1987, October 5, 1987, WHORM—Subject File, Ronald Reagan Presidential Library, Simi Valley, Calif.

82. As we have seen, Bork makes this argument passionately in *The Tempting of America*. He is not alone. Calling Bork's approach to the law "well within the mainstream of constitutional scholarship," Vieira and Gross fret that his rejection by the Senate creates a precedent for rejecting nominees on the basis of their judicial philosophy. See Vieira and Gross, *Supreme Court Appointments*, 247–48. The night of the Judiciary Committee vote against Bork, Meg Greenfield worried on ABC's *Nightline* that the hearings revealed a "cheapening [of] really complicated intellectual arguments" and suggested that there "should have been more restraint." See "Bork Nomination Bombs in Senate," ABC News, *Nightline*, October 6, 1987, 3.

83. See, for example, Pertschuk and Schaetzel, *People Rising*; and Gitenstein, *Matters of Principle*.

84. See Bronner, *Battle for Justice*, 151–53, 158–59.

85. "Bork Nomination Bombs in Senate," 3.

Chapter Seven. The Future of Supreme Court Confirmations: Beyond Bork

1. Typical of this escalating tension is the 2002–3 conflict over the Bush administration's appointment of Miguel Estrada to the D.C. Circuit Court of Appeals. Frustrated by the administration's unwillingness to release memoranda from the nominee's tenure in the solicitor general's office, Democratic senators filibustered the nomination. The president called the Senate's actions "a disgrace." See "President Bush Says Senate Filibuster Decision a 'Disgrace,'" March 6, 2003, available at http://www.whitehouse.gov/news/releases/2003/03/20030306 .html. For an analysis of Republican complicity in the shifting confirmation process, see Stephan O. Kline, "The Topsy-Turvy World of Judicial Confirmations in the Era of Hatch and Lott," *Dickinson Law Review* 103 (1999): 247–342.

2. "President Announces Plan for Timely Consideration of Judicial Nominees, October 30, 2002," available at http://www.whitehouse.gov/ news/releases/2002/10/ print/20021030.

3. See Vieira and Gross, *Supreme Court Appointments*, 182–85.

4. See Vieira and Gross, *Supreme Court Appointments*, 185–90. Vieira and Gross maintain that Kennedy's careful answers about a constitutional right to privacy and freedom of speech allayed the worries of liberal and moderate senators and contrasted well with the perceived extremism of Robert Bork, even as those views were substantively not that different from Bork's.

5. David G. Savage, *Turning Right: The Making of the Rehnquist Supreme Court* (New York: John Wiley and Sons, 1992), 355.

6. Abraham, *Justices, Presidents, and Senators*, 305.

7. Senate Committee on the Judiciary, *Nomination of David H. Souter to Be Associate Justice of the Supreme Court of the United States*, 101st Cong., 2nd sess., September 13–14, 17–19, 1986 (hereafter cited as *Souter Hearings*).

8. *Souter Hearings*, 60.

9. David A. Kaplan and Bob Cohn, "Presumed Competent," *Newsweek*, September 17, 1990, 32.

10. Bob Cohn, "The Soon-to-be Supreme," *Newsweek,* September 24, 1990, 27.

11. See S. Ashley Armstrong, "Arlen Specter and the Construction of Adversarial Discourse: Selective Representation in the Clarence Thomas–Anita Hill Hearings," *Argumentation and Advocacy* 32 (1995): 75–89; Karen Baker-Fletcher, "The Difference Race Makes: Sexual Harassment and the Law in the Thomas/Hill Hearings," *Journal of Feminist Studies in Religion* 10 (1994): 7–15; Joyce A. Baugh and Christopher E. Smith, "Doubting Thomas: Confirmation Veracity Meets Performance Reality," *Seattle University Law Review* 19 (1996): 455–96; Vanessa Bowles Beasley, "The Logic of Power in the Hill-Thomas Hearings: A Rhetorical Analysis," *Political Communication* 11 (1994): 287–97; William L. Benoit and Dawn M. Nill, "A Critical Analysis of Judge Clarence Thomas' Statement Before the Senate Judiciary Committee," *Communication Studies* 49 (1998): 179–95; Margaret A. Eisenhart and Nancy R. Lawrence, "Anita Hill, Clarence Thomas, and the Culture of Romance," in *Sexual Artifice: Persons, Images, Politics,* ed. Ann Kibbey, Kayann Short, and Abouali Farmanfarmaian, 94–124 (New York: New York University Press, 1994); Nancy Fraser, "Sex, Lies, and the Public Sphere: Some Reflections on the Confirmation of Clarence Thomas," *Critical Inquiry* 18 (1992): 595–612; Michael J. Gerhardt, "Divided Justice: A Commentary on the Nomination and Confirmation of Justice Thomas," *George Washington Law Review* 60 (1992): 969–96; Emma Coleman Jordan, "Race, Gender, and Social Class in the Thomas Sexual Harassment Hearings: The Hidden Fault Lines in Political Discourse," *Harvard Women's Law Journal* 15 (1992): 1–24; John Massaro, "President Bush's Management of the Thomas Nomination: Four Years, Several Books, Two Videos Later (And Still More to Come!)," *Presidential Studies Quarterly* 26 (1996): 816–27; Ken Masugi, "Natural Right and Oversight: The Use and Abuse of 'Natural Law' in the Clarence Thomas Hearings," *Political Communication* 9 (1992): 231–50; L. Martin Overby and Beth M. Henschen, "Race Trumps Gender? Women, African Americans, and the Senate Confirmation of Justice Clarence Thomas," *American Politics Quarterly* 22 (1994): 62–73; L. Marvin Overby, Beth M. Henschen, Michael H. Walsh, and Julie Strauss, "Courting Constituents? An Analysis of the Senate Confirmation Vote on Justice Clarence Thomas," *American Political Science Review* 86 (1992): 997–1003; Alison Regan, "Rhetoric and Political Process in the Hill-Thomas Hearings," *Political Communication* 11 (1994): 277–85; Dianne Rucinski, "Rush to

Judgment? Fast Reaction Polls in the Anita Hill-Clarence Thomas Controversy," *Public Opinion Quarterly* 57 (1993): 575–92; Dan Thomas, Craig McCoy, and Allan McBride, "Deconstructing the Political Spectacle: Sex, Race, and Subjectivity in Public Response to the Clarence Thomas/Anita Hill 'Sexual Harassment' Hearings," *American Journal of Political Science* 37 (1993): 699–720; and Gerald R. Webster, "Geography of a Senate Confirmation Vote," *Geographical Review* 82 (1992): 154–65. Special issues or sections of issues devoted to the Thomas nomination appear in the *Black Scholar* (vol. 22), *PS* (vol. 25), *Political Communication* (vol. 11), and the *Southern California Law Review* (vol. 65), among others. Symposiums and seminars were devoted to the nomination, and the media coverage of it was exhaustive.

12. The book-length treatments vary considerably, from essay collections and polemics to journalistic accounts of the events surrounding the nomination. See David Brock, *The Real Anita Hill: The Untold Story* (New York: Free Press, 1993); John C. Danforth, *Resurrection: The Confirmation of Clarence Thomas* (New York: Viking, 1994); Ronald Dworkin, *Freedom's Law: The Moral Reading of the American Constitution* (Cambridge, Mass.: Harvard University Press, 1996); Jane Flax, *The American Dream in Black and White: The Clarence Thomas Hearings* (Ithaca, N.Y.: Cornell University Press, 1998); Scott Douglas Gerber, *First Principles: The Jurisprudence of Clarence Thomas* (New York: New York University Press, 1999); Robin Tolmach Lakoff, *The Language War* (Berkeley and Los Angeles: University of California Press, 2000); Jane Mayer and Jill Abramson, *Strange Justice: The Selling of Clarence Thomas* (Boston: Houghton Mifflin, 1994); Toni Morrison, ed., *Race-ing Justice, En-gendering Power: Essays on Anita Hill, Clarence Thomas, and the Construction of Social Reality* (New York: Pantheon, 1992); James L. Nolan Jr., *The Therapeutic State: Justifying Government at Century's End* (New York: New York University Press, 1998); Phelps and Winternitz, *Capitol Games;* Sandra L. Ragan, Dianne G. Bystrom, Lynda Lee Kaid, and Christina S. Beck, eds., *The Lynching of Language: Gender, Politics, and Power in the Hill-Thomas Hearings* (Urbana: University of Illinois Press, 1996); Paul Siegel, ed., *Outsiders Looking In: A Communication Perspective on the Hill/Thomas Hearings* (Cresskill, N.J.: Hampton Press, 1996); Simon, *Advice and Consen;* Christopher E. Smith, *Critical Judicial Nominations and Political Change: The Impact of Clarence Thomas* (Westport, Conn.: Praeger, 1993); and Geneva Smitherman, ed., *African American*

Women Speak Out on Anita Hill–Clarence Thomas (Detroit: Wayne State University Press, 1995).

13. I will not list them here, but *Dissertation Abstracts* reveals that over twenty doctoral dissertations and masters theses have addressed these hearings since 1991.

14. I have developed this argument more fully in Trevor Parry-Giles, "Celebritized Justice, Civil Rights, and the Clarence Thomas Nomination," in *Civil Rights Rhetoric and the American Presidency*, ed. James Arnt Aune and Enrique Rigsby (College Station: Texas A&M University Press, in press).

15. Thomas remarked at Kennebunkport that as a child, he would never have imagined an appointment to the Supreme Court, and he thanked "all of those who have helped me along the way and who helped me to this point and this moment in my life, especially my grandparents, my mother, and the nuns, all of whom were adamant that I grow up to make something of myself." See "President's News Conference," 801.

16. Mayer and Abramson, *Strange Justice*, 30.

17. "Remarks Announcing the New American Schools Development Corporation Board, July 8, 1991," *Public Papers of the Presidents of the United States: George Bush, 1991*, Book 2 (Washington, D.C.: Government Printing Office, 1992), 830.

18. "Remarks at a Kickoff Ceremony for the Eighth Annual National Night Out Against Crime in Arlington, Virginia, August 6, 1991," *Public Papers of the Presidents of the United States: George Bush, 1991*, Book 2, 1027.

19. "Remarks in a Teleconference with the National Governors' Association in Seattle, Washington, August 18, 1991," *Public Papers of the Presidents of the United States: George Bush, 1991*, Book 2, 1052.

20. "Remarks to the National Association of Towns and Townships, September 6, 1991," *Public Papers of the Presidents of the United States: George Bush, 1991*, Book 2, 1118.

21. "Address to the Nation on the Supreme Court Nomination of Clarence Thomas, September 6, 1991," *Public Papers of the Presidents of the United States: George Bush, 1991*, Book 2, 1123.

22. "Remarks at a Fundraising Dinner for Senatorial Candidate Dick Thornburgh in Philadelphia, Pennsylvania, September 12, 1991," *Public Papers of the Presidents of the United States: George Bush, 1991*, Book 2, 1148.

23. *CBS News Special Report*, CBS, July 1, 1991.

24. *Nightline*, ABC, July 1, 1991.

25. *CBS Evening News*, CBS, July 2, 1991.

26. *Larry King Live*, CNN, July 8, 1991.

27. Lewis Grizzard, "Watching the Liberals Squirm," *Atlanta Journal-Constitution*, July 10, 1991.

28. ABC News, for instance, featured an individual at the NAACP convention that occurred a week after the nomination who said, "When I look at his beginnings, his background, he fits the ticket for me." See *World News Sunday*, ABC, July 7, 1991.

29. See Senate Committee on the Judiciary, *Nomination of Judge Clarence Thomas to Be Associate Justice of the Supreme Court of the United States*, pts. 1–3, 102nd Cong., 1st sess., September 10–13, 16–17, 19–20, 1991.

30. "Remarks Announcing the Nomination of Ruth Bader Ginsburg to Be a Supreme Court Associate Justice, June 14, 1993," *The Public Papers of the Presidents of the United States, William J. Clinton*, Book 1 (Washington, D.C.: Government Printing Office, 1994), 842–44.

31. Senate Committee on the Judiciary, *Nomination of Ruth Bader Ginsburg, to Be Associate Justice of the Supreme Court of the United States*, 103rd Cong., 1st sess., July 20–23, 1993, 41.

32. Senate Committee on the Judiciary, *Nomination of Ruth Bader Ginsburg*, 49–50.

33. "Reaction to Ginsburg Nomination Is Favorable," *National Public Radio*, June 15, 1993. See also Richard Davis, "Ginsburg Nomination and the Press," *Harvard International Journal of Press/Politics* 1 (1996): 78–99.

34. Richard L. Berke, "The Supreme Court: The Overview; Clinton Names Ruth Ginsburg, Advocate for Women, to Court," *New York Times*, June 14, 1993.

35. See Senate Committee on the Judiciary, *Nomination of Thurgood Marshall*, 90th Cong., 1st sess., July 1967; and Senate Committee on the Judiciary, *Nomination of Ruth Bader Ginsburg*.

36. Given the power of celebritizing rhetorics, it was hardly surprising when *Newsweek* reported that the Bush administration floated the name of Janice Rogers Brown as a possible nominee to the Supreme Court should a vacancy arise. A conservative member of California's Supreme Court, Brown is an African American woman who has voted against affirmative action and abortion rights who had been interviewed already by the White House as a possible nominee. *Newsweek* quoted a Washington lawyer who said, "An African-American female nominee is not going to be filibustered. . . . She

doesn't have a record that will stop Democrats in their tracks." See Daniel Klaidman, Debra Rosenberg and Tamara Lipper, "Moving On, Moving In, Moving Up," *Newsweek*, February 17, 2003, 9.

37. See George Stephanopoulos, *All Too Human: A Political Education* (Boston: Little, Brown, 1999), 166–68, 170–74.

38. See chapters 2 and 3; Simon, *Advice and Consent*, 254–56; and Mason, *Brandeis*, 466.

39. Tribe, *God Save This Honorable Court*, 136.

40. Senate Committee on the Judiciary, *Nomination of Stephen G. Breyer to Be an Associate Justice of the Supreme Court of the United States*, 103rd Cong., 2nd sess., July 12–15, 1994, 4 (emphasis added).

41. Senate Committee on the Judiciary, *Nomination of Stephen G. Breyer*, 8.

42. Senate Committee on the Judiciary, *Nomination of Stephen G. Breyer*, 20.

43. "Clinton Picks a New Justice," *Capital Gang*, CNN, May 14, 1994.

44. "Former Counsel to Senate Judiciary, Consensus Builder and Legal Scholar, Stephen Breyer to Breeze through Confirmation Process to Supreme Court," *CBS Evening News*, May 14, 1994.

45. "Opinions Regarding Judge Stephen Breyer," *All Things Considered*, National Public Radio, May 14, 1994.

46. See Abraham, *Justices, Presidents, and Senators*; Maltese, *Selling of Supreme Court Nominees*; and Jeffrey K. Tulis, "Constitutional Abdication: The Senate, The President, and Appointments to the Supreme Court," *Case Western Reserve Law Review* 47 (1997): 1331–57.

47. Keith E. Whittington, *Constitutional Construction: Divided Powers and Constitutional Meaning* (Cambridge, Mass.: Harvard University Press, 1999), 19.

Epilogue: Of Baseball Analogies, Crying Spouses, and the Erosion of Advice and Consent

1. Akhil Reed Amar, *America's Constitution: A Biography* (New York: Random House, 2005), 194.

2. Ronald Beiner, *Political Judgment* (Chicago: University of Chicago Press, 1983), 91.

3. All quotations from the Roberts and Alito confirmation hearings come from *The Washington Post*'s online archive of the hearing transcripts.

4. Several Republican senators even preempted Roberts's use of the analogy when they recounted this trope from private conversations they had had with the nominee. Both Senators Jeff Sessions and Sam Brownback spoke of their approval of the analogy in their opening remarks prior to Roberts's initial comments to the Committee.

5. "The Making of a Successful Justice," *Talk of the Nation*, National Public Radio, November 3, 2005; "Jeff Chamberlain Discusses Throwing Baseball Analogies from the Hot Seat," *Day to Day*, National Public Radio, September 14, 2005. All transcripts and news articles were accessed via the LexisNexis database.

6. "Despite Lingering Questions, Roberts Merits Confirmation," *USA Today*, September 22, 2005.

7. Jeff Jacoby, "Answer the Questions," *Boston Globe*, September 18, 2005.

8. "Umpire Roberts," *Boston Globe*, September 15, 2005.

9. "Letters to the Editor," *San Francisco Chronicle*, September 16, 2005.

10. "Judging John Roberts," *Washington Post*, September 23, 2005.

11. Samuel Alito's spouse is variously identified as Martha-Ann Alito and Martha-Ann Bomgardner.

12. Michael McAuliff, "Alito Wife Has a Battle Cry," *Daily News*, January 12, 2006.

13. "Battle Cry; Alito's Wife Breaks Down," *Good Morning America*, ABC, January 12, 2006.

14. "For Crying Out Loud, Leave Martha-Ann Alito Alone," *Washington Post*, January 21, 2006.

15. "We All Should Cry for Justice," *Chicago Sun-Times*, January 23, 2006.

16. George Washington, "Conference with a Committee of the United States Senate," August 8, 1789, in *The Papers of George Washington: Presidential Series*, Vol. 3, edited by W. W. Abbott (Charlottesville: University Press of Virginia, 1987), 401.

Bibliography

Archives and Manuscript Collections

Everett Dirksen Oral History, March 21, 1969. Lyndon B. Johnson Library, Austin, Texas.

Louis Martin Oral History, May 14, 1969. Lyndon B. Johnson Library, Austin, Texas.

Lyndon B. Johnson Handwriting File, 1967. Lyndon B. Johnson Library, Austin, Texas.

National Association for the Advancement of Colored People Records, Manuscript Division, Library of Congress, Washington, D.C.

Presidential Papers—Subject File, 1930. Herbert Hoover President Library, West Branch, Iowa.

Thurgood Marshall Oral History, July 10, 1969. Lyndon B. Johnson Library, Austin, Texas.

White House Special Files, Member and Office Files, Richard M. Nixon Materials Project, National Archives, College Park, Maryland.

WHORM—Subject File, Ronald Reagan Presidential Library, Simi Valley, California.

Cases

Abington School District v. Schempp 374 U.S. 203 (1963)

Adair v. United States 208 U.S. 161 (1908)

Adams v. Tanner 244 U.S. 590 (1917).

Adkins v. Children's Hospital 261 U.S. 525 (1923)

Augustus v. Board of Public Instruction of Escambia County 306 F.2d 862 (5th Circ. 1962)

Bailey v. Drexel Furniture Co. 259 U.S. 20 (1922)

Baker v. Carr 369 U.S. 186 (1962)

Bolling v. Sharpe 347 U.S. 497 (1954)

Brandenburg v. Ohio 395 U.S. 444 (1969)

Brown v. Board of Education 347 U.S. 483 (1954)

Brown v. Board of Education (Brown II) 349 U.S. 294 (1955)

Brunswick Corp. v. Long 392 F.2d 348 (4th Circ. 1968)

Bunting v. Oregon 243 U.S. 426 (1917)

Bush v. Gore 531 U.S. 98 (2000)

Coppage v. Kansas 236 U.S. 1 (1915)

Darlington Manufacturing Company v. National Labor Relations Board 325 F.2d 682 (4th Circ. 1963)

Dilliard v. School Board of Charlottesville 308 F.2d 920 (4th Circ. 1962)

Due vs. Tallahassee Theaters, Inc. 333 F.2d 630 (5th Circ. 1964).

Engel v. Vitale 370 U.S. 421 (1962)

Gideon v. Wainwright 372 U.S. 335 (1963)

Griffin v. Board of Supervisors of Prince Edward County 322 F.2d 332 (4th Circ. 1963)

Griffin v. County Board of Prince Edward County 377 U.S. 218 (1964)

Griswold v. Connecticut 381 U.S. 479 (1965)

Hammer v. Dagenhart 247 U.S. 251 (1918)

Hipolite Egg Co. v. United States 220 U.S. 45 (1911)

Hitchman Coal and Coke Co. v. Mitchell 245 U.S. 229 (1917)

International Organization, United Mine Workers of America, et al. v. Red Jacket Consolidated Coal and Coke Co. 18 F.2d 839 (4th Circ. 1927)

Liggett Co. v. Baldridge 278 U.S. 105 (1928)

Lochner v. New York 198 U.S. 45 (1905)

Mapp v. Ohio 367 U.S. 643 (1961)

Miranda v. Arizona 384 U.S. 436 (1966)

Muller v. Oregon 208 U.S. 412 (1908)

New York v. Galamison 342 F.2d 255 (2nd Circ. 1964)

Oil, Chemical, and Atomic Workers v. American Cyanamid 239 U.S. App. D.C. 222 (1984)

Plessy v. Ferguson 163 U.S. 537 (1896)

Reynolds v. Sims 377 U.S. 533 (1964)

Roe v. Wade 410 U.S. 113 (1973)

Scott v. Sandford 19 How. (60 U.S.) 393 (1857)

Second Employers' Liability Cases 223 U.S. 1 (1912)

South Carolina v. Katzenbach 383 U.S. 301 (1966)

United States v. Chandler-Dunbar Co. 229 U.S. 53 (1913)

Williams v. Standard Oil Co. 278 U.S. 235 (1929)

Youngblood v. Board of Public Instruction of Bay County, Florida 9 R.R.L.R. 1206 (1964)

Government Documents

Congressional Record. 64th Cong., 1st sess., 1916. Vol. 53, pts. 7–9.

———. 71st Cong., 2nd sess., 1930. Vol. 72, pts. 3–4, 7–8.

———. 90th Cong., 1st sess., 1967. Vol. 113, pts. 12–13, 18–19.

———. 91st Cong., 1st sess., 1969. Vol. 115, pts. 25–26.

———. 91st Cong., 2nd sess., 1970. Vol. 116, pts. 6, 8.

———. 100th Cong., 1st sess., 1987. Vol. 133, pt. 14.

Public Papers of the Presidents of the United States: George Bush, 1991. Book 2. Washington, D.C.: Government Printing Office, 1992.

Public Papers of the Presidents of the United States: Lyndon B. Johnson, 1967. Book 1. Washington, D.C.: Government Printing Office, 1968.

Public Papers of the Presidents of the United States: Richard M. Nixon, 1969. Washington, D.C.: Government Printing Office, 1971.

Public Papers of the Presidents of the United States: Richard M. Nixon, 1970. Washington, D.C.: Government Printing Office, 1971.

Public Papers of the Presidents of the United States: Ronald Reagan, 1987. Book 1. Washington, D.C.: Government Printing Office, 1989.

Public Papers of the Presidents of the United States: William J. Clinton, 1993. Book 1. Washington, D.C.: Government Printing Office, 1994.

Public Papers of the Presidents of the United States: William J. Clinton. Book 2. Washington, D.C.: Government Printing Office, 1999.

U.S. Congress. Senate. Committee on the Judiciary. *Clement F. Haynsworth, Jr.* 91st Cong., 1st sess., September 16–19, 23–26, 1969.

———. *George Harrold Carswell.* 91st Cong., 2nd sess., January 27–29 and February 2–3, 1970.

———. *Nomination of Abe Fortas: Report together with Individual Views.* 90th Cong., 2nd sess., September 20, 1968.

———. *Nomination of Clement F. Haynsworth, Jr.: Report together with Individual Views.* 91st Cong., 1st sess., November 12, 1969.

———. *Nomination of David H. Souter to be Associate Justice of the Supreme Court of the United States.* 101st Cong., 2nd sess., September 13–14, 17–19, 1986.

———. *Nomination of George Harrold Carswell: Report together with Individual Views.* 91st Cong., 2nd sess., February 27, 1970, Ex. Rept. No. 91–14.

———. *Nomination of Judge Antonin Scalia.* 99th Cong., 2nd sess., August 5–6, 1986.

_____. *Nomination of Judge Clarence Thomas to be Associate Justice of the Supreme Court of the United States*, pts. 1–4. 102nd Cong., 1st sess., September, 10–13, 16–17, 19–20, October 11–13, 1991.

_____. *Nomination of Justice William Hubbs Rehnquist.* 99th Cong., 2nd sess., July 29–31, August 1, 1986.

_____. *Nomination of Louis D. Brandeis: Report.* 64th Cong., 1st sess., June 1, 1916.

_____. *Nomination of Robert H. Bork to be Associate Justice of the Supreme Court of the United States*, pts. 1–5. 100th Cong., 1st sess., September 15–19, 21–23, 25, 28–30, 1987.

_____. *Nomination of Ruth Bader Ginsburg, to Be Associate Justice of the Supreme Court of the United States.* 103rd Cong., 1st sess., July 20–23, 1993.

_____. *Nomination of Sandra Day O'Connor.* 97th Cong., 1st sess., September 9–11, 1981.

_____. *Nomination of Stephen G. Breyer to be an Associate Justice of the Supreme Court of the United States.* 103rd Cong., 2nd sess., July 12–15, 1994.

_____. *Nomination of Thurgood Marshall.* 90th Cong., 1st sess., July 1967.

_____. *Nomination of Thurgood Marshall: Report Together with Minority Views.* 90th Cong., 1st sess., August 1967.

_____. *Nomination of Warren E. Burger.* 91st Cong., 1st sess., June 3, 1969.

_____. *Nomination of William Joseph Brennan, Jr.* 85th Cong., 1st sess., February 26–27, 1957.

_____. *Nominations of Abe Fortas and Homer Thornberry.* 90th Cong., 2nd sess., July 11–23, 1968.

U.S. Congress. Senate. Subcommittee of the Committee on the Judiciary. *Confirmation of Hon. John J. Parker to Be an Associate Justice of the Supreme Court of the United States.* 71st Cong., 2nd sess., April 5, 1930.

_____. *Executive Session on the Nomination of Earl Warren of California to Be Chief Justice of the United States.* February 20, 1954.

_____. *Hearings Before the Subcommittee of the Committee on the Judiciary United States Senate, on the Nomination of Louis D. Brandeis to Be an Associate Justice of the Supreme Court of the United States.* 2 vols. 64th Cong., 1st sess., 1916.

_____. *Nomination of Felix Frankfurter.* 76th Cong., 1st sess., January 11–12, 1939.

U.S. Department of Justice. *A Response to the Critics of Judge Robert H. Bork.* Washington, D.C.: U.S. Department of Justice, Office of Public Affairs, 1987.

Books, Periodicals, and Dissertations

Abraham, Henry J. *Justices, Presidents, and Senators: A History of the U.S. Supreme Court Appointments from Washington to Clinton.* New and rev. ed. Lanham, Md.: Rowman and Littlefield, 1999.

———. *Justice and Presidents: A Political History of Appointments to the Supreme Court.* 3rd ed. New York: Oxford University Press, 1992.

Adair, Douglass. "Fame and the Founding Fathers." In *Fame and the Founding Fathers: Essays,* edited by Trevor Colbourn, 3–24. New York: W. W. Norton, 1974.

Adams, John. *Discourses on Davila: A Series of Papers on Political History.* 1790. Reprint, New York: DaCapo, 1973.

Adelstein, Richard P. "'Islands of Conscious Power': Louis D. Brandeis and the Modern Corporation." *Business History Review* 63 (1989): 614–56.

Allen, Julia M. "'That Accursed Aesopian Language': Prosecutorial Framing of Linguistic Evidence in *U.S. v. Foster,* 1949." *Rhetoric and Public Affairs* 4 (2001): 109–34.

Ambrose, Stephen E. *Nixon: Volume 2, The Triumph of a Politician, 1962–1972.* New York: Simon and Schuster, 1989.

American Civil Liberties Union. *Report on the Civil Rights Record of Judge Robert H. Bork.* New York: American Civil Liberties Union, 1987.

Aristotle. *The "Art" of Rhetoric.* Loeb Classical Library, 1982.

Armstrong, S. Ashley. "Arlen Specter and the Construction of Adversarial Discourse: Selective Representation in the Clarence Thomas–Anita Hill Hearings." *Argumentation and Advocacy* 32 (1995): 75–89.

Avery, Sheldon. *Up from Washington: William Pickens and the Negro Struggle for Equality, 1900–1954.* Newark: University of Delaware Press, 1989.

Baker, Leonard. *Brandeis and Frankfurter: A Dual Biography.* New York: Harper and Row, 1984.

Baker, Liva. *Felix Frankfurter.* New York: Coward-McCann, 1969.

Baker, Ray Stannard. *Woodrow Wilson: Life and Letters, Facing War 1915–1917.* Vol. 6. Garden City, N.Y.: Doubleday, 1937.

Baker, Thomas N. *Sentiment and Celebrity: Nathaniel Parker Willis and the Trials of Literary Fame.* New York: Oxford University Press, 1999.

Baker-Fletcher, Karen. "The Difference Race Makes: Sexual Harassment and the Law in the Thomas/Hill Hearings." *Journal of Feminist Studies in Religion* 10 (1994): 7–15.

Ball, Howard. *A Defiant Life: Thurgood Marshall and the Persistence of Racism in America.* New York: Crown, 1998.

Ball, Terence, James Farr, and Russell L. Hanson. *Political Innovation and Conceptual Change*. Cambridge, U.K.: Cambridge University Press, 1989.

Baskerville, Stephen W. *Of Laws and Limitations: An Intellectual Portrait of Louis Dembitz Brandeis*. Rutherford, N.J.: Fairleigh Dickinson University Press, 1994.

Bates, Ernest Sutherland. *The Story of the Supreme Court*. Indianapolis, Ind.: Bobbs-Merrill, 1936.

Baugh, Joyce A., and Christopher E. Smith. "Doubting Thomas: Confirmation Veracity Meets Performance Reality." *Seattle University Law Review* 19 (1996): 455–96.

Baumlin, James S., and Tita French Baumlin, eds. *Ethos: New Essays in Rhetorical and Critical Theory*. Dallas: Southern Methodist University Press, 1994.

Beasley, Vanessa Bowles. "Logic of Power in the Hill-Thomas Hearings: A Rhetorical Analysis." *Political Communication* 11 (1994): 287–97.

Beiser, Edward N. "The Haynsworth Affair Reconsidered: The Significance of Conflicting Perceptions of the Judicial Role." *Vanderbilt Law Review* 23 (1970): 263–91.

Bell, Lauren Cohen. *Warring Factions: Interest Groups, Money, and the New Politics of Senate Confirmation*. Columbus: Ohio State University Press, 2002.

Benedict, Michael Les. "Laissez-Faire and Liberty: A Re-Evaluation of the Meaning and Origins of Laissez-Faire Constitutionalism." *Law and History Review* 3 (1985): 293–331.

Benoit, William L., and Dawn M. Nill. "A Critical Analysis of Judge Clarence Thomas' Statement Before the Senate Judiciary Committee." *Communication Studies* 49 (1998): 179–95.

Berman, William C. *America's Right Turn: From Nixon to Clinton*. 2nd ed. Baltimore: Johns Hopkins University Press, 1998.

Bickel, Alexander, M. *The Least Dangerous Branch: The Supreme Court at the Bar of Politics*. Indianapolis, Ind.: Bobbs-Merrill, 1962.

Bickel, Alexander M., and Benno C. Schmidt Jr. *The Judiciary and Responsible Government, 1910–21*. Vol. 9 of *History of the Supreme Court of the United States*. New York: Macmillan, 1984.

Biden, Joseph R., Jr. "The Constitution, the Senate, and the Court." *Wake Forest Law Review* 24 (1989): 951–58.

Bix, Brian. *Law, Language, and Legal Determinacy*. Oxford: Clarendon Press, 1993.

Black, Charles L., Jr. "A Note on Senatorial Consideration of Supreme Court Nominees." *Yale Law Journal* 79 (1970): 657–64.

Blum, John Morton. *The Progressive Presidents.* New York: W. W. Norton, 1980.

Bobbitt, Philip. *Constitutional Fate: Theory of the Constitution.* New York: Oxford University Press, 1982.

Bork, Robert. "Neutral Principles and Some First Amendment Problems." *Indiana Law Journal* 47 (1971): 1–19.

_____. *The Tempting of America: The Political Seduction of the Law.* New York: Free Press, 1990.

Boyte, Mary Katherine. "The Supreme Court Confirmation Process in Crisis: Is the System Defective, or Merely the Participants?" *Whittier Law Review* 14 (1993): 517–47.

Bracey, Christopher A. "Louis Brandeis and the Race Question." *Alabama Law Review* 52 (2001): 859–910.

Branch, Taylor. *Parting the Waters: America in the King Years, 1954–63.* New York: Simon and Schuster, 1988.

Brandeis, Louis D. "The Living Law." *Illinois Law Review* 10 (1916): 461–71.

Braudy, Leo. *The Frenzy of Renown: Fame and Its History.* New York: Oxford University Press, 1986.

Brest, Paul. "The Misconceived Quest for the Original Understanding." *Boston University Law Review* 60 (1980): 204–38.

Brock, David. *The Real Anita Hill: The Untold Story.* New York: Free Press, 1993.

Bronner, Ethan. *Battle for Justice: How the Bork Nomination Shook America.* New York: W. W. Norton, 1989.

Brooks, Peter, and Paul Gewirtz, eds. *Law's Stories: Narrative and Rhetoric in the Law.* New Haven, Conn.: Yale University Press, 1996.

Brummett, Barry. *Contemporary Apocalyptic Rhetoric.* New York: Praeger, 1991.

Burke, Kenneth. *A Grammar of Motives.* Berkeley and Los Angeles: University of California Press, 1969.

_____. *The Philosophy of Literary Form: Studies in Symbolic Action.* Berkeley and Los Angeles: University of California Press, 1973.

_____. *The Rhetoric of Religion: Studies in Logology.* Berkeley and Los Angeles: University of California Press, 1970.

Burris, William C. *Duty and the Law: Judge John J. Parker and the Constitution.* Bessemer, Ala.: Colonial Press, 1987.

_____. "John J. Parker and Supreme Court Policy: A Case Study in Judicial Control." Ph.D. diss., University of North Carolina, 1964

Burton, Michael John. "Propriety in Confirmation Questioning: The Appearance of Supreme Court Nominees Before the Senate Judiciary Committee." Ph.D. diss., University at Albany, State University of New York, 1995.

Bygrave, Stephen. *Kenneth Burke: Rhetoric and Ideology*. London: Routledge, 1993.

Caldeira, Gregory A., and John R. Wright. "Lobbying for Justice: Organized Interests, Supreme Court Nominations, and the United States Senate." *American Journal of Political Science* 42 (1998): 499–523.

Calluori, Joseph. "The Supreme Court Under Siege: The Battle over Nixon's Nominees." In *Richard M. Nixon: Politician, President, Administrator*, edited by Leon Friedman and William F. Levantrosser, 361-71. New York: Greenwood Press, 1991.

Cameron, Charles M., Albert D. Cover, and Jeffrey A. Segal. "Senate Voting on Supreme Court Nominees: A Neoinstitutional Model." *American Political Science Review* 84 (1990): 525–34.

Carcasson, Martín, and James Arnt Aune. "Klansman on the Court: Justice Hugo Black's 1937 Radio Address to the Nation." *Quarterly Journal of Speech* 89 (2003): 154–70.

Carey, George. *The Federalist: Design for a Constitutional Republic*. Urbana: University of Illinois Press, 1994.

Carter, Dan T. *George Wallace, Richard Nixon, and the Transformation of American Politics*. Waco, Tex.: Markham Press Fund, 1992.

Carter, Stephen L. *The Confirmation Mess: Cleaning up the Federal Appointments Process*. New York: Basic Books, 1994.

CBS News. *Face the Nation, 1969*. New York: Holt Information Systems, 1972.

———. *Face the Nation, 1970*. New York: Holt Information Systems, 1972.

Chafee, Zechariah, Jr. *Free Speech in the United States*. Cambridge, Mass.: Harvard University Press, 1946.

Charland, Maurice. "Constitutive Rhetoric: The Case of the *Peuple Québécois*." *Quarterly Journal of Speech* 73 (1987): 133–50.

[Cicero]. *Ad C. Herennium*. Loeb Classical Library, 1981.

Clark, Hunter R. *Justice Brennan: The Great Conciliator*. New York: Birch Lane Press, 1995.

Clayton, Mary Black. *Reminiscences of Jeremiah Sullivan Black*. St. Louis: Christian Publishing, 1887.

Cohodas, Nadine. *Strom Thurmond and the Politics of Southern Change*. New York: Simon and Schuster, 1993.

Cole, Kenneth C. "Judicial Affairs: The Rôle of the Senate in the Confirmation of Judicial Nominations." *American Political Science Review* 28 (1934): 875–94.

Comiskey, Michael. "Can the Senate Examine the Constitutional Philosophies of Supreme Court Nominees?" *PS: Political Science and Politics* 26 (1993): 495–500.

_____. "Not Guilty: The News Media in the Supreme Court Confirmation Process." *Journal of Law and Politics* 15 (1999): 1–36.

Condit, Celeste Michelle. *Decoding Abortion Rhetoric: Communicating Social Change*. Urbana: University of Illinois Press, 1990.

_____. "Democracy and Civil Rights: The Universalizing Influence of Public Argumentation." *Communication Monographs* 54 (1987): 1–18.

Condit, Celeste Michelle, and John Louis Lucaites. *Crafting Equality: America's Anglo-African Word*. Chicago: University of Chicago Press, 1993.

Confusione, Michael James. "Justice Ruth Bader Ginsburg and Justice Thurgood Marshall: A Misleading Comparison." *Rutgers Law Journal* 26 (1995): 887–907.

Conway, Glenda. "Inevitable Reconstructions: Voice and Ideology in Two Landmark U.S. Supreme Court Opinions." *Rhetoric and Public Affairs* 6 (2003): 487–507.

Cox, Archibald. *The Warren Court: Constitutional Decision as an Instrument of Reform*. Cambridge, Mass.: Harvard University Press, 1968.

Cray, Ed. *Chief Justice: A Biography of Earl Warren*. New York: Simon and Schuster, 1997.

Crenshaw, Carrie. "The Normality of Man and Female Otherness: (Re)Producing Patriarchal Lines of Argument in the Law and the News," *Argumentation and Advocacy* 32 (1996): 170–85.

_____. "The 'Protection' of 'Woman': A History of Legal Attitudes toward Women's Workplace Freedom." *Quarterly Journal of Speech* 81 (1995): 63–82.

Crockett-Smith, D. L. "Poetic Justice Thomas." *Black Scholar* 22 (1991–92): 156.

Cullis, Philip. "The Limits of Progressivism: Louis Brandeis, Democracy and the Corporation." *Journal of American Studies* 30 (1996): 381–404.

Danelski, David J. *A Supreme Court Justice Is Appointed*. New York: Random House, 1964.

Danelski, David J., and Joseph S. Tulchin, eds. *The Autobiographical Notes of Charles Evans Hughes*. Cambridge, Mass.: Harvard University Press, 1973.

Danforth, John C. *Resurrection: The Confirmation of Clarence Thomas.* New York: Viking, 1994.

Daniels, Josephus. *The Wilson Era: Years of Peace, 1910–1917.* 1944. Reprint. Westport, Conn.: Greenwood Press, 1974.

Daniels, William J. "The Geographic Factor in Appointments to the United States Supreme Court: 1789–1976." *Western Political Quarterly* 31 (1978): 226–37.

Davis, Michael D., and Hunter R. Clark. *Thurgood Marshall: Warrior at the Bar, Rebel on the Bench.* New York: Carol, 1992.

Davis, Richard. "Ginsburg Nomination and the Press." *Harvard International Journal of Press/Politics* 1 (1996): 78–99.

——. "Supreme Court Nominations and the News Media." *Albany Law Review* 57 (1994): 1061–79.

Davis, Richard, and Diana Owen. *New Media and American Politics.* New York: Oxford University Press, 1998.

Davis, Richard, and Vincent James Strickler. "The Invisible Dance: The Supreme Court and the Press." *Perspectives on Political Science* 29 (2000): 85–92.

Dean, John W. *The Rehnquist Choice: The Untold Story of the Nixon Appointment That Redefined the Supreme Court.* New York: Free Press, 2001.

Debord, Guy. *The Society of the Spectacle.* Trans. Donald Nicholson-Smith. New York: Zone Books, 1995.

Dellapenna, Joseph W., and Kathleen Farrell. "Law and the Language of Community: On the Contributions of James Boyd White." *Rhetoric Society Quarterly* 21 (1991): 38–58.

Denning, Brannon P. "The Judicial Appointments Process: The 'Blue Slip': Enforcing Norms of the Judicial Confirmation Process." *William and Mary Bill of Rights Journal* 10 (2001): 75–101.

Dent, Harry S. *The Prodigal South Returns to Power.* New York: John Wiley and Sons, 1978.

Diamond, Edwin, and Robert A. Silverman. *White House to Your House: Media and Politics in Virtual America.* Cambridge, Mass.: MIT Press, 1997.

Dixon, Wheeler Winston. *Disaster and Memory: Celebrity Culture and the Crisis of Hollywood Cinema.* New York: Columbia University Press, 1999.

Donnelly, Samuel J. M. *The Language and Uses of Rights: A Biopsy of American Jurisprudence in the Twentieth Century.* Lanham, Md.: University Press of America, 1994.

Douglas, William O. *The Court Years, 1939–1975: The Autobiography of William O. Douglas.* New York: Random House, 1980.

DuBois, W. E. B. "The Negro and Social Reconstruction." In *Against Racism: Unpublished Essays, Papers, Addresses, 1897–1961.* Edited by Herbert Aptheker, 103-58. Amherst: University of Massachusetts Press, 1985.

Dudziak, Mary L. *Cold War Civil Rights: Race and the Image of American Democracy.* Princeton, N.J.: Princeton University Press, 2000.

Dunne, Gerald T. *Hugo Black and the Judicial Revolution.* New York: Simon and Schuster, 1977.

Dunnington, Miles William. *Senator Thomas J. Walsh and the Vindication of Louis D. Brandeis.* Chicago: University of Chicago, 1943.

Dworkin, Ronald. *Freedom's Law: The Moral Reading of the American Constitution.* Cambridge, Mass.: Harvard University Press, 1996.

Dyson, Michael Eric. *I May Not Get There with You: The True Martin Luther King, Jr.* New York: Free Press, 2000.

Edelman, Murray. *Constructing the Political Spectacle.* Chicago: University of Chicago Press, 1988.

Ehrlichman, John. *Witness to Power: The Nixon Years.* New York: Pocket Books, 1982.

Eisenhart, Margaret A., and Nancy R. Lawrence. "Anita Hill, Clarence Thomas, and the Culture of Romance." In *Sexual Artifice: Persons, Images, Politics,* edited by Ann Kibbey, Kayann Short, and Abouali Farmanfarmaian, 94–124. New York: New York University Press, 1994.

Ely, John Hart. *Democracy and Distrust: A Theory of Judicial Review.* Cambridge, Mass.: Harvard University Press, 1980.

Entin, Jonathan L. "Judicial Selection and Political Culture." *Capital University Law Review* 30 (2002): 523–57.

Epstein, David F. *The Political Theory of the Federalist.* Chicago: University of Chicago Press, 1984.

Ervin, Sam J., Jr. *Preserving the Constitution: The Autobiography of Senator Sam J. Ervin, Jr.* Charlottesville, Va.: Michie, 1984.

"Essays on the Supreme Court Appointment Process." *Harvard Law Review* 101 (1988): 1146–229.

Evans, Rowland, Jr., and Robert D. Novak. *Nixon in the White House: The Frustration of Power.* New York: Random House, 1971.

Ewbank, Henry L. "The Constitution: Burkeian, Brandeisian, and Borkian Perspectives." *Southern Communication Journal* 61 (1996): 220–32.

Fallows, James. *Breaking the News: How the Media Undermine American Democracy.* New York: Vintage Books, 1997.

Farber, Daniel A. "Reinventing Brandeis: Legal Pragmatism for the Twenty-First Century." *University of Illinois Law Review* 1995 (1995): 163–90.

Faria, Joseph, and David Markey. "Supreme Court Appointments After the Thomas Nomination: Reforming the Confirmation Process." *St. John's Journal of Legal Commentary* 7 (1991): 389–416.

Farrell, Thomas B. *Norms of Rhetorical Culture.* New Haven, Conn.: Yale University Press, 1993.

Fausold, Martin L. *The Presidency of Herbert C. Hoover.* Lawrence: University Press of Kansas, 1985.

Felice, John D., and Herbert F. Weisberg. "The Changing Importance of Ideology, Party, and Region in Confirmation of Supreme Court Nominees, 1953–1988." *Kentucky Law Journal* 77 (1988–89): 509–30.

Ferguson, Robert. "Ideology and the Framing of the Constitution." *Early American Literature* 22 (1987): 157–65.

———. "The Judicial Opinion as Literary Genre." *Yale Journal of Law and the Humanities* 2 (1990): 201–19.

Fish, Peter G. "The Hushed Case against a Supreme Court Appointment: Judge Parker's 'New South' Constitutional Jurisprudence, 1925–1933." *Duke Law Magazine* 9 (1990): 12–21.

———. "*Red Jacket* Revisited: The Case That Unraveled John J. Parker's Supreme Court Appointment." *Law and History Review* 5 (1987): 51–104.

———. "Torchbearer for Pre–New Deal Southern Economic Development: Judge John J. Parker of the U.S. Court of Appeals for the Fourth Circuit." In *An Uncertain Tradition: Constitutionalism and the History of the South,* edited by Kermit L. Hall and James W. Ely Jr., 253–95. Athens: University of Georgia Press, 1989.

———. "William Howard Taft and Charles Evans Hughes: Conservative Politicians as Chief Judicial Reformers." In *The Supreme Court Review 1975,* edited by Philip B. Kurland, 123–45. Chicago: University of Chicago Press, 1976.

Fisher, Walter. *Human Communication as Narration: Toward a Philosophy of Reason, Value, and Action.* Columbia: University of South Carolina Press, 1987.

Flax, Jane. *The American Dream in Black and White: The Clarence Thomas Hearings.* Ithaca, N.Y.: Cornell University Press, 1998.

Flynt, Wayne. *Duncan Upshaw Fletcher: Dixie's Reluctant Progressive.* Tallahassee: Florida State University Press, 1971.

Fowles, Jib. *Starstruck: Celebrity Performers and the American Public.* Washington, D.C.: Smithsonian Institution Press, 1992.

Frank, John P. "The Appointment of Supreme Court Justices: Prestige, Principles and Politics." *Wisconsin Law Review* 1941 (1941): 172–210, 343–79, 461–512.

———. *Clement Haynsworth, the Senate, and the Supreme Court.* Charlottesville: University Press of Virginia, 1991.

———. "The Legal Ethics of Louis D. Brandeis." *Stanford Law Review* 17 (1965): 683–709.

Frank, John P., and Julie Katz. "The Appointment of Earl Warren as Chief Justice of the United States." *Arizona State Law Journal* 23 (1991): 725–32.

Frankfurter, Felix. "The United States Supreme Court Molding the Constitution." *Current History* (May 1930): 235–40.

Fraser, Nancy. "Sex, Lies, and the Public Sphere: Some Reflections on the Confirmation of Clarence Thomas." *Critical Inquiry* 18 (1992): 595–612

Freedman, Eric M. "Why Constitutional Lawyers and Historians Should Take a Fresh Look at the Emergence of the Constitution from the Confederation Period: The Case of the Drafting of the Articles of Confederation." *Tennessee Law Review* 60 (1993): 783–839.

Freedman, Max, comp. and ann. *Roosevelt and Frankfurter: Their Correspondence, 1928–1945.* Boston: Little, Brown, 1967.

Freeman, Jody. "Constitutive Rhetoric: Law as a Literary Activity." *Harvard Women's Law Journal* 14 (1991): 305–25.

Freund, Paul A. "Appointment of Justices: Some Historical Perspectives." *Harvard Law Review* 101 (1988): 1146–63.

Friedlander, Robert A. "Judicial Selection and the Constitution: What Did the Framers Originally Intend?" *Saint Louis University Public Law Review* 8 (1989): 1–11.

Friedman, Richard D. "Tribal Myths: Ideology and the Confirmation of Supreme Court Nominations." *Yale Law Journal* 95 (1986): 1283–320.

Frug, Jerry. "Argument as Character." *Stanford Law Review* 40 (1988): 869–927.

Furtwangler, Albert. *The Authority of Publius: A Reading of the Federalist Papers.* Ithaca, N.Y.: Cornell University Press, 1984.

Gabler, Neal. *Winchell: Gossip, Power, and the Culture of Celebrity.* New York: Knopf, 1994.

Gale, Fredric G. *Political Literacy: Rhetoric, Ideology, and the Possibility of Justice.* Albany: State University of New York Press, 1994.

Gannon, Katherine M. "The Template-Driven Construal Model: An Application to Decision Making of the Senate Judiciary Committee in

Supreme Court Justice Nomination Hearings." Ph.D. diss., Ohio State University, 1995.

Garcia, George F. "Black Disaffection from the Republican Party during the Presidency of Herbert Hoover, 1928–1932." *Annals of Iowa* 45 (1981): 462–77.

Garver, Eugene. *Aristotle's Rhetoric: An Art of Character*. Chicago: University of Chicago Press, 1994.

Gauch, James E. "The Intended Role of the Senate in Supreme Court Appointments." *University of Chicago Law Review* 56 (1989): 337–65.

Genovese, Michael A. *The Nixon Presidency: Power and Politics in Turbulent Times*. New York: Greenwood Press, 1990.

Gerber, Scott Douglas. *First Principles: The Jurisprudence of Clarence Thomas*. New York: New York University Press, 1999.

Gerhardt, Michael J. "The Confirmation Mystery." *Georgetown Law Journal* 83 (1994): 395–431.

_____. "Divided Justice: A Commentary on the Nomination and Confirmation of Justice Thomas." *George Washington Law Review* 60 (1992): 969–96.

_____. *The Federal Appointments Process: A Constitutional and Historical Analysis*. Durham, N.C.: Duke University Press, 2000.

_____. "The Rhetoric of Judicial Critique: From Judicial Restraint to the Virtual Bill of Rights." *William and Mary Bill of Rights Journal* 10 (2002): 585–645.

Ginsburg, Ruth Bader. "Confirming Supreme Court Justices: Thoughts on the Second Opinion Rendered by the Senate." *University of Illinois Law Review* 1988 (1988): 101–17.

Gitenstein, Mark. *Matters of Principle: An Insider's Account of America's Rejection of Robert Bork's Nomination to the Supreme Court*. New York: Simon and Schuster, 1992.

Gitlin, Todd. *The Sixties: Years of Hope, Days of Rage*. New York: Bantam, 1987.

Goings, Kenneth W. *"The NAACP Comes of Age": The Defeat of Judge John J. Parker*. Bloomington: Indiana University Press, 1990.

Goodrich, Peter. *Legal Discourse: Studies in Linguistics, Rhetoric and Legal Analysis*. New York: St. Martin's, 1987.

Grantham, Dewey W., Jr. *Hoke Smith and the Politics of the New South*. Baton Rouge: Louisiana State University Press, 1958.

Greene, John Robert. *The Limits of Power: The Nixon and Ford Administrations*. Bloomington: Indiana University Press, 1992.

Greene, Linda S. "The Confirmation of Thurgood Marshall to the Supreme Court." *Harvard Blackletter Journal* 6 (Spring 1989): 27–50.

Gronbeck, Bruce E. "Characterological Argument in Bush's and Clinton's Convention Films." In *Argument and the Postmodern Challenge: Proceedings of the Eighth SCA/AFA Conference on Argumentation,* edited by Raymie E. McKerrow, 392–97. Annandale, Va.: Speech Communication Association, 1993.

Grossman, Joel B., and Stephen L. Wasby. "Haynsworth and Parker: History Does Live Again." *South Carolina Law Review* 23 (1971): 345–59.

———. "The Senate and Supreme Court Nominations: Some Reflections." *Duke Law Journal* 1972 (1972): 557–91.

Guliuzza, Frank, III, Daniel J. Reagan, and David M. Barrett. "Character, Competency, and Constitutionalism: Did the Bork Nomination Represent a Fundamental Shift in Confirmation Criteria?" *Marquette Law Review* 75 (1992): 409–37.

———. "The Senate Judiciary Committee and Supreme Court Nominees: Measuring the Dynamics of Confirmation Criteria." *Journal of Politics* 56 (1994): 773–87.

Gunther, Gerald. *Constitutional Law.* 11th ed. Mineola, N.Y.: Foundation Press, 1985.

Haldeman, H. R. *The Haldeman Diaries: Inside the Nixon White House.* New York: G. P. Putnam's Sons, 1994.

Hall, Jacquelyn Dowd. *Revolt against Chivalry: Jessie Daniel Ames and the Women's Campaign against Lynching.* New York: Columbia University Press, 1993.

Hariman, Robert. *Political Style: The Artistry of Power.* Chicago: University of Chicago Press, 1995.

Harris, Joseph P. *The Advice and Consent of the Senate: A Study of the Confirmation of Appointments by the United States Senate.* Berkeley: University of California Press, 1953.

Harris, Richard. *Decision.* New York: E. P. Dutton, 1971.

Hart, Roderick P. *Seducing America: How Television Charms the Modern Voter.* New York: Oxford University Press, 1994.

Hasian, Marouf, Jr. "Critical Legal Rhetorics: The Theory and Practice of Law in a Postmodern World." *Southern Communication Journal* 60 (1994): 44–56.

———. *Legal Memories and Amnesias in America's Rhetorical Culture.* Boulder, Colo.: Westview, 2000.

———. "The Public Addresses of Meese and Brennan: Voices in the American Legal Wilderness." *Communication Studies* 44 (1993): 299–319.

———. *The Rhetoric of Eugenics in Anglo-American Thought*. Athens: University of Georgia Press, 1996.

Hasian, Marouf, Jr., Celeste Michelle Condit, and John Louis Lucaites. "The Rhetorical Boundaries of 'the Law': A Consideration of the Rhetorical Culture of Legal Practice and the Case of the 'Separate but Equal' Doctrine." *Quarterly Journal of Speech* 82 (1996): 323–42.

Hasian, Marouf, Jr., and Earl Croasmun. "Rhetoric's Revenge: The Prospect of a Critical Legal Rhetoric." *Philosophy and Rhetoric* 29 (1996): 384–99.

Hatch, Orrin G. "More Marbury Myths." *Cincinnati Law Review* 57 (1989): 891–901.

Haverkamp, Anselm. "Rhetoric, Law, and the Poetics of Memory." *Cardozo Law Review* 13 (1992): 1639–53.

The Haynsworth Nomination: An Analysis by the AFL-CIO. Washington, D.C.: AFL-CIO, 1970

Heath, Robert L. *Realism and Relativism: A Perspective on Kenneth Burke*. Macon, Ga.: Mercer University Press, 1986.

Hertsgaard, Mark. *On Bended Knee: The Press and the Reagan Presidency*. New York: Farrar, Strauss, Giroux, 1988.

Hill, Forbes. "Conventional Wisdom—Traditional Form—The President's Message of November 3, 1969." *Quarterly Journal of Speech* 58 (1972): 373–86.

Hine, Darlene Clark. "The NAACP and the Supreme Court: Walter F. White and the Defeat of Judge John J. Parker." *Negro History Bulletin* 40 (1977): 753–57.

Hoff, Joan. *Nixon Reconsidered*. New York: Basic Books, 1994.

Hoffert, Robert W. *A Politics of Tensions: The Articles of Confederation and American Political Ideas*. Niwot: University Press of Colorado, 1992.

Hogan, J. Michael. *The Nuclear Freeze Campaign: Rhetoric and Foreign Policy in the Telepolitical Age*. East Lansing: Michigan State University Press, 1994.

Hoover, Herbert C. *The Memoirs of Herbert Hoover: The Cabinet and the Presidency, 1920–1933*. New York: Macmillan, 1952.

Horwitz, Morton J. "The Bork Nomination and American Constitutional History." *Syracuse Law Review* 39 (1988): 1029-39.

Hyde, Michael J., and Craig R. Smith. "Hermeneutics and Rhetoric: A Seen but Unobserved Relationship." *Quarterly Journal of Speech* 65 (1979): 347–63.

Jamieson, Kathleen Hall. *Packaging the Presidency: A History and Criticism of Presidential Campaign Advertising*. 3rd ed. New York: Oxford University Press, 1996.

Jasinski, James. "The Feminization of Liberty, Domesticated Virtue, and the Reconstitution of Power and Authority in Early American Political Discourse." *Quarterly Journal of Speech* 79 (1993): 146–64.

———. "(Re)constituting Community through Narrative Argument: *Eros* and *Philia* in *The Big Chill*." *Quarterly Journal of Speech* 79 (1993): 467–86.

Jensen, Merrill. *The Articles of Confederation*. Madison: University of Wisconsin Press, 1940.

Johnson, Claudius O. *Borah of Idaho*. New York: Longmans, Green, 1936.

Johnson, Lyndon Baines. *The Vantage Point: Perspectives on the Presidency, 1963–1969*. New York: Holt, Rinehart and Winston, 1971.

Jones, Hugh David. "The Confirmation of Charles Evans Hughes as Chief Justice of the Supreme Court of the United States." A.M. thesis, Duke University, 1962.

Jones, Nathaniel R. "Whither Goest Judicial Nominations, *Brown* or *Plessy?*—Advice and Consent Revisited." *SMU Law Review* 46 (1992): 735–49.

Jordan, Emma Coleman. "Race, Gender, and Social Class in the Thomas Sexual Harassment Hearings: The Hidden Fault Lines in Political Discourse." *Harvard Women's Law Journal* 15 (1992): 1–24.

Judge Bork's Views Regarding Supreme Court Constitutional Precedents: A Report of the NAACP Legal Defense and Educational Fund, Inc. and People for the American Way Action Fund. N.p.: n.p., 1987.

Judis, John B., and Ruy Teixeira. *The Emerging Democratic Majority*. New York: Scribner, 2002.

Kagan, Elena. "Confirmation Messes, Old and New." *University of Chicago Law Review* 62 (1995): 919–42.

Kahn, Michael A. "Shattering the Myth about President Eisenhower's Supreme Court Appointments." *Presidential Studies Quarterly* 22 (1992): 47–56.

Kahn, Victoria. "Rhetoric and the Law." *Diacritics* 19 (1989): 21–34.

Kalk, Bruce H. "The Carswell Affair: The Politics of a Supreme Court Nomination in the Nixon Administration." *American Journal of Legal History* 42 (1998): 261–87.

———. "Wormley's Hotel Revisited: Richard Nixon's Southern Strategy and the End of the Second Reconstruction." *North Carolina Historical Review* 71 (1994): 85–105.

Karfunkel, Thomas, and Thomas W. Ryley. *The Jewish Seat: Anti-Semitism and the Appointment of Jews to the Supreme Court.* Hicksville, N.Y.: Exposition Press, 1978.

Karl, Barry D. *The Uneasy State.* Chicago: University of Chicago Press, 1983.

Kaufman, Andrew L. *Cardozo.* Cambridge, Mass.: Harvard University Press, 1998.

Keller, Morton. *Regulating a New Society: Public Policy and Social Change in America, 1900–1933.* Cambridge, Mass.: Harvard University Press.

Klarman, Michael J. *From Jim Crow to Civil Rights: The Supreme Court and the Struggle for Racial Equality.* New York: Oxford University Press, 2004.

Kleindienst, Richard G. *Justice: The Memoirs of Attorney General Richard Kleindienst.* Ottawa, Ill.: Jameson Books, 1985.

Klinck, Dennis R. *The Word of the Law.* Ottawa, Canada: Carleton University Press, 1992.

Kline, Stephan O. "The Topsy-Turvy World of Judicial Confirmations in the Era of Hatch and Lott." *Dickinson Law Review* 103 (1999): 247–342.

Klinger, Geoffrey. "Law as Communicative *Praxis:* Toward a Rhetorical Jurisprudence." *Argumentation and Advocacy* 30 (1994): 236–47.

Kluger, Richard. *Simple Justice.* New York: Knopf, 1975.

Kohlmeier, Louis M., Jr. *"God Save This Honorable Court!"* New York: Charles Scribner's Sons, 1972.

Kotlowski, Dean J. "Trial by Error: Nixon, the Senate, and the Haynsworth Nomination." *Presidential Studies Quarterly* 26 (1996): 71-91.

Kurland, Philip B. *Politics, the Constitution, and the Warren Court.* Chicago: University of Chicago Press, 1970.

Lakoff, Robin Tolmach. *The Language War.* Berkeley and Los Angeles: University of California Press, 2000.

Lambert, Oscar Doane. *Presidential Politics in the United States, 1841–1844.* Durham, N.C.: Duke University Press, 1936.

Landever, Arthur R. "Those Indispensable Articles of Confederation—Stage in Constitutionalism, Passage for the Framers, and Clue to the Nature of the Constitution." *Arizona Law Review* 31 (1989): 79–125.

Larisa, Joseph S., Jr. "Popular Mythology: The Framers' Intent, the Constitution, and Ideological Review of Supreme Court Nominees." *Boston College Law Review* 30 (1989): 969–86.

LaRue, L. H. *Constitutional Law as Fiction: Narrative in the Rhetoric of Authority.* University Park: Pennsylvania State University Press, 1995.

Lawlor, John M. "Court Packing Revisited: A Proposal for Rationalizing the Timing of Appointments to the Supreme Court." *University of Pennsylvania Law Review* 134 (1986): 967–1000.

Lee, Emery G., III. "The Federalist in an Age of Faction: Rethinking Federalist No. 76 on the Senate's Role in the Judicial Confirmations Process." *Ohio Northern Law Review* 30 (2004): 235–66.

Leiter, Brian. "Intellectual Voyeurism in Legal Scholarship." *Yale Journal of Law and the Humanities* 4 (1992): 79–104.

Lerner, Max. "The Social Thought of Mr. Justice Brandeis." In *Mr. Justice Brandeis,* edited by Felix Frankfurter, 7–46. 1932. Reprint. New York: DaCapo, 1972.

Leubsdorf, John. "Deconstructing the Constitution." *Stanford Law Review* 40 (1987): 181–201.

Leuchtenburg, William E. "A Klansman Joins the Court: The Appointment of Hugo L. Black." *University of Chicago Law Review* 41 (1973): 1–31.

_____. *The Perils of Prosperity, 1914–1932.* Chicago: University of Chicago Press, 1958.

_____. *The Supreme Court Reborn: The Constitutional Revolution in the Age of Roosevelt.* New York: Oxford University Press, 1995.

Levinson, Sanford. "'The Constitution' in American Civil Religion." In *The Supreme Court Review 1979,* edited by Philip B. Kurland and Gerhard Casper, 123–51. Chicago: University of Chicago Press, 1979.

Levinson, Sanford, and Steven Mailloux, eds. *Interpreting Law and Literature: A Hermeneutic Reader.* Evanston, Ill.: Northwestern University Press, 1988.

Levy, David W. "Brandeis and the Progressive Movement." In *Brandeis and America,* edited by Nelson L. Dawson, 99–117. Lexington: University Press of Kentucky, 1989.

Lewis, William. "Law's Tragedy." *Rhetoric Society Quarterly* 21 (1991): 11–21.

_____. "Of Innocence, Exclusion, and the Burning of Flags: The Romantic Realism of the Law." *Southern Communication Journal* 60 (1994): 4–21.

Lief, Alfred. *Brandeis: The Personal History of an American Ideal.* New York: Stackpole Sons, 1936.

Link, Arthur S. *Woodrow Wilson and the Progressive Era, 1910-1917.* New York: Harper and Brothers, 1954.

_____. ed. *The Papers of Woodrow Wilson.* Vol. 36. Princeton, N.J.: Princeton University Press, 1981.

Lisio, Donald J. *Hoover, Blacks, and Lily-Whites: A Study of Southern Strategies.* Chapel Hill: University of North Carolina Press, 1985.

Lively, Donald E. "The Supreme Court Appointment Process: In Search of Constitutional Roles and Responsibilities." *Southern California Law Review* 59 (1986): 551–79.

Logue, Cal M., and Eugene F. Miller. "Rhetorical Status: A Study of Its Origins, Functions, and Consequences." *Quarterly Journal of Speech* 81 (1995): 20–47.

Longmore, Paul K. *The Invention of George Washington*. Charlottesville: University Press of Virginia, 1999.

Lucaites, John Louis. "Between Rhetoric and 'the Law': Power, Legitimacy, and Social Change." *Quarterly Journal of Speech* 76 (1990): 435–49.

Lucaites, John Louis, and Maurice Charland. "The Legacy of [Liberty]: Rhetoric, Ideology, and Aesthetics in the Postmodern Condition." *Canadian Journal of Political and Social Theory* 8 (1989): 31–48.

Lucaites, John Louis, and Celeste Michelle Condit. "Reconstructing <Equality>: Culturetypal and Counter-Cultural Rhetorics in the Martyred Black Vision." *Communication Monographs* 57 (1990): 5–24.

Luke, Timothy. *Screens of Power: Ideology, Domination, and Resistance in Informational Society*. Urbana: University of Illinois Press, 1989.

Lusted, David. "The Glut of Personality." In *Stardom: Industry of Desire*, edited by Christine Gledhill, 251-58. London: Routledge, 1990.

Lutz, Donald S. "The Articles of Confederation as the Background to the Federal Republic." *Publius* 20 (1990): 55–70.

MacIntyre, Alasdair. *After Virtue: A Study in Moral Theory*. Notre Dame, Ind.: University of Notre Dame Press, 1981.

Mackenzie, G. Calvin, ed. *Innocent Until Nominated: The Breakdown of the Presidential Appointments Process*. Washington, D.C.: Brookings Institution Press, 2001.

Madison, James, Alexander Hamilton, and John Jay. *The Federalist Papers*. Edited by Issac Kramnick. Middlesex, U.K.: Penguin, 1987.

Maltese, John Anthony. *The Selling of Supreme Court Nominees*. Baltimore: Johns Hopkins University Press, 1995.

Manoloff, Richard D. "The Advice and Consent of Congress: Toward a Supreme Court Appointment Process for Our Time." *Ohio State Law Journal* 54 (1993): 1087-107.

Marcotte, Matthew D. "Advice and Consent: A Historical Argument for Substantive Senatorial Involvement in Judicial Nominations." *NYU Journal of Legislation and Public Policy* 5 (2001/2): 519–62.

Marcus, Maeva, and James R. Perry, eds. *The Documentary History of the Supreme Court of the United States, 1789–1800.* Vol. 1, Part 2. New York: Columbia University Press, 1985.

Marshall, P. David. *Celebrity and Power: Fame in Contemporary Culture.* Minneapolis: University of Minnesota Press, 1997.

Marshall, Thomas R. *Public Opinion and the Supreme Court.* Boston: Unwin Hyman, 1989.

Mason, Alpheus Thomas. *Brandeis: A Free Man's Life.* New York: Viking, 1946.

———. *Harlan Fiske Stone: Pillar of the Law.* New York: Viking, 1956.

———. *The Supreme Court from Taft to Burger.* 3rd ed. Baton Rouge: Louisiana State University Press, 1979.

———. *The Supreme Court from Taft to Warren.* Baton Rouge: Louisiana State University Press, 1958.

Massaro, John. "President Bush's Management of the Thomas Nomination: Four Years, Several Books, Two Videos Later (And Still More to Come!)." *Presidential Studies Quarterly* 26 (1996): 816–27.

Massey, Calvin R. "Getting There: A Brief History of the Politics of Supreme Court Appointments." *Hastings Constitutional Law Quarterly* 19 (1991): 1–21.

Masugi, Ken. "Natural Right and Oversight: The Use and Abuse of 'Natural Law' in the Clarence Thomas Hearings." *Political Communication* 9 (1992): 231–50.

Mayer, Jane, and Jill Abramson. *Strange Justice: The Selling of Clarence Thomas.* Boston: Houghton Mifflin, 1994.

McCraw, Thomas K. "Louis D. Brandeis Reappraised." *American Scholar* 54 (1985): 525–36.

———. *Prophets of Regulation: Charles Francis Adams, Louis D. Brandeis, James M. Landis, Alfred E. Kahn.* Cambridge, Mass.: Belknap Press, 1984.

McDonald, Forrest. *Novus Ordo Seclorum: The Intellectual Origins of the Constitution.* Lawrence: University Press of Kansas, 1985.

McDorman, Todd F. "Challenging Constitutional Authority: African American Responses to *Scott v. Sanford.*" *Quarterly Journal of Speech* 83 (1997): 192–210.

———. "Uniting Legal Doctrine and Discourse to Rethink Women's Workplace Rights." *Women's Studies in Communication* 21 (1998): 27–55.

McFeeley, Neil D. *Appointment of Judges: The Johnson Presidency.* Austin: University of Texas Press, 1987.

McGee, Michael Calvin. "The 'Ideograph': A Link Between Rhetoric and Ideology." *Quarterly Journal of Speech* 66 (1980): 1–16.

———. "In Search of 'The People': A Rhetorical Alternative." *Quarterly Journal of Speech* 61 (1975): 235–49.

———. "Text, Context, and the Fragmentation of Contemporary Culture." *Western Journal of Speech Communication* 54 (1990): 274–89.

Medina, Harold. "John Johnston Parker 1885–1958." *North Carolina Law Review* 38 (1960): 299–306.

Meisenhelder, Thomas. "Law as Symbolic Action: Kenneth Burke's Sociology of Law." *Symbolic Interaction* 4 (1981): 43–57.

Melone, Albert P. "The Senate's Confirmation Role in Supreme Court Nominations and the Politics of Ideology versus Impartiality." *Judicature* 75, no. 2 (1991): 68–79.

Meyrowitz, Joshua. *No Sense of Place: The Impact of Electronic Media on Social Behavior*. New York: Oxford University Press, 1985.

Millican, Edward. *One United People: The Federalist Papers and the National Idea*. Lexington: University Press of Kentucky, 1990.

Minow, Martha. "Law Turning Outward." *Telos* 73 (1987): 79–100.

Mitzner, Adam. "The Evolving Role of the Senate in Judicial Nominations." *Journal of Law and Politics* 5 (1989): 387–428.

Monroe, Dan. *The Republican Vision of John Tyler*. College Station: Texas A&M University Press, 2003.

Morgan, Edmund S. *Inventing the People: The Rise of Popular Sovereignty in England and America*. New York: W. W. Norton, 1988.

Morgan, Robert J. *A Whig Embattled: The Presidency under John Tyler*. Lincoln: University of Nebraska Press, 1954.

Morris, Madeline. "The Grammar of Advice and Consent: Senate Confirmation of Supreme Court Nominees." *Drake Law Review* 38 (1988–89): 863–87.

Morrison, Toni, ed. *Race-ing Justice, En-gendering Power: Essays on Anita Hill, Clarence Thomas, and the Construction of Social Reality*. New York: Pantheon, 1992.

Murphy, Bruce Allen. *Fortas: The Rise and Ruin of a Supreme Court Justice*. New York: William Morrow, 1988.

Murphy, John M. "Knowing the President: The Dialogic Evolution of the Campaign History." *Quarterly Journal of Speech* 84 (1998): 23–40.

Nakayama, Thomas K., and Robert L. Krizek. "Whiteness: A Strategic Rhetoric." *Quarterly Journal of Speech* 81 (1995): 291–310.

Nerhot, Patrick, ed. *Law, Interpretation, and Reality: Essays in Epistemology, Hermeneutics and Jurisprudence*. Dordrecht, The Netherlands: Kluwer Academic, 1990.

Neuberger, Richard L., and Stephen B. Kahn. *Integrity: The Life of George W. Norris*. New York: Vanguard Press, 1937.

Nevins, Allan, ed. *Letters of Grover Cleveland, 1850–1908*. Boston: Houghton Mifflin, 1933.

Newman, Roger K. *Hugo Black: A Biography*. New York: Pantheon Books, 1994.

Nixon, Richard M. "Acceptance Speech: Candidate for President." *Vital Speeches of the Day* 34 (September 1, 1968): 674–77.

———. *RN: The Memoirs of Richard Nixon*. Vol. 1. New York: Warner Books, 1978.

Nolan, James L., Jr. *The Therapeutic State: Justifying Government at Century's End*. New York: New York University Press, 1998.

O'Brien, Francis Wilson. "Bicentennial Reflections on Herbert Hoover and the Supreme Court." *Iowa Law Review* 61 (1975): 397–417.

O'Keane, Josephine. *Thomas J. Walsh, a Senator from Montana*. Francestown, N.H.: Marshall Jones, 1955.

O'Leary, Stephen D. *Arguing the Apocalypse: A Theory of Millenial Rhetoric*. New York: Oxford University Press, 1994.

O'Reilly, Kenneth. *Nixon's Piano: Presidents and Racial Politics from Washington to Clinton*. New York: Free Press, 1995.

Overby, L. Marvin, and Beth M. Henschen. "Race Trumps Gender? Women, African Americans, and the Senate Confirmation of Justice Clarence Thomas." *American Politics Quarterly* 22 (1994): 62–73.

Overby, L. Marvin, Beth M. Henschen, Julie Strauss, and Michael H. Walsh. "African-American Constituents and Supreme Court Nominees: An Examination of the Senate Confirmation of Thurgood Marshall." *Political Research Quarterly* 47 (1994): 839–55.

Overby, L. Marvin, Beth M. Henschen, Michael H. Walsh, and Julie Strauss. "Courting Constituents? An Analysis of the Senate Confirmation Vote on Justice Clarence Thomas." *American Political Science Review* 86 (1992): 997–1003.

Pacelle, Richard L., Jr. *The Transformation of the Supreme Court's Agenda*. Boulder, Colo.: Westview, 1991.

Pacher, Daniela K. "Aesthetics and Ideology: The Motives behind 'Law and Literature.'" *Columbia-VLA Journal of Law and the Arts* 14 (1990): 587–614.

Palmer, Jan. "Senate Confirmation of Appointments to the U.S. Supreme Court." *Review of Social Economy* 41 (1983): 152–62.

Parry-Giles, Shawn J. "The Rhetorical Tension Between 'Propaganda' and 'Democracy': Blending Competing Conceptions of Ideology and Theory." *Communication Studies* 44 (1993): 117–31.

Parry-Giles, Trevor. "Celebritized Justice, Civil Rights, and the Clarence Thomas Nomination." In *Civil Rights Rhetoric and the American Presidency*, edited by James Arnt Aune and Enrique Rigsby. College Station: Texas A&M University Press, in press.

———. "Character, the Constitution, and the Ideological Embodiment of 'Civil Rights' in the 1967 Nomination of Thurgood Marshall to the Supreme Court." *Quarterly Journal of Speech* 82 (1996): 364–82.

Parry-Giles, Trevor, and Shawn J. Parry-Giles. "Political Scopophilia, Presidential Campaigning, and the Intimacy of American Politics." *Communication Studies* 47 (1996): 191–205.

Paulsen, Michael Stokes. "Straightening Out *The Confirmation Mess*." *Yale Law Journal* 105 (1995): 549–79.

People for the American Way. *Robert Bork: The Wrong Man, the Wrong Place, the Wrong Time: Editorial Memorandum*. Washington, D.C.: People for the American Way, 1987.

Percy, Charles H. "Advice and Consent: A Reevaluation." *Southern Illinois University Law Journal* 1978 (1978): 31–43.

Peretti, Terri Jennings. "Restoring the Balance of Power: The Struggle for Control of the Supreme Court." *Hastings Constitutional Law Quarterly* 20 (1992): 69–103.

Perry, Barbara A. *A "Representative" Supreme Court? The Impact of Race, Religion, and Gender on Appointments*. New York: Greenwood, 1991.

Pertschuk, Michael, and Wendy Schaetzel. *The People Rising: The Campaign against the Bork Nomination*. New York: Thunder's Mouth Press, 1989.

Pfeffer, Leo. *This Honorable Court: A History of the United States Supreme Court*. Boston: Beacon Press, 1965.

Phelps, Timothy M., and Helen Winternitz. *Capitol Games: Clarence Thomas, Anita Hill, and the Story of a Supreme Court Nomination*. New York: Hyperion, 1992.

Pierce, Carl A. "A Vacancy on the Supreme Court: The Politics of Judicial Appointment 1893–94." *Tennessee Law Review* 39 (1972): 555–612.

Pilotta, Joseph, John W. Murphy, Elizabeth A Wilson, and Tricia S. Jones. "The Contemporary Rhetoric of the Social Theories of Law." *Central States Speech Journal* 34 (1983): 211–20.

Polk, James K. *The Diary of a President, 1845–1849*. Edited by Allan Nevins. London: Longmans, Green, 1929.

Posner, Richard A. *An Affair of State: The Investigation, Impeachment, and Trial of President Clinton*. Cambridge, Mass.: Harvard University Press, 1999.

Pound, Arthur, and Samuel Taylor Moore, eds. *They Told Barron: Conversations and Revelations of an American Pepys in Wall Street*. New York: Harper and Brothers, 1930.

Pringle, Henry F. *The Life and Times of William Howard Taft*. 2 vols. New York: Farrar and Rinehart, 1939.

Prosise, Theodore O., and Craig R. Smith. "The Supreme Court's Ruling in *Bush v. Gore*: A Rhetoric of Inconsistency." *Rhetoric and Public Affairs* 4 (2001): 605–32.

Pusey, Merlo J. *Charles Evans Hughes*. 2 vols. New York: Columbia University Press, 1963.

Ragan, Sandra L., Dianne G. Bystrom, Lynda Lee Kaid, and Christina S. Beck, eds. *The Lynching of Language: Gender, Politics, and Power in the Hill-Thomas Hearings*. Urbana: University of Illinois Press, 1996.

Rees Grover, III. "Questions for Supreme Court Nominees at Confirmation Hearings: Excluding the Constitution." *Georgia Law Review* 17 (1983): 913–67.

"Reflections on the Ginsburg and Breyer Nominations." *Journal of Law and Politics* 12 (1996): 459–79.

Regan, Alison. "Rhetoric and Political Process in the Hill-Thomas Hearings." *Political Communication* 11 (1994): 277–85.

Revesz, Richard L. "Thurgood Marshall's Struggle." *New York University Law Review* 68 (1993): 237–64.

Richardson, James, D., ed. *A Compilation of the Messages and Papers of the Presidents, 1789–1897*. 10 vols. Washington, D.C.: Government Printing Office, 1897.

Rodgers, Daniel T. "In Search of Progressivism." *Reviews in American History* 10 (1982): 113–32.

Romine, Ronald Hale. "The 'Politics' of Supreme Court Nominations from Theodore Roosevelt to Ronald Reagan: The Construction of a 'Politicization Index.'" Ph.D. diss., University of South Carolina, 1984.

Ross, Barbara J. *J. E. Spingarn and the Rise of the NAACP, 1911–1939*. New York: Atheneum, 1972.

Ross, William G. "The Functions, Roles, and Duties of the Senate in the Supreme Court Appointment Process." *William and Mary Law Review* 28 (1987): 633–82.

———. "The Supreme Court Appointment Process: A Search for a Synthesis." *Albany Law Review* 57 (1994): 993–1042.

Rotunda, Ronald D. "Innovations Disguised as Traditions: A Historical Review of the Supreme Court Nominations Process." *University of Illinois Law Review* 1995 (1995): 123–31.

Rovere, Richard. "Walter Lippmann." *American Scholar* 44 (1975): 585–603.

Rowan, Carl T. *Dream Makers, Dream Breakers: The World of Justice Thurgood Marshall*. Boston: Little, Brown, 1993.

Rucinski, Dianne. "Rush to Judgment? Fast Reaction Polls in the Anita Hill-Clarence Thomas Controversy." *Public Opinion Quarterly* 57 (1993): 575–92.

Ruckman, P. S., Jr. "The Supreme Court, Critical Nominations, and the Senate Confirmation Process." *Journal of Politics* 55 (1993): 793–805.

Ryther, Scott R. "Advice and Consent: The Senate's Political Role in the Supreme Court Appointment Process." *Utah Law Review* 1988 (1988): 411–33.

Safire, William. *Before the Fall: An Inside View of the Pre-Watergate White House*. New York: Ballantine Books, 1977.

Sapiro, Virginia, and Joe Soss. "Spectacular Politics, Dramatic Interpretations: Multiple Meanings in the Thomas/Hill Hearings." *Political Communication* 16 (1999): 285–314.

Sarat, Austin, and Thomas R. Kearns, eds. *The Rhetoric of Law*. Ann Arbor: University of Michigan Press, 1994.

Savage, David G. *Turning Right: The Making of the Rehnquist Supreme Court*. New York: John Wiley and Sons, 1992.

Scallen, Eileen A., William Wiethoff, Warren Sandmann, and James Arnt Aune. "Rhetorical Criticism of Legal Texts: Four Rhetoricians on *Lochner v. New York*." *Hastings Constitutional Law Quarterly* 23 (1996): 621–70.

Schaller, Michael. *Reckoning with Reagan: America and Its President in the 1980s*. New York: Oxford University Press, 1992.

Schickel, Richard. *Intimate Strangers: The Culture of Celebrity*. Garden City, N.Y.: Doubleday, 1986.

Schram, Sanford F. "The Post-Modern Presidency and the Grammar of Electronic Electioneering." *Critical Studies in Mass Communication* 8 (1991): 210–16.

Schudson, Michael. *The Good Citizen: A History of American Civic Life*. New York: Martin Kessler Books, 1998.

Schwartz Bernard. *The New Right and the Constitution: Turning Back the Legal Clock*. Boston: Northeastern University Press, 1990.

Segal, Jeffrey A. "Senate Confirmation of Supreme Court Justices: Partisan and Institutional Politics." *Journal of Politics* 49 (1987): 998–1015.

Segal, Jeffrey A., and Albert D. Cover. "Ideological Values and the Votes of U.S. Supreme Court Justices." *American Political Science Review* 83 (1989): 559–65.

Shapiro, Yonathan. "American Jews in Politics: The Case of Louis D. Brandeis." *American Jewish Historical Quarterly* 15 (1965): 199–211.

Siegel, Paul, ed. *Outsiders Looking In: A Communication Perspective on the Hill/Thomas Hearings*. Cresskill, N.J.: Hampton Press, 1996.

Siegworth, Greg. "The Distance Between Me and You: Madonna and Celestial Navigation (or You Can Be My *Lucky Star*)." In *The Madonna Connection: Representational Politics, Subcultural Identities, and Cultural Theory*, edited by Cathy Schwichtenberg, 291–318. Boulder, Colo.: Westview, 1993.

Silverstein, Mark. *Judicious Choices: The New Politics of Supreme Court Confirmations*. New York: W. W. Norton, 1994.

Silverstein, Mark, and William Haltom. "You Can't Always Get What You Want: Reflections on the Ginsburg and Breyer Nominations." *Journal of Law and Politics* 12 (1996): 459–79.

Simon, James F. *The Center Holds: The Power Struggle Inside the Rehnquist Court*. New York: Simon and Schuster, 1995.

———. *In His Own Image: The Supreme Court in Richard Nixon's America*. New York: David McKay, 1973.

Simon, John Y., ed. *The Papers of Ulysses S. Grant*. 28 vols. Carbondale: Southern Illinois University Press, 1995.

Simon, Paul. *Advice and Consent: Clarence Thomas, Robert Bork and the Intriguing History of the Supreme Court's Nomination Battles*. Washington, D.C.: National Press Books, 1992.

Simson, Gary J. "Mired in the Confirmation Mess." *University of Pennsylvania Law Review* 143 (1995): 1035–63.

Smith, Bob. *They Closed Their Schools*. Chapel Hill: University of North Carolina Press, 1965.

Smith, Christopher E. *Critical Judicial Nominations and Political Change: The Impact of Clarence Thomas*. Westport, Conn.: Praeger, 1993.

Smith, Christopher E., and Thomas R. Hensley. "Unfulfilled Aspirations: The Court-Packing Efforts of Presidents Reagan and Bush." *Albany Law Review* 57 (1994): 1111–31.

Smith, K. L. "The Radicalization of Martin Luther King, Jr.: The Last Three Years." *Journal of Ecumenical Studies* 26 (1989): 270–88.

Smitherman, Geneva, ed. *African American Women Speak Out on Anita Hill-Clarence Thomas*. Detroit: Wayne State University Press, 1995.

Songer, Donald R. "The Relevance of Policy Values for the Confirmation of Supreme Court Nominees." *Law and Society* 13 (1979): 927–48.

Soper, Morris, Fred B. Helms, and Orie L. Phillips. "A Tribute to Judge John J. Parker—'The Gladsome Light of Jurisprudence.'" *North Carolina Law Review* 37 (1958): 1–16.

Spillenger, Clyde. "Elusive Advocate: Reconsidering Brandeis as People's Lawyer." *Yale Law Journal* 105 (1996): 1445–535.

Stahl, Roger. "Carving Up Free Exercise: Dissociation and 'Religion' in Supreme Court Jurisprudence." *Rhetoric and Public Affairs* 5 (2002): 439–58.

Stephanopoulos, George. *All Too Human: A Political Education*. Boston: Little, Brown, 1999.

Stephenson, Donald Grier, Jr. *Campaigns and the Court: The U.S. Supreme Court in Presidential Elections*. New York: Columbia University Press, 1999.

Storey, Moorfield, and Edward W. Emerson. *Ebenezer Rockwood Hoar: A Memoir*. Boston: Houghton Mifflin, 1911.

Strauss, David A., and Cass R. Sunstein. "The Senate, the Constitution, and the Confirmation Process." *Yale Law Journal* 101 (1992): 1491–524.

Strum, Philippa. *Brandeis: Beyond Progressivism*. Lawrence: University Press of Kansas, 1993.

———. "Louis Brandeis: Lawyer and Judge." *Journal of Supreme Court History* 1993 (1993): 29–40.

———. "Louis D. Brandeis, the New Freedom and the State." *Mid-America* 69 (1987): 105–24.

Swindler, William F. "John Tyler's Nominations: 'Robin Hood,' Congress, and the Court." *Yearbook of the Supreme Court Historical Society* (1977): 39–43.

"Symposium, Confirmation Controversy: The Selection of a Supreme Court Justice." *Northwestern University Law Review* 84 (1990): 832–1046.

"Symposium: Rhetoric and Skepticism." *Iowa Law Review* 74 (1989): 755–836.

"Symposium Issue: The Selection of Judges in the United States." *Kentucky Law Journal* 77 (1988–89): 481–644.

Teger, Stuart E. "Presidential Strategy for the Appointment of Supreme Court Justices." Ph.D. diss., University of Rochester, 1976.

Thomas, Brook. "Reflections on the Law and Literature Revival." *Critical Inquiry* 17 (1991): 510–39.

Thomas, Dan, Craig McCoy, and Allan McBride. "Deconstructing the Political Spectacle: Sex, Race, and Subjectivity in Public Response to the Clarence Thomas/Anita Hill 'Sexual Harassment' Hearings." *American Journal of Political Science* 37 (1993): 699–720.

Thompson, John B. *Ideology and Modern Culture.* Stanford, Calif.: Stanford University Press, 1990.

———. *Political Scandal: Power and Visibility in the Media Age.* Cambridge: Polity, 2000.

Todd, A. L. *Justice on Trial: The Case of Louis D. Brandeis.* Chicago: University of Chicago Press, 1964.

Tonn, Mari Boor. "Donning Sackcloth and Ashes: *Webster vs. Reproductive Health Services* and Moral Agony in Abortion Rights Rhetoric." *Communication Quarterly* 44 (1996): 265–79.

Tribe, Laurence H. *God Save This Honorable Court: How the Choice of Supreme Court Justices Shapes Our History.* New York: Random House, 1985.

Tulis, Jeffrey K. "Constitutional Abdication: The Senate, the President, and Appointments to the Supreme Court." *Case Western Reserve Law Review* 47 (1997): 1331–57.

Tushnet, Mark V. *The NAACP's Legal Strategy against Segregated Education, 1925–1950.* Chapel Hill: University of North Carolina Press, 1987.

———, ed. *Thurgood Marshall: His Speeches, Writings, Arguments, Opinions, and Reminiscences.* Chicago: Lawrence Hill Books, 2001.

Twentieth Century Fund. *Judicial Roulette: Report of the Twentieth Century Fund Task Force on Judicial Selection.* New York: Priority, 1988.

Ulrich, Walter. "The Creation of a Legacy: Brandeis' Concurring Opinion in *Whitney v. California." Southern Speech Communication Journal* 50 (1985): 143–55.

Urofsky, Melvin I. *Louis D. Brandeis and the Progressive Tradition.* Boston: Little, Brown, 1981.

———. *A Mind of One Piece: Brandeis and American Reform.* New York: Charles Scribner's Sons, 1971.

———. "The 'Outrageous' Brandeis Nomination." In *Supreme Court Historical Society Yearbook 1979,* edited by William F. Swindler, 8–19. Washington, D.C.: Supreme Court Historical Society, 1980.

Urofsky, Melvin I., and David W. Levy. *Letters of Louis D. Brandeis.* Vol. 4. Albany: State University of New York Press, 1975.

Vargyas, Ellen J., Suzanne E. Meeker, Marcia D. Greenberger, and Nancy Duff Campbell. *Setting the Record Straight: Judge Bork and the Future of Women's Rights.* N.p.: National Women's Law Center, 1987.

Vatz Richard E., and Theodore Otto Windt Jr. "The Defeats of Judges Haynsworth and Carswell: Rejection of Supreme Court Nominees." *Quarterly Journal of Speech* 60 (1974): 477-88.

Vieira, Norman, and Leonard E. Gross. "The Appointments Clause: Judge Bork and the Role of Ideology in Judicial Confirmations." *Journal of Legal History* 11 (1990): 311–52.

———. *Supreme Court Appointments: Judge Bork and the Politicization of Senate Confirmations.* Carbondale: Southern Illinois University Press, 1998.

Walpin, Gerald. "Take Obstructionism Out of the Judicial Nominations Confirmation Process." *Texas Review of Law and Politics* 8 (2003): 89–112.

Warren, Charles. "The Progressiveness of the United States Supreme Court." *Columbia Law Review* 13 (1913): 294–313.

Warren, Earl. *The Memoirs of Earl Warren.* Garden City, N.Y.: Doubleday, 1977.

Wasby, Stephen L., and Joel B. Grossman. "Judge Clement F. Haynsworth, Jr.: New Perspective on His Nomination to the Supreme Court." *Duke Law Journal* 1990 (1990): 74–80.

Waterhouse, David L. *The Progressive Movement of 1924 and the Development of Interest Group Liberalism.* New York: Garland, 1991.

Watson, Richard L., Jr. "The Defeat of Judge Parker: A Study in Pressure Groups and Politics." *Mississippi Valley Historical Review* 50 (1963): 213–34.

Webster, Gerald R. "Geography of a Senate Confirmation Vote." *Geographical Review* 82 (1992): 154–65.

Weisberg, Robert. "The Law-Literature Enterprise." *Yale Journal of Law and the Humanities* 1 (1988): 1–67.

Welch, Richard E., Jr. *The Presidencies of Grover Cleveland.* Lawrence: University Press of Kansas, 1988.

Wetlaufer, Gerald B. "Rhetoric and Its Denial in Legal Discourse." *Virginia Law Review* 76 (1990): 1545–97.

White, G. Edward. "The Canonization of Holmes and Brandeis: Epistemology and Judicial Reputations." *New York University Law Review* 70 (1995): 576–621.

———. *Earl Warren: A Public Life.* New York: Oxford University Press, 1982.

White, James Boyd. *Heracles' Bow: Essays on the Rhetoric and Poetics of the Law.* Madison: University of Wisconsin Press, 1985.

———. *Justice as Translation.* Chicago: University of Chicago Press, 1990.

White, Theodore H. *The Making of the President, 1968.* New York: Atheneum, 1969.

White, Walter. *A Man Called White: The Autobiography of Walter White*. New York: Viking, 1948.

Whittington, Keith E. *Constitutional Construction: Divided Powers and Constitutional Meaning*. Cambridge, Mass.: Harvard University Press, 1999.

———. "Taking What They Give Us: Explaining the Court's Federalism Offensive." *Duke Law Journal* 51 (2001): 477–520.

Wilkins, Roy. *Standing Fast: The Autobiography of Roy Wilkins*. New York: Viking, 1982.

Wilkinson J. Harvie, III. *From Brown to Bakke: The Supreme Court and School Integration, 1954–1978*. New York: Oxford University Press, 1979.

Williams, Juan. *Thurgood Marshall: American Revolutionary*. New York: Times Books, 1998.

Williamson, Joel. "Wounds Not Scars: Lynching, the National Conscience, and the American Historian." *Journal of American History* 83 (1997): 1221–53.

Wise, Henry A. *Seven Decades of Union*. Philadelphia: J. B. Lippincott, 1881.

Witt, Elder. *A Different Justice: Reagan and the Supreme Court*. Washington, D.C.: Congressional Quarterly, 1986.

Wolfe, Christopher. "The Senate's Power to Give 'Advice and Consent' in Judicial Appointments." *Marquette Law Review* 82 (1999): 355–79.

Wolin, Sheldon S. *The Presence of the Past: Essays on the State and the Constitution*. Baltimore: Johns Hopkins University Press, 1989.

Wolters, Raymond. *The Burden of Brown: Thirty Years of School Desegregation*. Knoxville: University of Tennessee Press, 1984.

Woodward, Bob, and Scott Armstrong. *The Brethren*. New York: Simon and Schuster, 1979.

Yalof, David Alistair. *Pursuit of Justices: Presidential Politics and the Selection of Supreme Court Nominee*. Chicago: University of Chicago Press, 1999.

Yarbrough, Tinsley E. "Reagan and the Courts." In *The Reagan Presidency: An Incomplete Revolution?* edited by Dilys M. Hill, Raymond A. Moore, and Phil Williams, 68–94. New York: St. Martin's, 1990.

———. *The Rehnquist Court and the Constitution*. New York: Oxford University Press, 2000.

Zangrando, Raymond L. *The NAACP Crusade against Lynching, 1909–1950*. Philadelphia: Temple University Press, 1980.

Zarefsky, David. *President Johnson's War on Poverty: Rhetoric and History*. University: University of Alabama Press, 1986.

Index

Index

Michigan State University Press is committed to preserving ancient forests and natural resources. We elected to print this title on 55# Natures Natural, which is 50% recycled (50% post consumer recycled) and processed chlorine free. As a result of our paper choice, Michigan State University Press has saved the following natural resources*:

5	Trees (40' feet in height)
2,133	Gallons of water
858	Kilowatt-hours of Electricity
462	Pounds of Greenhouse Gases

Both Michigan State University Press and our printer, Thomson-Shore, Inc., are members of the Green Press Initiative - a nonprofit program dedicated to supporting book publishers, authors, and suppliers in maximizing their use of fiber that is not sourced from ancient or endangered forests. For more information about the Green Press Initiative and the use of recycled paper in book publishing, please visit *www.greenpressinitiative.org*

* Environmental benefits were calculated based on research provided by Conservatree and Californians Against Waste.